Out Of The Darkness
The Story of Mary Ellen Wilson

BY

ERIC A. SHELMAN
and
STEPHEN LAZORITZ, M.D.

First printing 1999
Second printing 2000

Whatever Happened To Mary Ellen, by Stephen Lazoritz, reprinted from CHILD ABUSE AND NEGLECT, September 1989, with permission from Elsevier Science.

Out of the Darkness was written with the intention of entertaining and informing, and should be considered "based on a true story". The dramatic format in which it was written may classify it as historical fiction, but for the purposes of this book, we, the authors, did not want to present it as a dry documentary. Using every piece of information available, we have filled small gaps in the story with likely characters and scenarios; with the wealth of information we've accumulated over the years, it's very likely we're not far off. Letters, newspaper articles, and conversations with Mary Ellen's descendants support much of the creative license taken here. Where dates are used, they are accurate. We assume no responsibility for errors, inaccuracies, omissions or any other inconsistency herein. Some fictitious characters were introduced for the purposes of story continuity, but they do not distort the factual information presented. Any slights against people or organizations are unintentional, and any resemblance of fictional characters to actual living persons is entirely coincidental.

ISBN 0-9669400-0-8

Library of Congress Catalog Card Number 98-89460

Cover design and computer photo enhancement by Stephen Tokai.
Edited and Indexed by Jean Middleton, *Index Empire Indexing*, Riverside, CA
All photographs courtesy of the Shelman & Lazoritz collections unless otherwise noted.

ATTENTION ANIMAL AND CHILD PROTECTION AGENCIES:

Quantity discounts are available on bulk purchases of this book for fund raising purposes. For information, contact Dolphin Moon Publishing, P.O. Box 568, Lake Forest, California, 92630. Phone or FAX: (949) 380-7212. Email sales@dolphinmoon.com

Here's what people are saying about
Out of the Darkness: The Story of Mary Ellen Wilson

"*Out of the Darkness* brings one of America's most important, but least known stories to the public's attention. Shelman and Lazoritz have pulled together the most comprehensive collection of sources available to tell the dramatic story of Mary Ellen Wilson and her rescue from an abusive home."

~ Stephen Zawistowski, Ph.D.
American Society for the Prevention of Cruelty to Animals (ASPCA)

"I highly recommend *Out Of The Darkness* to all. A vivid depiction of child and animal abuse as it so commonly existed, the book traces the paths of Henry Bergh and Mary Ellen until their predestined meeting in April 1874. With realistic descriptions of orphans in the Hell's Kitchen tenements of New York City, the book also includes rare photographs of Mary Ellen, Etta Wheeler, and even Henry Bergh, who was rarely photographed."

~ Charles William Bergh
Cofounder of Animal Rescue Foundation (ARF), Dana Point, California, and columnist for the Dana Point Sentinel. He's also the great, great nephew of Henry Bergh, founder of the American Society for the Prevention of Cruelty to Animals. (ASPCA)

"Mary Ellen's story is riveting and filled with passion and pathos. Readers will fall in love with her in infancy and struggle with her through a cruel and often inhumane youth, breathing a sigh of relief upon her rescue by the ASPCA. This forceful story is one that should have a place in the history books."

~ Marilyn Kammer
Columnist, Saddleback Valley Voice

"A moving and powerful story . . . Mary Ellen is not just a child of her times, she is a child for all times."

~ Anne Reiniger, M.S.W., J.D.
Executive Director, The New York Society for the Prevention of Cruelty to Children
(NYSPCC)

This book is dedicated to past and present victims of abuse,
be they children or animals, living or dead.

Acknowledgments

The authors thank the following who assisted in the research and pursuit of historical data required to write this book:

First and foremost, we offer our sincere gratitude to the late **Shirley Mehlenbacher** and her husband, **Frank**. Shirley was Mary Ellen's granddaughter, and without her written authorization, many crucial documents could not have been obtained. We also express our condolences to Shirley's family for their loss. We thank **Nick DeSante**, not only for his help, but for his undying faith in the book from the first time he heard of Mary Ellen's story; **Jean Middleton** for editing the book and creating the index; **Jessica Heineman-Pieper** for her undergraduate thesis on the subject, which she sent to us all the way from Oxford University just on the strength of a phone call from a stranger. We very much appreciate **Stephen L. Zawistowski** Ph.D., Senior Vice President and Science Advisor for the American Society for the Prevention of Cruelty to Animals, for *everything* he contributed, especially the unpublished notes of **Edward P. Buffett**; We are also indebted to **Kenneth Cobb**, Director of the New York City Municipal Archives Department, for the information he was able to supply; and **Anne Reiniger,** Executive Director of the New York Society for the Prevention of Cruelty to Children, for her assistance and cooperation; **Joseph Gleason**, Archives Director of the New York Society for the Prevention of Cruelty to Children, for his assistance and cooperation, and especially for access granted the authors to the George Sim Johnston Archives.

A special thank you to **Stephen Tokai**, who worked for hours on cover design and computer enhancing the photos.

For moral support and other "miscellaneous" support, we must thank our wives, **Linda Shelman** and **Mary Lazoritz** for putting up with us throughout this mission. Though Linda had only to put up with Eric's disappearance into his computer for three years, poor Mary has lived Steve's obsession with this case for more than fifteen years. We hasten to say that it couldn't have been done with less understanding partners at our sides. Eric also thanks **Amelia Lewis** for everything she did to help him along the way, and **Roger Mangrum,** for running around book stores and dragging people over to hear Eric talk about the book. Steve would like to acknowledge the help of his father, **Louis**

Lazoritz, without whose intervention and guidance he insists he would be a worthless bum. Another thank you must go out to Steve's children, many of whom read the book and offered their own critiques as it moved toward completion.

Several others made valuable contributions both during and after the writing of this book. Special thanks to **Nicole Porter** for all the scanning and photo retouching work she did. Another big thanks to **Marilyn Kammer** and **Mary Ann Foster** for the articles they wrote about Mary Ellen and *Out of the Darkness* for the *Saddleback Valley News* and the *Saddleback Valley Voice*, both publications out of Orange County, California. Special appreciation to **Wendy Oglesbee** for asking Eric to speak about the book at Irvine's University High School. The more young people who know about Mary Ellen's plight, the better off the world will be.

Thanks to **Dolphin Moon Publishing** for their faith and dedication to this project, and for seeing the book through when others just couldn't grasp what an important piece of history Mary Ellen's story is.

Last, **Eric** and **Stephen**, the two men who wrote this book over the vast expanses of the internet, from different states and different time zones, would like to thank each other. Each has given the other the opportunity to bring the story of Mary Ellen, Etta Wheeler, and Henry Bergh's ASPCA to the world for the first time in more than a century.

May the story of Mary Ellen never be forgotten again.

Prologue

"Stop crying, Mary Ellen!"

"Mama . . . I love my little strings," Mary Ellen pleaded. "I . . . play with them." Even as she said the words, she knew it was useless.

"That's stupid. These aren't toys, child. They're garbage and should be in the garbage can for the ragpickers to gather."

"No, Mama!" she shouted in her panic. "Please, please let me keep them. I'll never ask for anything else, I promise."

Mama laughed, and the sound of it frightened her. "Why . . . you may ask if you like, Mary Ellen. You know what you'll get for it, don't you?"

Mary Ellen didn't remember seeing the rawhide whip packed in the boxes yet, but she knew very well it was kept high in the kitchen cupboard. She watched Mama storm into the kitchen, and Mary Ellen slumped to the floor and cried. It would never stop. Even when she just wanted to help, she did the wrong thing. "Mama, please," she cried, "don't hurt me!" The cupboard door creaked as Mama opened it, the sound slow and terrifying to her ears.

"No, Mama! Please . . . I'll be good, I promise! I don't want the strings!"

Mama walked toward her with the whip in her hand. Her knuckles were white from gripping the handle, her mouth set in a hard, thin line. "Get up!"

Mary Ellen didn't even try to obey her command. There was no strength left in her legs, no strength in her heart.

"I said get up!" Mama screamed, lashing at her with the leather crop. Mary Ellen didn't move or try to cover her exposed flesh with her hands. Instead, she tried hard to drift into her safe place. As the stained leather strands tore at her pale, tender skin, Mary Ellen remained motionless, staring straight ahead, not at the bunch of colorful threads her mama had dropped on the floor, but at something beyond them, somewhere deep in the warmest, safest parts of her imagination.

* * * * *

1

May 1864
Cold Harbor, Virginia
The Wilderness Campaign

Thomas Wilson stretched out on his bedroll, his muscles sore from the long marches, but more firm than he ever remembered before. Today the entire winter encampment would be broken down, as General Hancock had gotten word out that once the site was dismantled, the 69th Irish Brigade would move toward the swift Rapidan River. It was the final barrier the corps would cross before marching on to Richmond.

Tom yawned, his mind wide awake now with the thoughts of war. He shook the cobwebs from his head and imagined what lay ahead. Getting to the Rapidan, much less crossing it, would not be easy, for somewhere between where they now camped and Richmond, Virginia, Lee's army would provide a formidable resistance. After all the battles Tom had fought, the possibility of more to come still made him shudder. Home felt so close, and thinking of his wife made it feel that much closer. Each contact with the enemy increased the odds that he might not make it back to her.

Frances Wilson, the wife he called Fanny, awaited him in New York City. They had married in 1861, just before Tom volunteered to fight for his new country. Fanny begged him not to go, but Tom knew that not to join the "Fighting 69th", would be a betrayal of the oath he made to America when he stepped on her shores. He had abandoned Ireland when he fled during the potato famine, when people were dying in hoards of disease and starvation. Could he live with himself if he were to abandon a brigade of his own people?

The 69th Brigade was an entirely Irish unit, and Tom was proud to serve with them. Most had been killed and only a fraction of the original soldiers remained. Tom loved Fanny with all his heart, but serving in the brigade was a matter of devotion and honor to his new country and his old countrymen.

Tom sat up in his tent and scratched the rough growth of beard on his face. It comes off this morning, he thought. Cold Harbor should have been called Hot Harbor. Sweltering heat diminished a man's alertness, even at night. This was no place to wear a beard on his face.

Tom reached into his haversack to find his straightedge, but instead his hand fell upon the only image of Fanny that he owned. He pulled out the worn photograph and ran his fingers over her face. God she's beautiful, he thought, smiling to himself.

He first met Fanny at the St. Nicholas Hotel in New York City. He had started there as an oyster shucker, and noticed Fanny, a hotel laundress, the first day. He soon learned she was born Frances Connor, she was twenty years old at the time, and the most wonderful woman Tom had ever met. Her crisp English accent was the first thing to draw him in, but her sparkling brown eyes and dark, wavy hair ensured that he fell in love the moment he saw her standing there in the kitchen of the St. Nicholas. It took Tom only a few months to convince Fanny she could not live without him, either.

Tom slid the picture carefully back into his pack and sighed, removing the letter he had yet to open. He had been on picket duty all night, a nerve-wracking task. No clear view of the enemy's front line here, in this dense brush. The troops had not yet reached the stifling area called the Wilderness, but the thickets here were so close that Tom found it hard to imagine they could get much worse. A man couldn't see much farther than fifteen or twenty feet in front of him, and the slightest rustle in the distance put nerves on end and sent many a musket firing by mistake. The false discharges only served to put the enemy on notice that Union soldiers were nearby.

Some nights drained Tom more than others, and with the clinging heat and night insects, he was more than exhausted. After his picket duty, he had collapsed in his tent and slept like death itself.

As the morning light filtered through the thick material of his tent, Tom leaned back again, drifting in and out of thoughts of Fanny and the child he had yet to meet. He toyed with the letter in his hands, knowing it would speak to him in Fanny's voice; that she would tell him whether their baby was a boy or a girl. Tom stared at the tattered envelope, anxious, but saddened to open it and have nothing more to look forward to. The sounds of busy soldiers packing their tents and other belongings kept bringing him back to the present, an unwelcome beckoning.

The letter was still fragrant from the perfume Fanny splashed on her communications, and Tom breathed it in for a long moment, then finally tore it open. Now, having rested all he could, he would savor every word. Not much mail made it through the battle lines, and the letter inside was dated two months earlier:

March 10, 1864

Dearest Thomas,

This letter shall begin with the announcement of the birth of our beautiful daughter, Mary Ellen . She has dark hair like me, and her eyes appear to be a bluish green, but will probably turn brown like mine. She looks so much like you though, her nose particularly resembling yours, and there is a little of my younger sister Ellen in her mouth and chin. Mother and daughter are both in fine condition. As I feared would happen, the landlord, Mrs. Cobb, finalized the sale of the building two days ago, and the first thing the new owner, Mr. Kelsko, did was to announce to all tenants that he would expect payment upon the due date with no exceptions. He also emphasized that he would have no trouble filling a vacancy if anyone were to become unable to pay on time. The housing has become so bad in the city, I'm positive he is correct, but I won't dwell on it, as I'm sure there will be no problem. I am paid up for the next month in any event. I would like to have a likeness taken of Mary Ellen so you won't have to wait until you return home to see her, but spending the money now might be foolish, for I must keep her fed and clothed first. Perhaps when you send more money I will have it taken. I will close this letter by thanking you, Thomas. You have given me a daughter, and she is the pride of my life. I know she will be yours, too. Please come home and see her, darling. You will fall in love with her. She makes it so easy to do.

All my love, Fanny

Tom jumped up and tossed the letter on his mat. With the tune of "The Irish Washerwoman" playing in his head, he hunched over and danced a little jig right around the small tent.

"I'm a father!" he shouted to the walls of the tent. "You got that? A father!" The sound of his words made him dance faster still, until a distant bugle blew, interrupting his jig. Tom dropped back to the mat and picked up the letter again, running his fingers over the words, lost in thought.

A daughter, and nearly two months old already! She would be waiting for him when he arrived home, his own flesh and blood. The Wilson family would live on in Mary Ellen, as well as the other children he and Fanny would have. Maybe four or five more!

Tom had seen many places on his journey through the war where they could build a big house and escape the congestion of New York City for the scenery of the country. He might even decide to farm potatoes as his family once had in Ireland. He wouldn't be content to shuck oysters at the St. Nicholas, that was certain. Now that he had begun his family, he would need a decent income to support them, and whatever he chose to do, Fanny and his baby girl would be right beside him.

Money. Tom frowned. Fanny's words made it seem she needed more money, though he had sent another forty-seven dollars to her a month ago. At

12

least she was already paid up on a month's board. In any case, if she hadn't gotten it yet, it was either stolen or would arrive at a time when she could desperately use it. As for the new landlord, it was probably just her imagination getting the better of her.

A young soldier stuck his head inside the tent. "Tom did you hear—"

"Sully!" Tom yelled, jumping back to his feet and renewing his jig. "Come on in and celebrate with me, I'm a new father! My little Mary Ellen was born back in March! A little girl, Sully!"

"Bless you and your family, Tom! That's the best kind of news a soldier can get!"

"Aye, it is, Sully. I can't believe it!" He danced some more as his friend looked on, a smile on his face.

"I can understand how you're feeling Tom, but we're breaking camp. Probably ought to start collecting your belongings and get the tent dropped."

"Aye, thanks Sully," Tom sighed, not wanting to leave the excitement behind him. "I heard the call." The young man clapped him on the shoulder again and ducked out of the tent. The word from the Generals wasn't always carved into stone, but men had been burning the winter's accumulation of wood all night during his picket, so he knew they would be marching today. Tom got up, stretched, and stepped outside the Sibley tent.

The men packed supplies into the white-topped wagons, and the haze of smoke hung thickly in the air from the night's burning. Things moved along quickly, and Tom knew his work needed to be done as well. He went back inside, arranged his haversack, and broke down the tent.

By eleven that morning, they were on the march. They would keep on all day, probably reaching the Rapidan sometime late that evening. They would no doubt camp on the north bank for the night, crossing first thing in the morning when the dawn's light would offer visibility and a chance to spy the enemy should he be lying in wait.

As the sun glinted off the raised muskets of the weary but enthusiastic soldiers, the train of wagons lumbered precariously over the uneven terrain. The men who walked beside them were watchful, not only of Confederate soldiers, but of the wagons themselves, having seen more than one man crushed when a wagon tipped over on top of him.

In spite of the dangers, the day turned out clear, only moderately hot, and beautiful. Bands played lively airs, and could be heard from all directions. Banners waved as regiments, brigades, and divisions fell into line. Even to eyes long familiar with military fanfare, the scene was one of astounding grandeur.

The colors of the different brigades held high, the Army of the Potomac and the other forty thousand Yankees marched steadily on toward Richmond, Virginia.

* * * * *

Fanny sat in front of the Singer machine, pumping the foot pedal by lamp light. Her knotted brown hair was now coming undone, and every few minutes she brushed the falling strands away from her face. She yawned and stretched, taking a momentary respite.

Making foot stockings at four bits per pair was a lot of work for little money, but she needed the income. A friend from the hotel, Alanna Cavanagh, had let her borrow the new Singer machine to help out with her finances, but Fanny knew she wasn't a very good seamstress, with or without the fancy machine. Still, it was impossible to know when the next letter would arrive from Thomas, or if it would contain any money to help see her through the month's board. Most of his letters had, but Thomas told her there was no way to guarantee a letter would arrive safely to her after leaving his hands. Many soldiers reported letters never making it home—particularly the ones containing money.

Behind Fanny, Mary Ellen slept in the makeshift crib a neighbor downstairs had built for her, her breathing steady, but occasionally interrupted by the small, sweet sounds of an infant's dreams. At each tiny noise Fanny smiled. She didn't realize how it affected her—it came as a natural reflex to the contentment of their precious, new daughter.

At a few minutes past midnight the lamp flickered, throwing eerie, dancing shadows upon the wall, then the yellow luminescence faded to black.

"Idiot," she said aloud, realizing she had used the last of the lard oil, and now she would be forced to work only by the light of day until she could afford more. She put her sewing down and shook her head. Fanny hadn't even thought of running out of oil, but she had been sewing by the lamp a lot lately. It was much easier, with Mary Ellen's feeding and sleeping schedule, to sew at night rather than during the day. With Mary Ellen sleeping, Fanny could get far more work done. When the infant babbled and cooed, Fanny was drawn to her, unable to concentrate on anything else.

In the wee hours of the early spring morning, as her baby explored the new world of dreams, Fanny sat in the dark and worried about Thomas. He had been gone so long it made her heart ache. Of course she was independent, at least as much as she could be. She had traveled to America with a worthless uncle who had abandoned her as soon as they reached Castle Garden, but she did not give up. She found work through her own efforts, and the St. Nicholas is where she met Thomas. Things had happened for a reason, and now she only wished he would return soon. She was strong, though. She'd proven it before. Thomas was strong, too. Before long he would walk through that door and take his daughter in his arms.

The moonlight shone on Mary Ellen's crib, and Fanny rocked it gently, fingering the smooth curvature of the ring that hung from the thin chain around her neck. Her mother had given the ornate gold band to her when she departed England, a symbol of her love, she had said. One day, Fanny would pass the ring on to Mary Ellen, named after her mother and sister whom she missed so much.

Fanny felt a wave of guilt; her parents must be wondering what had become of her by now. She had not written them since she learned of her pregnancy, though it was not for a lack of trying. Each time she put pen to paper, the letter ended up being to Thomas! That wasn't fair to her sister, Ellen, who would be fifteen now. Fifteen! Was it really possible?

The foggy day Fanny set sail, her mother stood there on the dock, her face red and swollen. Fanny remembered Mary Connor's quivering lip as she tried so hard to be strong. The desperate feeling in her mother's embrace—it was love, given unconditionally, as only a mother can.

Sitting in her cramped room in the quiet of the New York City night, rocked with memories of her mother, Fanny resolved to do whatever was necessary to take care of her daughter. Mary Ellen deserved that.

As her mind returned to Mary Ellen, the baby stirred, then awoke. Her little mouth opened in the soft cry Fanny had come to cherish, and she lifted her from the crib. "Okay, little one," Fanny said. It was time for her feeding, and she was as accurate as a wristwatch. In response to her cry, milk leaked from Fanny's right breast, a reaction that still surprised her. She smiled and moved aside the thin material of her robe, moving her daughter to her breast. Mary Ellen's mouth opened wide as she searched for nourishment.

"Oh, you're just like a little baby bird." She brushed her nipple across Mary Ellen's mouth twice, then the child took over, her tiny hands pressing against Fanny's breasts as she suckled fervently, the sweet, warm milk satisfying her hunger.

* * * * *

As night gripped the outskirts of Wilderness, the exhausted Union troops reached the rushing waters of the Rapidan. Here they would stop and rest for the night, replenishing a portion of their energy for the battles yet to come. At the first light of dawn, the pontoniers would begin to apply their craft; cutting and strapping, fitting and laying the pontoon bridge that would serve as another stepping stone in the Union's pathway to victory over the Rebels.

Tom didn't allow his eyes to close more than a few moments at a time, and that made for a long night. On his back he stared up at the stars visible through the scrub brush that had become increasingly thicker as they neared the river. They had not set up tents, as this was nothing more than a rest stop. He reached down and loosened the laces on his boots, which were a size too small, then leaned back once more.

In this, his second tour of duty, Tom had served the Union longer than many of the others, and had become well known as an expert marksman. During the stretches of time with no enemy contact, the soldiers would sometimes hold casual shooting competitions, and he usually came out the champion, firing his musket with deadly accuracy three times in the span of one minute. He had won numerous pairs of boots and coats that way—he only competed when he needed supplies—but his shooting was so exceptional that his commander replaced his musket with a sixteen shot, breech loading 'Henry' rifle as soon as it became available.

Tom accepted it with mixed emotions. The Henry would likely save his life, but it also took him out of the musket firing competition unless someone was willing to lend him one—and that would only be likely if the musket's

16

owner didn't plan to join the games. If the Union had its way, all Federal soldiers would carry the Henry, but the cost was prohibitive. At under fifteen dollars each, the Springfield rifle was more affordable, though even the most experienced veteran soldier—except for Tom Wilson, it seemed—could fire the weapon only twice per minute due to the complicated loading procedure. Loading the gun became even more difficult under enemy return fire.

Tom glanced over at Sully, a few feet to his left. The young man's cap rested over his eyes, and he was sound asleep. His full name was Ryan Sullivan and he was a few years Tom's junior. He fell in with the company at Brandy Station in December, and at first he looked typical enough; a young, curly haired soldier anxious to taste victory over Johnny Reb. At first, Tom had put him in the same category as the other greenhorns.

Before Sully finished his first month of duty though, Tom knew he was special; different from the other recruits. Using good sense more refined than his years, Sully's talent with a rifle and intelligence on the battlefield caused him to be easily accepted by the veteran soldiers. Tom found him good company, despite his reservations about making friends here.

There had been another friend Tom made in the war, a man named Alex Purcell. Alex died in Gettysburg, and Tom had been right beside him, unaware he was mortally injured. Tom might have been able to save him if he'd have paid more attention and watched out for him, but that's not how it turned out. Alex's death was not quick, and Tom blamed himself for each moment of the boy's agony.

Tom now kept mostly to himself. This *was* war and men were expected to die, but if he didn't know them, he could deal with it. Whether it was a solitary man lying a few feet from him with a hole in his chest, or hundreds of bodies everywhere, Tom just kept fighting. After all, he didn't know their families, their wives and children. It was a lottery; everyone had the chance to die, and those things, along with the smell of blood and smoke, were just part of this hell, and it wasn't personal.

The odor of death he almost no longer noticed—he had become immune to it. After the first couple of years he began to imagine the many bodies were nothing more than old logs, or piles of leaves. He wouldn't have kept his sanity if he thought of them as dead husbands and fathers. As long as he didn't allow himself to know them he could hold it inside.

Now he had risked his own mandated detachment by befriending Ryan Sullivan, a fine young man who spoke of his own parents often, and of his sisters and brother. The possibility still haunted Tom. Would Sully die beside him, leaving his loved ones behind?

Not if he could stop it.

Tom closed his eyes and mentally prepared for the night, the comforting sounds of strangers all around him.

* * * * *

The next morning, as the faint light of dawn pierced the overgrowth, the soldiers got to work. While the pontoniers worked diligently on the bridge across the Rapidan River, pickets supplied protection for them, scouting several hundred yards out in the brush. No musket fire was heard throughout the operation, and to the engineers laying the bridge it was a welcomed silence.

The other soldiers took breakfast, cleaned their muskets, and repaired wagons. They refreshed tired horses, patched worn shoes, and prepared to move south upon completion of the bridge. Once over the Rapidan, they would enter the twisted, tangled thickets of the true Wilderness.

2

Fanny made her way down Franklin Street, turning left on Baxter. She stayed to the west side of the street so as not to pass too near the filthy tenements of Mulberry Bend, the site of some of the most horrible living conditions she had ever witnessed. The people there were living in a way that even rats would detest, and she would never have chosen to walk the street had it not been the shortest route to the casualty postings. Mary Ellen had grown quickly, and she was a burdensome load now, feeling all the heavier with each step Fanny took.

Unlike the wealthy, society women downtown, Fanny couldn't afford a fancy baby carriage to tote the child around in. Instead, she had sewed herself a sling—she learned this by watching the Chinese women—and carried Mary Ellen on her back. It was much easier than holding her in her arms, and it left her free to carry other things.

The smell drifting from the Mulberry Bend warrens across the street reminded her of the stench aboard the *India Star* halfway through her journey to America. It was a sickening blend of rotted food and decaying feces, and she felt herself gag at the mere thought of it. The steerage compartment, as horrifying as it was, did not reek of such foulness. Fanny quickened her step as she saw Canal Street up ahead, where the war casualties would be posted.

As usual, a small group of people—mostly women—stood before the postings. Today, two of them were sobbing, one of the poor ladies down on her knees, her head pressed against the ground as she wailed in anguish.

Fanny cringed. *That won't be me*, she thought. *Thomas's name will not be on this list.*

Looking at the list of dead was difficult for Fanny, and it was easier to do it quickly and with no hesitation. She approached the sheets without pause, ran her eyes over them, and came to the end without seeing Thomas's name. Just to be sure, she started again at the top, reviewing it more slowly. No, Thomas Wilson was, at this printing, still alive. Satisfied, she stepped around the weeping woman and walked away.

A few months ago, Fanny might have stopped to comfort her. Now, having had luck on her side for so long, she had come to believe that contact with the bereaved could only bring her luck to an end. Instinct told her to offer consolation, but she was determined to distance herself from the sorrow of others until Thomas was safely back in New York, where he could take care of his wife and daughter. It was foolish, but she couldn't bring herself to abandon the belief.

Wiping away the tears that had formed in her eyes, Fanny fought the urge to run. Money was lower than ever before. She must make some decisions to preserve her future, not to mention Mary Ellen's.

There's no time like the present, she thought. She would go to the St. Nicholas and inquire as to whether they could use her services as a laundress again. Alanna Cavanagh, a friend from her days as a laundress at the hotel, still labored there as a chambermaid when she last visited. Perhaps Alanna could help her obtain a position again. "I'll be earning money to feed you with, Mary Ellen," Fanny said aloud. "We mustn't sit and wait for a post from your father. Mummy can simply do as she did before."

Fanny walked the two blocks to Grand Street, then waved down a passing omnibus. The coachman pulled the reins firmly, and the huge, lumbering carriage drew to a stop a few feet in front of her.

"Will your route put you near the St. Nicholas Hotel, driver?" Fanny asked.

The plump old gentleman nodded. "Just about a block from there," he

20

grumbled. "C'mon now. Get in and have a short bit ready."

Fanny went to the rear of the vehicle and up the steps. Edging sideways to the front of the bus, she thrust her ten cents through the hole in the roof behind the driver's seat, then moved Mary Ellen around into her arms.

She sat and checked her coin purse, taking note that she would probably have to walk home from the St. Nicholas. If she afforded herself the luxury of riding home as well, she would have to sew another pair of stockings to recover the bus fare. It was a lot of work for the convenience, and her legs were strong, after all.

As the cobblestone-paved thoroughfare shook the old carriage to its frame and caused her teeth to chatter, Fanny held onto the side rail and said a prayer for her husband. She looked at Mary Ellen and saw that the very bumpiness that irritated most passengers seemed to be quite all right with her, for the vibration had sent her right off to sleep.

Fanny smiled, closed her eyes, and pressed Mary Ellen close to her breast. Perhaps with a little effort, she could enjoy the bumpy ride into town as well.

* * * * *

"What do you think the Rebs are gonna do, Tom?" Sully asked, staring off into the thicket. "They gonna give up soon?"

Tom looked at the young soldier, who looked more haggard by the minute. The changes had come over him the last few weeks, and Tom was worried. He'd seen many a young soldier either harden or waste away before his eyes. "That's just wishful thinkin', Sully," he said, smiling in spite of his concerns. "Goin' by what they've done so far, I'd guess the Rebs are gonna fight like the devil before they let us march into Richmond and plant a Union flag."

Sully rubbed his eyes with the back of one scraped hand. "Yeah, I thought as much," he said, his eyes hollow and sunken.

"You sleepin' all right, lad?"

"Good as anyone, I reckon," Sully said. "From what I've seen, you don't sleep that good yourself."

"Aye, but I'm used to it, Sully. I've been doin' it for a long time now." He hoisted his rifle up on his shoulder and scanned the clearing from left to right, taking in all he could see. No sign of the enemy so far today, and it was already past noon.

General Grant had ordered the masses of soldiers to bivouac on the south bank of the Rapidan until the exact position of Lee's troops could be determined. The scouts had left hours ago on horseback to try to locate the rebel troops. With good reports, Grant would most likely decide to flank to either side of Lee's Confederates in an attempt to surround them before engaging them in battle.

Tom knew the strategy—it didn't change much as the war progressed. With a quick, unexpected strike, Grant could buy time and avoid a huge, organized battle and a massive loss of life. If they could get closer to Richmond before engaging, such a battle would be less likely to affect the Union's final advance on the Southern capital.

The newspapers Tom read were few, but clearly the armies on both sides were huge. If they were anywhere in the same vicinity, they could not avoid touching, and each contact of the armies would result in scores of corpses on both sides. Tom had seen it before, too many times.

The crossing of the Rapidan River had been what nobody expected; uneventful. There was some sniper fire from a distance, but it was unlikely that it came from Confederate soldiers. The shots probably came from local hunters for whom the area was a source of food, and who didn't appreciate the presence of the large army.

"Lee's men are out there somewhere, Sully," Tom said. "I think the battles we'll be fightin' in the days ahead will be the most troublesome of the war." He turned to face his fellow soldier. "God, I miss my wife, and I'd give anything to hold my little girl."

Sully gripped his shoulder with a rough hand. "It's gotta be hard, Tom. I miss my mother and father more than I reckoned I would. Just takes being out here for a while to figure out what's important and what don't amount to a hill of beans." He smiled as he looked out at the shadowy woods, then turned back to face Tom. "You've got yourself a pretty lady there, Tom, judging by the likeness she sent you. I'm sure your little girl was lucky enough to get her looks instead of yours."

"If you like the taste of boot soles, keep on."

Both men laughed.

The rest of the evening's picket duty was quiet, and the remaining predawn hours supplied both Tom Wilson and Ryan Sullivan a restful night's sleep.

But as the hazy light of the Virginia morning touched the faraway tops of the thick branches that served as their shelter, Tom Wilson and Ryan Sullivan awoke with the roar of musketry ringing in their ears.

* * * * *

Fanny started work before sunrise, making her rounds at the St. Nicholas. She was happy to be working again. Taking care of Mary Ellen was rewarding—indeed, her only real pleasure these days—but if she were unable to feed her daughter, she was not fit to be a mother.

Her arms full of sheets, Fanny made her way toward the washroom.

"Mrs. Wilson, do come here, please."

Fanny turned, and her heart froze. It was Ellis Gilmour. He had hired Fanny on Alanna's recommendation and did all the coordinating of the staff and firing as well. His round, deeply lined face was red with anger and Fanny thought she knew why.

"Yes, Mr. Gilmour?"

"What's that on your back?" he asked, his voice booming as he glared at Mary Ellen.

Fanny shook like a frightened child as she answered. "My baby, Mr. Gilmour. But it's only for today. Mrs. Cavanagh—"

"Why, I *know* it's only for today, Mrs. Wilson, because that is exactly how long you'll have your situation here."

Fanny bit her lip as she fought back tears, then spotted Alanna Cavanagh coming out of a nearby room behind Gilmour. The look on her face told Fanny she had overheard his angry words.

Alanna walked without hesitation and stood between them, facing Gilmour. "Excuse me, Mr. Gilmour," Alanna said, "but I'm arranging for the child to be watched after today. I'm taking her with me after work, and she'll not be back tomorrow."

Fanny breathed a sigh of relief. Thank God for Alanna! She had been frozen on her feet!

Gilmour shook his head frantically. "I've stated my position clearly, Mrs.

Cavanagh! There are regulations, *my* regulations—"

"I'm aware of that, Mr. Gilmour, and Mrs. Wilson is aware of it as well. She is a fine laundress, and after today, you will be happy you hired her. The child will be gone tomorrow."

He appeared reluctant to give in, but the redness soon drained from his face. "Well . . . just for today, then," he said. He looked hard at Fanny again. "And need I remind you, Mrs. Wilson, there will be no more children at the St. Nicholas. Is that understood?"

"Yes, sir. Thank you, sir." She hurried away, and Alanna followed her to the washroom where Fanny stood cradling Mary Ellen in her arms. The baby cooed and looked at her mother with an infant's innocence.

"Fanny, I know of a woman named Martha Score who cares for children for a fee. She can take Mary Ellen for a time, at least until your mister comes home. I think her fee is two dollars a week."

"Two dollars!" Fanny said. "It might as well be ten. I can't afford to pay it." She brushed her brown hair from her eyes, and wiped the perspiration from her forehead. "I'm in trouble, Alanna."

Alanna waved her off. "Nonsense. Miss Score will keep her for you until you have the money to care for her again. For that she'll feed and house her, Fanny. You should not be able do it for less, and still afford to keep your lodging, much less your situation here."

Thoughts whirled in Fanny's head, but none held any solutions other than what Alanna had suggested. Thomas had not sent money in a long time, and Fanny could no longer rely on it. There was no choice in the matter.

"All right, then," Fanny said, touching Alanna's arm. "It will break my heart to let her go for even a moment—"

"I know that," Alanna said. "It's the right thing to do for her and for yourself."

"Thank you for helping me. I've needed a friend . . . it's been a trial, really."

Alanna shrugged. "That's what friends do, and besides, I like having you here. In case you haven't noticed, I don't fancy many of the other ladies who work here. Now let's see how we'll do this," she said. "I'm through here in three hours. I can take the little darling to Mrs. Score's this afternoon and you can bring her clothes tomorrow."

Fanny laughed. "All of her things?" Fanny hesitated, then added "There's not much, you understand. Only two little dresses and some wraps."

"Yes, bring what she has. From what I understand, Mrs. Score has some extra things. She's been taking in children for some time. I'll spend the rest of the day with Mary Ellen and drop her off on my way home this evening. I've got some errands to run this afternoon so I won't be going straight home, but with this sling of yours, it shouldn't be a problem taking her along."

"Where does Mrs. Score live?"

"On Mulberry Street, between Park and Bayard. Two buildings from my own. We used to be in the same building. That's how I came to know her."

Fanny bit her lip and held Mary Ellen closer, as the baby tried to find her breast through her dress. "Alanna . . . I had no idea that's where you lived. Aren't they those awful tenement buildings at Mulberry Bend?"

"Fanny, it's only until your husband comes home. The war's nearly over, so the papers say. You'll have her back in a wink. Besides, those buildings aren't as bad as people say. A lot depends upon those who live within, and my home, for one, is kept quite nicely. You know how folks talk things up."

Fanny remembered the smell as she walked by the Bend on her way to the postings. Still, she supposed Alanna was right. People usually made things sound far worse than they were. She would know, wouldn't she? Of course. She lived there and had seen them firsthand. Perhaps Fanny would go by and see for herself in a few days. If she didn't approve, she would look for something else.

"Okay, Alanna. I know you're right. And as you said, it's only for a short time."

* * * * *

Hundreds of deadly steel projectiles whizzed overhead like angry bees as Tom and Sully lay pinned on their bedrolls for nearly half an hour. The attack was unrelenting, and each time one of the men tried to move, more fire sprayed in their direction as the powder smoke thickened. Trees on either side of them splintered and exploded, sending wood chips raining down on them. Other unseen soldiers returned fire on both sides of them.

"We've got to get our weapons, Sully!" Tom said, angry at himself for not

25

having the rifle by his side during the night. Both he and Sully had gone to relieve themselves the night before and had left their guns leaning against a tree fifteen feet away. It may as well have been a mile. If only his rifle were at hand, he was sure he could hit some of the snipers; enough to allow Sully to get to his gun. What a fool he was!

Soldiers were dying, and a risk had to be taken.

"Stay here, Sully," Tom ordered. Suddenly, he sprung from the mat and crouched low, scrambling through the thick brush. Bushes beside him danced under Rebel fire as he dropped low and used his elbows to crawl to his gun. Now he could see some of the others in his Company. Many of the soldiers were dead already, others were busy engaging the enemy in battle.

He was finally there. Tom snatched up his Henry, knowing he had left it with a full cartridge for just such an occasion, now glad he did. The gun smoke permeated the air quickly, and Tom found he could not see beyond a few yards. He crawled forward, keeping low, beneath the hanging cloud. When he was as sure as he could be that the front of the battle line lay before him, he rested on his stomach, his gun in firing position and called, "C'mon, Sully! I'll keep 'em down for you, lad!"

Firing several shots toward the yellow spurts of flame that flared up from the thatch of trees beyond, he glanced occasionally in Sully's direction as his friend crawled on his belly toward him.

Sully reached his weapon, grabbed it, and crouched as he made his way over to Tom. He dropped down beside him.

"Good work, Sully."

"Couldn't have done it without you, Tom."

Tom nodded. "Load your weapon, man. This ain't gonna end soon." *I can feel my heart pounding*, he thought. *But it means I'm still alive.* Then, without warning, his mind drifted. *What does Mary Ellen look like? Does she have Fanny's eyes? Her dimples? They're probably resting now, or perhaps Fanny's taking her for a morning stroll. Oh, how I wish I were with them.*

Sully's voice drew him back. "How'd they surprise us like that, Tom?" he asked, his voice trembling.

"They must've ambushed the pickets," Tom said, straining to be heard over the relentless, furious blasts.

"Could've been us, Tom," Sully said.

"Could've been anyone, lad. Remember that."

Sully tore the corner from the paper cartridge containing the rifle ball and powder with his teeth, and said, "But there's at least two men at each picket! How in God's name could they surprise both of 'em?"

Tom shook his head. He wasn't absolutely sure how, but he knew from the dead soldiers in Union uniforms that this was an unexpected charge. The pickets on duty most likely had fallen asleep and were killed with a silent bayonet thrust. If they lived and turned up after the battle, Hancock would order them shot, but Tom was pretty sure the Confederates had already seen to that.

Tom's rifle was already reloaded, but Sully's hands shook as he loaded his. Tom realized his young friend was frightened out of his mind. Despite the early hour, the heat was unbearable, made even worse by the thick, hot smoke that hung thick in the air.

Joining his company and allowing Sully to fall in when he finished loading his weapon was the proper thing to do, but instead, Tom waited. Sully finally drew the ramrod and pushed the projectile down into the barrel. He slid the percussion cap on the nib, pulled back the hammer, and said, "Well, Corporal Wilson, it ain't a Henry, but it can sure as hell kill a Johnny Reb."

"Aye, Sully," Tom said. "With you at the sight it can. Our men are there." He pointed to the west, where, through the cacophony of artillery and musketry, familiar voices could be heard shouting orders, primarily the strong voice of their immediate commander, Colonel Kelly. He was a fine soldier and leader from the Eighty-eighth New York. Tom, as did most of the veteran soldiers, recognized Patrick Kelly as a man who would someday become a great General—if he lived long enough to achieve it. He was a brave man— almost foolishly so—and it could someday be his downfall.

Tom patted Sully on the back and said, "They're waitin' lad. Let's get this task done and get home."

Together, the two soldiers fell in with their corps. Colonel Kelly directed them farther to the east, where a huge gap had formed in the opposing line. They followed his orders, the Union soldiers forcing the fighting, the Confederates reeling from the charge. The smoke thickened as the corpses mounted.

All day, the fighting went on. As Tom watched Sully's confidence grow, he also became more comfortable with the young soldier's focus. He was loading his weapon with skill and speed, and firing it with the same traits.

He's overcoming his fear, Tom thought. That's good. He can't afford to be frightened here. Fear is our enemy, too.

* * * * *

The evening came quickly, and the Confederates had yet to retreat beyond a few hundred yards. Tom had expected the battle to be short once the Union gained the upper hand, but the Confederate army was far more determined than he had given them credit for. In thickets such as this, all advantages were in favor of the defense.

"Ready bayonets!" Kelly shouted. The sound of metal locking onto metal followed all around.

As they forged into the Wilderness, the underbrush and saplings grew wilder still, the smoke unbearable, as thick as fog in the unmoving air. It was as though night had fallen. The Union troops may as well have been fighting blindfolded.

General Hancock's voice could be heard from the rear, his excited voice booming, commanding: "Colonel Kelly, charge forward! Jefferson Davis awaits us in Richmond!"

Kelly responded with, "I'll lead the charge!"

We're making an error, Tom thought. We can't even see the enemy.

The bugle sounded and the division started forward, the hundreds of voices raised along with their rifles. Among them, Tom Wilson and Ryan Sullivan advanced bravely, blindly.

Through the smoky darkness they charged, their bayonets held high. With Sully to his left, Tom could not see more than three feet in front of him. The low branches and leaves tore across his face, and his eyes burned from the heat. He heard men screaming from his left and his right, then suddenly, from out of the fog, felt a sharp, stabbing pain in his left shoulder. He screamed and fell backward, coming to rest against a prickly bush, then saw the Confederate soldier standing right in front of him holding the embedded rifle, trying to get his finger on the trigger. With a swift reaction, Tom kicked out at him, and the soldier tumbled backward, pulling the bayonet from Tom's shoulder as his hands slipped from the gun.

With stunned surprise, Tom realized the Henry was still in his hands. As the Rebel soldier scrambled to his feet, Tom pointed the weapon at his head and fired. The man's face disintegrated and the body convulsed, falling to the ground in a heap. Sweat poured from Tom's forehead into his eyes, and as another soldier ran toward him from the heavy brush, Tom raised his weapon to fire again. His finger squeezed the trigger, and just before the hammer fell—he stopped.

It was Sully. He had almost shot him.

"Are you all right, Tom? God man, I saw that Johnny stab you, but I had another one to deal with!" With shaking hands, Sully ripped a large strip from the sleeve of his uniform, wrapped it twice, and then tied it around Tom's shoulder.

Tom kept his eyes peeled on the thicket behind his friend. "Aye, Sully. I told you to take care of yourself first, and I meant it." He winced as Sully tightened the knot. It felt better. "Help me up, lad."

Sully gave him a hand up. "You'd better go back."

Gritting his teeth, Tom moved his arm in a large circle. "See? I'm fine. Come on now."

He crouched low and began the advance again, Sully beside him. "You're a great soldier, Tom," he said.

"Just a fool, lad."

Small fires had broken out within the forest, and spreading pools of flame ran along hillsides and into ravines. Tom and Sully heard men screaming, possibly wounded and now trapped in the flames, being burned alive. They still could not tell where the battle lines were, but tried to use the thunder of musketry to determine it. That failed them, as the exploding guns seemed to be everywhere, creating a rampart of sound that transformed the battleground into a smoke-filled haze full of invisible dangers.

Moments later, Tom lost sight of Sully yet again. His senses were dulled, from the ringing of his ears to his lack of sight, and he probably wouldn't hear Sully if he cried out. The only thing to do was to find him quickly. Frantic, he ran a few yards to the west and saw his friend on the ground.

He was loading his rifle.

"Why didn't you do that when we were back in safer territory?" Tom asked.

Sully tore the corner from the cartridge. "I was thinking of getting you taken care of, Tom." He poured the powder in the barrel and pressed the ball in with his thumb.

Tom shook his head. "Worry about yourself, lad. I'll take care of Tom Wilson."

Sully drew the ramrod and slid it down the barrel, pushing the projectile down. His young friend was becoming an expert with the weapon now, and he was glad of it.

Suddenly, two Confederate soldiers burst out of the brush. They stumbled to an abrupt halt, their eyes wild. They had undoubtedly been tearing through the trees as blindly as the Union soldiers. The dirty-faced blonde soldier looked all of seventeen years old, while the other dark-haired soldier wasn't much older. Still they both held rifles, which made them dangerous no matter what their ages.

Tom instinctively dropped to the ground, jarring his wounded shoulder. He fought the pain, swung the rifle toward the men and released a shot, missing badly. He had succeeded in drawing their attention away from Sully, though, and both young Rebels now trained their weapons upon Tom.

Tom glanced quickly at Sully, his hands shaking as he struggled to place the percussion cap beneath the hammer of his Springfield.

Tom fired again, killing the dirty-faced blonde soldier instantly. If not for his Henry rifle, he and Sully would have both been dead. He swung the barrel of his gun toward the other man, but before he could pull the trigger, an explosion met his ears. His arms went numb, and a curtain of blackness fell over his eyes.

* * * * *

His arms heavy with sorrow, Sully raised his loaded musket toward the remaining Rebel soldier. The boy had used his minié ball on Tom—he had seen that Sully wasn't prepared to fire at him. The young soldier's bayonet was his only hope, but Sully wouldn't give him the opportunity to use it. He fired and watched the Confederate soldier fall at his feet.

Sully puked onto the ground beside the dead man, then stared at his lifeless body, waiting to see if it moved. It didn't. It never would again, and he was glad. The young Rebel's last living act had been to shoot a man Sully respected; a true friend he had grown to love.

He turned his attention toward the thicket for a few moments before scooting toward Tom, whose blood soaked uniform rose and fell with his ragged breath. Sully glanced at the gaping wound and knew he could do nothing to save him. He leaned close to his friend and gently slipped his hand beneath his head. Tom's eyelids lifted and closed again.

"Tom?"

Open. Frantic eyes darted from side to side. Tom's shaking hand crawled slowly up to his chest, and his fingers sank into the gushing hole from which his life now drained.

"Sully? Sully . . . are you . . . here?" he moaned.

Sully's eyes filled with tears as he leaned closer to hear Tom's feeble voice. The air everywhere in and around the Wilderness was still alive with the crackle of distant fires, the screams of wounded men, and the dissonance of exploding muskets. None of it mattered. As far as Sully was concerned, there was no one, nothing more important than Corporal Tom Wilson. "Yeah, Tom. I'm here."

For one brief moment, Tom's eyes swam into full focus, and he looked hard into the young man's eyes. "I want you to . . . write Fanny," he choked through blood and bile. "Will you do . . . that for me . . . please Sully?"

"You know I will, Tom," he said. "I'll do anything you ask."

Sully glanced behind him at the smoky shadows, watching for approaching Rebels. He would not be able to do anything at all, for Tom or himself, if he were killed.

"Are . . . are you wounded?" Tom's voice was fading like the last remnants of an echo.

"No, Tom. Thanks to you, I'm not." Tears rolled down his face, but he didn't bother wiping them away.

"Tell . . . Fanny that I . . . love her, and to . . . to kiss Mar. . ."

Tom released his last breath. His chest fell still.

Ryan Sullivan stared at Tom's body for a long time, hearing his friend's last words over and over in his head. Then he finished the sentence Tom could not.

"Kiss Mary Ellen for you," Sully whispered. "I'll tell Fanny to kiss your new baby for you, Tom." He passed his hand gently over Tom's eyelids, closing them. His musket lay upon the ground next to him, but Tom's Henry was there also. He picked it up and checked the cartridge. Several unused rounds of ammunition remained. In Tom's pack he found more ammunition for the Henry, along with Fanny's address in New York and paper on which to write. He also found seven dollars, which he would put inside the letter, too.

"God bless you, Tom," Sully said. "I didn't understand why you took the trouble to show me how to use this rifle. Now I know." He knelt down beside Tom's body and recited the few words he knew of the Lord's Prayer, then stood and wiped his swollen eyes with his tattered sleeve. In his heart and soul, he was certain of one thing.

He would not die today, thanks to his friend, Tom Wilson.

3

The flat on the second floor of the building at 235 Mulberry Street, situated in the very crook of Mulberry Bend's elbow, didn't distinguish itself from any other, except perhaps for the number of children who lived there. Martha Score passed out crusty bread topped with a piece of dried beef to the five children old enough to eat it, and mixed porridge for the four who weren't. She had drawn a pail of water from the public faucet downstairs earlier that morning, and prepared tea for the children to drink with their lunch.

When they finished eating, she sent the older children outside to play among the peddlers and thieves, and the younger ones took a nap. Martha prepared a bottle of warm goat's milk for her newest—and youngest—visitant, a child named Mary Ellen, just over twelve weeks old. This alert, wispy-haired infant didn't want to sleep, and Martha didn't mind one bit. She enjoyed caring for the little ones.

As Mary Ellen lay in her lap, Martha ran her fingers across the smooth skin of the baby's plump cheeks. Her big, curious eyes took in everything around her, and occasionally they would linger on Martha for a moment before moving on to other things new to her.

The second morning of Mary Ellen's stay, as Martha cradled her in her arms, the baby sought to suckle her breast, and to her amazement, Martha had pulled aside the fabric of her dingy blouse and given her nipple to her. As Mary Ellen's mouth found it, and her little hands pressed against her breast, Martha felt guilty and elated at the same time.

There was no milk to be taken from these breasts; there never had been. Still, a longing within her needed to know what it felt like to hold and nurse a child. Martha closed her eyes as the baby suckled, her heart aching for what would never be. She cried along with Mary Ellen, her own painful sorrow felt along with the infant's disappointment that these useless breasts would not feed her.

Martha Score, now twenty-six years old, had finally admitted to herself after two years of fruitless marriage that she would never be able to bear children. Her husband, James, whom she loved with all her heart, had known it also. He left her one horrible day without uttering a word—but then, words were hardly necessary, were they? Could she blame him for wanting a family with his wife? She didn't. She blamed herself.

She had been a good mother to James's three children. They loved her, too, and all of them cried the day he packed up their things. Their mother died from diphtheria only a year before Martha and James were married, and Martha filled the void in their lives, caring for them as if they were her own. The youngest had been four, the oldest, six. Standing in the window watching them leave, Martha had never felt more alone than on that day.

Martha had always been a pretty girl, with a small but full figure that men favored. She also had ringlets of light brown hair, hazel eyes, and smooth olive skin. Despite all these attributes, she was nothing more than an ornament for viewing and toying with, for she could not conceive a child. This made her not want to be touched, for on the inside, she felt deformed.

Following James's departure, she met with such difficult times that she considered prostitution as a means of supporting herself, but in the end could not bring herself to participate in such a servile profession. Her only real skills were sewing and cooking, and one day, while she was searching for work as a seamstress, an acquaintance mentioned that taking in children for a fee could supply her a decent wage—especially if she took in many of them.

She had begun immediately, initially soliciting to women who worked at the hotels in town. Now she had been doing it for two full years. It didn't take long before the need to look for new children to take in was replaced by word-of-mouth, and Martha soon found herself turning children away.

Despite the poverty around her and the rundown condition of the building in which she lived, the work provided her a decent living, and the children who stayed in her care received the best that she could provide. It was wise to keep her distance emotionally, trying not to become too attached to the children, but inevitably, some of them captured her heart.

Like little Mary Ellen. She was so warm, so new, the youngest she had taken in for some time. She quickly found herself pretending she was her own baby, and when she held her and rocked her, Martha could almost allow herself to believe it.

* * * * *

June 1864

Fanny had not seen Mary Ellen for over a week. She intended to go to Mulberry Street to see Martha Score and find out how well she tended to the children she kept, but her work hours were long, and she finished the days exhausted. The constant pain in her full breasts added to her discomfort, and her exhaustion was compounded by the fact that Mr. Gilmour had been quietly making lewd comments and improper advances toward her. She was a respectable, married woman, and though she was frightened of making him angry, Fanny managed to steer clear of him and avoid his confrontations. And she thought the time he admonished her about Mary Ellen had been bad!

It made her feel sick to her stomach when Mr. Gilmour commented on the size of her breasts or the roundness of her bottom.

"Ignore him, sweetheart," Alanna had replied when Fanny told her about it. "He's a perfect fool who probably hasn't had a beautiful woman in all his life!"

"And I'm to suffer for that?" At nearly fifty and not very attractive, Alanna wasn't—and likely, never had been—the object of the superintendent's desire.

"It's not like the men on the street, Alanna. I don't mind a tip of the hat or a smile in the slightest! It feels absolutely dirty!"

"You'll simply tell Thomas when he returns, and he'll punch the vile man in the nose," Alanna laughed.

"Oh, I like that," Fanny had replied. "I *do* like that!"

Fanny wrung the rinse water from the bed sheet, then hung it carefully from the line that strung from one side of the small courtyard to the other. This was the area she most loved to work, as the sun could find her there and it was an area that Mr. Gilmour rarely visited. She usually encountered him in the hallways and rooms. The rooms were the worst, as he was more aggressive when he knew nobody else was about. Thank goodness she was a laundress, not a chambermaid!

Fanny's mood faded again when she pondered the fact that a month had gone by since she last received a letter from Thomas. That one contained forty-seven dollars, most of which went to pay Mr. Kelsko's increased rent payment of fourteen dollars per month. Fourteen dollars! It was only a dollar less than she made in a whole month at the St. Nicholas! She had sent two months advance payment to Martha Score through Alanna, and after paying an equal amount of board, she had been left with only three dollars with which to buy food. She missed Mary Ellen terribly, but it became more clear each day that she would not have been able to survive and take care of her, too.

She stepped back into the building, and noticed it was after six o' clock, the end of her shift. She had begun work at eight that morning, but the work was constant, and when Mr. Gilmour wasn't around, the hours flew by. She dreaded the walk home; not because she was frightened of the city, but because her feet already ached by then from being on them all day. The thirty minutes it took to walk home could seem as long as the entire ten hours of work! The omnibus was out of the question, as even a short bit could mean the difference between a meal and no meal, or a lighted lamp and darkness.

Fanny left the hotel, stepping onto the ever-busy streets of New York. A handsome couple strolled by her, the gentleman wearing a stovepipe hat, along with a dashing, store-bought suit. His hair was slicked back, and Fanny could smell the fragrant macassar oil as he passed. The lady with him wore a fashionable Zouave jacket with its military-style braiding, and beneath that, a lovely red silk, ankle-length dress. Her hair was done in a chignon, the silk net over it matching her dress perfectly, and curls of her dark, shiny hair hung over her ears.

This was a society couple, the kind whose noses usually stayed pointed toward the sky, and who had little to say to someone like Fanny. Still, she enjoyed watching them, imagining where they must be going, and what they talked about as they strolled along.

As she passed, she smiled at a lamp lighter who kept pace with her as he began his rounds. She watched as the young man hooked his ladder on the lamp-irons, ran up and ignited the lamp, then scurried back down to repeat the process on the next lamp.

There were no lamps on Fanny's street, so nights in the alley remained dark unless a lighted carriage happened by, or perhaps a policeman with his lantern, trying to cast illumination upon a runaway thief or ruffian. She thought the lamps were romantic and remembered walking with Thomas along the boulevard next to Central Park one evening, the lamps flickering in the light wind, the many extravagant coaches passing by carrying unseen passengers of unimaginable wealth.

She and Thomas had talked about how they would one day live in one of the states like Virginia, of which Thomas had spoken, and he would grow so many different kinds of vegetables , she wouldn't even presume to try to name them all. Potatoes. He would surely grow potatoes like his father and his grandfather before him. He would be so proud.

To her surprise, she realized she was already home. She stopped at the mailbox, opened it, and saw a letter inside. Finally! It had to be from Thomas! She plucked it from the box, looked at it, then furrowed her brow. The envelope was the same, but the handwriting wasn't, and Thomas's name wasn't on it either.

It was from a man named Ryan Sullivan. Her heartbeat rose to her throat as she carried the letter up the stairs and into her apartment. Fanny walked into her room, removed her light summer wrap, and dropped into the only chair she and Thomas owned. It was the chair in which she sat when she sewed, and it was the chair she used when she nursed Mary Ellen.

Her precious Mary Ellen. Fanny looked at the envelope again, afraid to open it, her fingernails white from gripping it so tightly. Tears rolled down her cheeks. She didn't need to open the letter to know what it meant, but she had to read it for herself. With shaking hands, Fanny tore the envelope open and her eyes fell upon the uneven handwriting of Private Ryan Sullivan, Union

Army. This letter, which had arrived faster than many of the rest, was dated three weeks earlier:

May 7, 1864
Dear Mrs. Wilson,

I will call you Fanny, because that is the name I heard Tom use when he spoke about you. My name is Ryan Sullivan, and as your husband's friend, I believe I need to tell you that yesterday he was killed in battle. I met your husband at Brandy Station, Virginia only a short time ago, but war can make time pass slowly. While those long hours passed, I came to know a lot about Corporal Tom Wilson. I learned he was a good man, a man who loved his wife and new little daughter more than anything else in this world. Writing this now is like writing a friend, for in his words and thoughts I came to know you pretty well. When he talked about you, he would smile and go on for hours. I didn't mind. It gave me a hankering for a good, loving wife myself. Fanny, though I was a new soldier, Tom treated me with respect. I can say without any question that he was my best friend and the soldier I most respected in this great Army, including General U.S. Grant.

Tom was a man of courage and dedication, and he displayed those traits on the battlefield right up until the second he died. For that, I owe him my life. I made a foolish error, and was at the mercy of two Confederate soldiers. Tom drew their muskets away from me and saved my life, he himself dying in the process. I killed the rebel who shot Tom, Fanny. Just in case you wanted to know.

I sent you all the money in his pack, and I believe you will receive a pension, if that comforts you some. Before he died, Tom asked me to tell you that he loves you, and to have you give Mary Ellen a kiss for him.

I'll miss him a lot, Fanny. He really was my friend, and

friends are harder to come by as the years pass. I suppose I don't have anything more to say, except that I'm sorry.

And please, give Mary Ellen a kiss for me, too.

Thoughtfully,
Ryan Sullivan

Fanny let the letter slip from her fingers onto the floor, and slumped in the chair. Her loving Thomas was dead, and she and Mary Ellen were alone in the world. Fanny's heart palpitated as a sudden panic overwhelmed her. She sprang from the chair and ran toward the door. She had to see Mary Ellen *now.*

Tears streaming down her flushed cheeks, she flew down the steps two at a time, charging out into the alley below, where the shadows of twilight tucked themselves into every corner. The sun had dropped behind the multistory buildings, and a gloom similar to the one in her soul consumed the last light of day. She ran, despite her aching feet. She ran to escape the tragedy that had befallen her.

Fanny ran because she didn't know what else to do.

She kept on until she could run no more, then slowed to a walk as she crossed Elm, then finally, Centre Street. The night draped itself over the city now, and the tiny crescent moon did little to penetrate the darkness. A slurred voice came from somewhere off to her right as a hand reached out from behind an ash barrel to brush across her ankle. Fanny screamed and started to run again, having no idea where she was until she reached Baxter Street, where the warrens of Mulberry Bend loomed before her. She should be afraid, but grief blurred all logic. She needed to find her daughter, needed to hold Thomas' child in her arms.

She reached Bayard and turned right, her lungs burning in her chest. Her legs trembled as she turned down Mulberry Street and slowed to a walk. The sidewalks alongside the brick-paved street were littered with overflowing ash cans and slimy vegetable husks and sausage skins, and the stench was horrid, stronger than she remembered the day she walked by. There were several shopkeepers pulling in the last of their wares for the night before retiring to the back rooms to sleep.

In the crowded tenement buildings that loomed over her on both sides of the street, the lower floors were makeshift stores of varying kinds, the many signs advertising services such as horseshoing, knife sharpening, tailoring, and blacksmithing. As Fanny drew by some of the shop windows, she saw rotted vegetables in crates—probably taken from the trash barrels of better markets that would no longer sell them—and bloody-aproned butchers worked late in their shops, carving meats whose animal origins were a mystery when compared with those sold in the upscale butcher shops of the city proper. Here, in the heart of the slums, the smell pressed in on Fanny, permeating her nostrils like a wretched perfume, making her stomach churn.

Thomas's voice echoed in her head, though he had never spoken the words. *Find Mary Ellen. Find our daughter, Fanny, and bring her home.*

Mary Ellen was here somewhere, but the many dilapidated buildings were as large as hers, yet no space separated them from each other, and there were endless rows of them. Her little girl could be anywhere. She had been foolish to come here. The tears came again, and as she struggled to choke them down, Fanny heard the helpless wail of a baby coming from the building behind her.

She turned and rushed up the steps of the building at 237 Mulberry, and screamed, "Mary Ellen! Mrs. Score, are you here? It's Fanny Wilson!" Spinning around in circles, she screamed, "Bring my baby to me, please! I miss her so much, please bring her to me!" The baby continued to cry, and a moment later, another infant's frustrated cries could be heard.

Fanny fell to her knees on the dirty floor of the hall. It was not Mary Ellen. Indeed, she could hear children crying everywhere, now that she was inside. As she listened, she realized it sounded as if there were a thousand babies in that very building, crying, one and all. Sobbing heavily, she turned and walked back down the stairs, holding the rail for support. A rat scurried across the step in front of her, but Fanny hardly noticed, so great was her depression. She collapsed midway down and buried her face in her hands.

When she looked up, a man crouched on the steps in front of her. He thrust his rough, unshaven face into hers, and his hand grabbed her neck, pressing her head back into the stairs. "What you doing here? You don't live here!" he said, the liquor on his breath horrid in her face.

Fanny couldn't draw a breath as he squeezed her windpipe with a firm hand. She trembled under his strong grip, all too aware of the roughness of his hands, the stench of decay rising through the reek of alcohol.

She tried to utter something to satisfy him. "Please . . . I'll . . . give you whatever . . . you want!"

"Shut up, you whore! I could lay you over them steps right now and— hey, what the hell is this?" His fingers curled around the gold chain that hung from her neck. The ring her mother had given her was in his hand. With one yank, he broke the chain.

"No!" she screamed. He slapped her hard in the face and she fell back, her head spinning. He held the chain and ring to his cloudy eyes as he examined it and said, "This is gold, ain't it? I ought to be able to get me a couple coins for —"

With a guttural scream, Fanny brought her foot up into the man's groin. Thomas had once told her that if she ever found herself being attacked, to use her foot, and use it hard. Oh, how right he had been! The man bellowed in pain and tumbled backward, his head smacking the hard floor at the bottom of the stairs. He lay there unmoving except for his rising and falling chest. Fanny watched him, holding her breath, until she was convinced he was unconscious.

Shaking off her dizziness, she scrambled to her feet, turning as a door behind her opened and a voice called out. Fanny ignored it as she stuttered down the steps toward the dazed drunkard and rolled him aside, her fingers ready to drag across his eyes should he move. He didn't. She saw the chain and ring beside him, snatched them up and charged out of the building, never once looking back. If anyone tried to attack her again, she knew what to do.

Fanny struggled against her exhaustion to keep up a quick pace until she was out of the Bend, the ring and chain held tightly in her balled fist. The tension that ran through her body eased as she reached her building, and after she climbed the steps to the second floor and entered her apartment, she locked the door behind her as Thomas had always told her to do.

Her face and neck were sore from the hoodlum's abuses, and as she slowly undressed, she felt her exhaustion. Without lighting a lamp, she sat on the bed she and Thomas once shared and stared into the darkness. She would not struggle against the many tears tonight; she would let them come. Thomas had been a good husband, an able soldier. He deserved her tears, a flood of them.

Tomorrow she would ask Alanna where to find Mary Ellen, and Fanny and her daughter would begin their lives again.

* * * * *

Before the start of her work shift at ten o' clock, Fanny walked to the St. Nicholas, dropping a letter off at the post office along the way. She would ask for the day off so she could spend it with her daughter.

"I don't know what to say, Fanny," Alanna said. "I'm so sorry."

Fanny nodded, knowing she would cry if she looked Alanna in the eyes. "I must go see Mr. Gilmour. Thank you for being a friend."

She turned and walked toward Gilmour's office. It would be the first time she stepped inside voluntarily.

"Come in, Fanny."

He sat at his desk smoking a pipe, a cloud of the smoke gathered at the top of the small, cramped room. Sweat glistened on his forehead, and he looked unusually cheerful. "Have a seat." His hand directed her toward a chair.

Fanny sat, uncomfortable. "I've come to tell you that my husband was killed in the war," she said. "I should like to take today off to spend the time with my daughter, if that's acceptable."

"I'm sorry to hear of your loss, Fanny," he said. "I hold the greatest respect for our soldiers, though I can't say I agree with their cause."

Fanny said nothing.

Tapping his pipe on the ashtray on his desk, Gilmour said, "I'll do better than just letting you have today off. He stood and leaned forward on the desk. "You shall take the rest of the week off. Of course you won't be paid for it, but I insist you take the time."

"I'm . . . afraid I couldn't afford that, Mr. Gilmour," she said, her heart sinking further.

He took her hands gently in his and said, "Now Fanny, you'll need this time to adjust to your loss."

Gilmour's concern made her uncomfortable. It wasn't his style, and each word he spoke seemed contrived. Fanny did not want too much time off work. It would only be more time to dwell on the fact that Thomas was gone forever. She shook her head. "I'll decide after today, Mr. Gilmour. Perhaps I'll need more time, but plan on having me back tomorrow."

As she turned to leave, Gilmour stepped forward and squeezed her buttocks hard with both hands. Fanny turned quickly to face him, disgusted. "Don't you ever touch me like that again!" she screamed. To her surprise, she slapped him on the face, hard. In her fury she would have hit him again, but Gilmour seized her wrist in mid-swing and gripped it tight. Fanny whimpered in pain, but he squeezed tighter and bent her arm backward, a malicious smile touching his lips.

"I'll overlook that idiotic move this time, Fanny," he said, rubbing his stinging face with one hand. "Have a pleasant rest, and I'll be here waiting when you return."

He released her arm with a little push and Fanny ran down the hall, a flood of tears blurring her vision. Alanna stepped out from one of the rooms, but Fanny ignored her, turning sideways and slipping past her. Alanna had already given her Martha Score's address, and she wanted only to get to Mary Ellen as soon as possible.

Suddenly a man stepped into the hall and Fanny ran dead into him. "Whoa!" he said, holding her arms, "You should slow down a bit."

Fanny pushed away from him, her eyes puffy and swollen. "Let me by," she said, her fists clenched. She would not be able to skirt past him as she had Alanna. He was quite a large man and he stood in the center of the hall, with no apparent intention of moving. He wore a tailored frock coat on his six-foot plus frame, and he filled it with little room to spare.

"Are you all right, Miss? Is there anything I can do?"

She tried to hold back her tears, but it was pointless. She stood before the gentleman and wept like a frightened child, but when she turned away, she saw Gilmour standing outside his office at the other end of the hall. His face was still angry and red, but now there was a different look there, too. Gilmour turned and walked away without looking back. Fanny tried to push past the big man again, but he wouldn't allow it.

"Now, now, Miss. I insist on knowing what's upset you so."

Through her tears Fanny replied, "I . . . don't wish to discuss it, especially with a perfect stranger. Please allow me to pass."

He laughed, and Fanny found it to be a kind laugh. "Just a moment now. Have you any idea who I am?" he asked, smiling.

She looked at him carefully for a moment, then realized she *did* know who he was. "Excuse me, sir," she said lamely, "but I didn't recognize you and—"

"Lindsey," he said, holding out his hand. "Douglas Lindsey. And you have to tell me what's disturbed you so, because I run the St. Nicholas. I can't have any of my guests upset now, can I? Now, what was that look you gave Mr. Gilmour there?"

Oh, my God, Fanny thought. *I'm not wearing my uniform and he thinks I'm a guest! Once he discovers I work here, he'll brush me off like an insect!* Better to come out with it and get it over with. "Excuse me, Mr. Lindsey, I'm not a guest of the St. Nicholas. I'm an employee."

Lindsey seemed taken aback for a moment, then he laughed aloud. "Oh, my, that's somewhat of a relief! I thought we'd lost a customer for life!" A moment later his face grew serious again. "No matter, though. I still want to know if and how Mr. Gilmour upset you, if you don't mind. We must keep our employees happy as well."

Fanny smiled and nodded, but didn't know what to say. This was Mr. Gilmour's boss, and if she were to report him, she may be fired. After all, Mr. Gilmour was *her* boss. "He's . . . well, nothing really, Mr. Lindsey. I've just received some news . . . about my husband." Her lip quivered, and she realized she was going to cry again. She tried, but couldn't stop the tears.

The man slapped his head and said, "I'm sorry, Madam. I've got a knack for upsetting women unintentionally." Lindsey removed a silk handkerchief from his breast pocket and gave it to Fanny. Suddenly, a shamed look swept over his face. He looked embarrassed for a moment, then said, "Oh, my. You must accept my apology. Was your husband a casualty of the war, Mrs.—"

She nodded, taking the handkerchief. Fanny's dress was black, and though not exactly proper for mourning, it was the only one she owned. She had put it on this morning without really thinking. "Wilson. I'm Frances Wilson." She held out her hand and he shook it gently. "And yes, you were correct. My husband was killed three weeks ago, Mr. Lindsey. I just learned of it yesterday."

"My deepest condolences," he muttered clumsily. "Inadequate as that may be. Mrs. Wilson, is there anything I can do for you?"

Fanny shook her head. "No, thank you. Mr. Gilmour offered me several days leave, but I'll need to work every day if I'm to keep my apartment."

"Did he not offer you paid time off?" Lindsey was clearly angry. His eyes flashed down the hall, but Gilmour was nowhere to be seen. Douglas Lindsey returned his gaze to Fanny.

"No, he said I wouldn't collect pay for the time off—"

"Nonsense. I specifically told my managing staff that war-related absentees were to be given up to a full week of paid leave if need be. Did you know the War Department is using this hotel as its headquarters?"

Fanny shook her head. She had noticed the soldier guarding the door to the employees entrance, but she wasn't familiar with wartime procedures. She assumed it was for the general safety of the guests.

"Well, it is, and they do pay for the usage of the building, though not much. I imagine the owner, Mr. Hawk, will allow me to recover some of your leave pay through them, if I so choose." He smiled again, and tossed his coarse brown hair away from his eyes. He didn't use macassar oil, and as a result, his unruly hair gave him a somewhat boyish look.

"I . . . don't know what to say, Mr. Lindsey. Thank you so much."

"Please, don't mention it. I'm sure your husband was a valiant soldier, and I feel I owe him a debt of gratitude. If I can repay it by helping you, then so be it." He appeared to be lost in thought for a moment, then said, "I'll take care of arranging your pay, and you can pick up your check on Monday as usual."

"Thank you again, Mr. Lindsey," Fanny said. "Thank you so very much."

4

Martha Score sat in a chair outside her building, keeping an eye on the children playing in the street. They played tag amidst the hustle bustle of the shopkeepers and patrons while the younger children napped on their mattresses inside. In Martha's arms, Mary Ellen worked on a bottle. As infants went, Martha was impressed with this one; the little girl never cried without good reason and usually slept through the night. More and more, she wished the child were her own.

"There we are Mary Ellen," she said. "That's my angel." She looked up to see a woman coming down the street toward her. Her dress, while not upper class by any means, was more upscale than normal for Mulberry Street. Martha smiled and rocked Mary Ellen as the pretty woman approached her.

"Hello," Martha said, smiling.

The woman did not respond. She leaned over, looked at the child in Martha's arms, and a look of relief formed on her face. "Mary Ellen!" she said, reaching for the baby.

Martha instinctively pulled the child away. Holding Mary Ellen close to her breast, she said, "I'm sorry Miss, but I've no idea who you are." But she *did* know. Judging from the woman's accent, she was English, and Alanna had told her that much about the child's mother.

"I am Mary Ellen's mother," she said, her voice trembling with anger. "I presume you're Mrs. Score, and if that is true, you know very well that Alanna Cavanagh brought her here for me, and I would appreciate it if you would give my child to me this instant!"

A dagger pierced Martha's heart. This woman was going to take Mary Ellen away. "You're Mrs. Wilson, then?" she asked.

"Yes, I am," she replied, softer than before. "Now please . . . give me my baby."

Martha held her up and Mrs. Wilson lifted the child from her arms. Drained and empty, Martha let go of the infant, admitting to herself that she had broken her own rule; she had grown to love the child. "I've taken good care of her, Mrs. Wilson," she said.

The woman didn't seem to hear, just held and kissed the child, tears in her eyes. Martha fidgeted and tried not to stare, but finally stood and put her arm around the woman's shoulders. "Please, don't cry. I told you I've taken good care of her. You can see she's perfectly well."

Mary Ellen's mother looked at her, dabbing her eyes with a blue silk handkerchief. "I know, Mrs. Score. She looks wonderful, just fine. I'm crying because her father . . . he's been killed in the war, and I've no idea what we'll do now."

The woman was beleaguered, and understandably so. Martha had felt just that way once, when her husband deserted her. She patted the woman's back and said, "Come upstairs for a bit, and we'll talk. You can see where Mary Ellen has been staying."

Before entering the building, Martha called to the street, "Children!" They stopped playing and looked at her. When she had their attention, she said, "I'll be right upstairs for a moment. You may continue to play, but don't wander past the butcher shop or the cobbler's on either side, do you hear?" The children all nodded, then played on.

Martha led the woman up the stairs and through the hallway, trying to see the building as Mrs. Wilson, or any stranger would. The wallpaper hung down in peeling ribbons, many of the aged floorboards were broken and shoddily patched. There was no trash on the floor, and Martha hoped Mrs. Wilson would recognize that this was one of the better buildings on the street. Many of them were rat infested and dangerous. Hers was not.

Martha opened the door, imagining she were seeing her flat for the first time. Lined side by side on the floor beneath the window were ten thin, bare mattresses. The first three were occupied by sleeping children ranging from two to four years old, but none awakened as Martha and her guest entered the room. At the top of each empty mattress was a cloth bag stuffed with straw, used as pillows. One thin blanket was folded neatly at the bottom of each empty mattress—Martha insisted that the older children take the responsibility to leave their beds neat—and the room itself was generally clean.

At one end of the room was a partition separating it from the rooms next door, and beyond that, a tiny kitchen that inhabitants of both rooms used.

"We'll need to speak softly, Mrs. Wilson, so as not to wake the children," Martha said. She looked around and added, "You can see I keep it tidy. I bathe Mary Ellen at least twice a week, and I keep her changed as well."

The woman nodded. "Yes, Mrs. Score, I see it's quite orderly. I was afraid . . . well, I had an experience on this street last night that was terrifying. I had just received news of my husband's death . . . and I feared all the worst about everything, especially Mary Ellen."

"You were here last night? In the Bend?" Martha shook her head. "Mrs. Wilson, that can be dangerous. Why, there's an alley nearby known as Bandit's Roost, and for good reason. Thieves and hoodlums gather there."

"I was frantic, Mrs. Score. When I got the news about . . . my husband, I just . . ." The woman's voice trailed off, and she squeezed her daughter to her breast.

"Please, call me Martha, and know that I . . . I understand how you feel. My husband, too, is gone." She didn't add that he deserted her. Better to let Mrs. Wilson believe she was a widow too, rather than a woman unworthy of a husband.

"Thank you, Martha. Please call me Fanny."

"Will you be taking Mary Ellen with you?" Martha had to ask. The pain of not knowing was unbearable.

Fanny seemed to ponder the question, then shook her head slowly, the sadness returning to her eyes. "No . . . not just now. I only knew I needed to hold my baby," she said. "I also needed to see that she was safe, and . . . cared for."

"Oh, Fanny, she is," Martha said, relieved. "I've cared for her as if she were my . . . well, I've treated her special." Martha was hesitant to say anything that might strike a possessive chord in Fanny Wilson. She didn't want to lose the child—or the income—over a foolish slip of the tongue.

"She is a special baby, Martha." Fanny looked at Mary Ellen and said, "I think she just smiled."

"I thought so myself, earlier today," Martha said. "What will you do now, Fanny?"

"I'm not at all sure. I've written some close friends in St. Paul, Minnesota to see if they have room for me. I'll need to save for my fare, though, and that . . . well, it may take some time. Will you be able to keep her a while longer?"

Martha's heart soared. "Of course, Fanny. I can keep her as long as you need." She hesitated, then added, "I'll need payment, Fanny. I know it will be difficult for you, but I'm afraid I wouldn't be able to afford to care for Mary Ellen without it."

Fanny nodded slowly. "Yes, I suppose there's some sort of widow's pension due me, but I haven't even begun to think about that yet. I'll want her to stay with you, Martha. Mary Ellen is in good care here, and your home is neat and clean."

After visiting a while longer, Fanny left. Martha stood in the window holding Mary Ellen and watched her walk away. She liked Fanny Wilson. Knowing she was a good woman would make it less painful when she eventually came back to take Mary Ellen home.

* * * * *

As Fanny walked away from Martha Score's apartment, she glanced back. Martha was still visible in her window, cradling Mary Ellen in her arms, and the knowledge that she was a decent, well-intentioned woman soothed Fanny. She also shared a common bond with Martha—she lost her husband, too. She was surrounded by slums, but Martha was a sincere woman, her own flat clean and well-kept. The older children Martha cared for listened to and obeyed her. When Fanny left, all of them were still in the street, well within the limits Martha set earlier. It was a relief to have met her. Her feelings of guilt for leaving Mary Ellen eased considerably, she could now stop worrying about her so much. Her daughter was in good hands.

As she turned down Franklin Street, she heard the familiar cry of the street vendors selling newspapers and bread, and her fingers stroked the fine silk handkerchief she still clutched in her hand. A young, dirty-faced boy appeared on the sidewalk outside a place identified as *Murphy's Pub.* "Come on in and have a drink, lady," he said.

Fanny glared at the boy and stepped around him, then stopped. She could use something to calm her nerves. She'd been through a lot, after all, and a bit of alcohol might just be what she needed to forget her pain for a while. She turned back toward the boy.

"Are women allowed in this pub?"

"Sure, Murph lets 'em all come in. Even proper ladies like yourself," the boy said with a grin.

"I believe I will, young man," she said, and pushed the door open, stepping into the small, gloomy room lined with small, square tables. Tobacco smoke swirled in the air as she walked in, and the low ceiling gave Fanny a nervous feeling she hadn't experienced since she first stepped down into the close-quartered steerage compartment of the *India Star*, the vessel that brought her to America.

She turned to leave.

"Wait! What do you want, m'lady?" the bartender asked.

Fanny stopped and looked at him. His eyes were indeed, smiling. "Why, I supposed I'd like a drink," she replied.

The bartender rolled his eyes. "Aye, I *know* that. What kind of a drink is it you'd be wantin'?"

Fanny shrugged. "What do you suggest?" She found she liked listening to the Irish bartender's voice. It reminded her of Thomas.

"Well, now. That depends entirely upon what you're aimin' for. If you're celebratin', and I don't think so by the looks of you, then it would be champagne. On the other hand, if you've got a heavy heart, then maybe a martini would suit you."

Fanny smiled and said, "Martini, then."

The bartender prepared the drink. "I'll go easy on the vermouth, then. You'll want to ease the pain as quickly as you can."

"Thanks, uh . . ."

"Terry Murphy. And you better call me Terry."

"Thank you, Terry. I'm Fanny Wilson. It's nice to make your acquaintance."

He gave her the drink and Fanny took a sip. Her eyes filled with water and she choked the strong drink down with a gasp.

"First one's the hardest," Terry said, laughing.

She looked at him and smiled, his laugh so reminded her of Thomas. Not much more about him, though. His curly hair was almost the same color as Thomas' but the top of Terry's head was completely bald, and he had an overgrown mustache. The space between his two front teeth also set him apart from Thomas, but he was every bit as cheerful, and that made Fanny feel good.

He finished preparing the drink and slid it to her. "Try this, lass."

To her surprise, the second one *was* easier. The third one was child's play.

* * * * *

The weeks passed, and Fanny found it more and more difficult to concentrate on her work. Since Thomas died, everything else in the world seemed unimportant. She carried the sheets, newly dried on the line, to the open counter by the kitchen and put them in a neat stack. Across the room, she saw the same stool that Thomas once used as he pried open the hotel's oysters, and the tears began anew. She dropped into a chair just inside the kitchen and sobbed.

Ellis Gilmour passed by the kitchen and she hurriedly got up. He mumbled something Fanny didn't understand, then walked off in a huff. He had not spoken harshly or made any advances whatsoever toward her since the day she stumbled into Mr. Lindsey, and she was relieved. Apparently, whatever he'd said to him had done the trick. She noticed Mr. Gilmour was still harsh with Alanna, though. Maybe she would speak to Mr. Lindsey about that, too.

Fanny wondered for the hundredth time when she and her daughter would once again sleep under the same roof.

* * * * *

51

January 1865

"C'mon . . . just one more . . . that's wonderful!"

Martha laughed as Mary Ellen stumbled into her open arms and said in her small voice, "Da!"

"Hello yourself, little one! Your first steps and look how far you've gone!" She squeezed her and picked up the eleven-month-old. Mary Ellen struggled in her arms. "Oh, I see you want to do that again," Martha said, laughing. "There'll be enough time for that later, of course."

Martha let her go anyway, and she tottered across the floor and fell upon one of the mattresses. Martha laughed, but Mary Ellen didn't think it was funny in the least. The child wanted to cry, but couldn't seem to force the tears as she struggled to right herself. Martha helped her back to her feet and she wobbled toward the door with short, unsteady steps.

"Now that you've begun to walk you're bound to become troublesome, aren't you? I'll have to put the chairs in front of the stove again, that's a certainty. I won't have you burning those curious little hands of yours."

Martha's thoughts drifted to Fanny, as they always did when the little girl achieved another milestone. When she first started to crawl, three months ago, Martha was surprised to find that she was ambiguous about Fanny seeing it. She was so proud of Mary Ellen's accomplishments and wanted Fanny to share in them, yet she always worried that each visit would end with Fanny taking away the child she had come to love so deeply. And yet, Fanny hadn't mentioned—not even in passing—that she might take Mary Ellen home soon.

She always seemed so happy when she first arrived for her visits, then became melancholy after spending a few moments with her daughter. Martha knew what it was—she had seen it all too often. Fanny Wilson was feeling guilty for having left her child for so long, and she realized that Mary Ellen now loved Martha more than her own mother.

The toddler wasn't tiring. She would walk until her wobbly little legs collapsed, then cry out in frustration, plop her hands flat on the floor, and stand up to do it all over again, a six-toothed grin spreading from ear to ear.

Martha grinned with her.

* * * * *

Fanny was inebriated, her speech incoherent. Martha reached out to catch her before she fell down in the hallway. Martha almost gagged when Fanny fell into her arms. Her breath reeked of alcohol.

"What in God's name has happened to you, Fanny? Your face . . . the bruises! And you stink of liquor!"

"Of course I do," Fanny said, laughing. "I've been to Terry's pub. He's my friend, you know, Terry Murphy. He's a very nice Irish—"

Martha took her arm and pulled her inside her apartment. "You don't need friends like him Fanny, and please don't make a scene for my neighbors." Martha led her to a chair, sat her down, and looked at Mary Ellen, who had stopped playing with her doll, her eyelids heavy. Fanny hadn't spotted her yet, but it couldn't be long before she would. Martha hoped Mary Ellen would fall asleep before Fanny got the idea of holding her in her condition. She would have to forbid it.

Fanny sat quietly, swaying slightly in the chair. She stared out the dirty windows toward the buildings across the street and spoke softly, as though to herself: "I've . . . lost everything that's ever meant anything to me. First it was my family, then Thomas. Now I'm losing my daughter. I must have angered God horribly to receive such punishment."

"What do you mean?" Martha asked. "You're not losing Mary Ellen."

Fanny nodded, her mind seemingly elsewhere. "Andrew and I could have been so happy," she said. "Oh . . . did I tell you about Andrew?"

Martha shook her head and poured Fanny a glass of water, who took one sip of it and put on the table.

"When I was seventeen, I thought Andrew was my prince, but it wasn't true," Fanny muttered, staring into space. "He started seeing another girl, and left me. He was supposed to be my suitor. The whore he betrayed me with was his cousin!"

Martha stood and brushed off her apron. "I have to speak to you, Fanny, but you must be in a better state of mind before I do. It's important, and you mustn't miss one word." Martha took her by the arm and lifted her up. Fanny conceded reluctantly, allowing Martha to help her to the bed. Once on the mattress, Fanny drifted off, sleeping for just over two hours.

It was seven o' clock in the evening when Fanny awoke. "Come now, up we go," Martha said, leading Fanny back to the table where she could sit up and drink a glass of water. "Feeling better?"

"Yes, I think so," Fanny said. "A drink would be good, though."

"I want to talk to you about that, dear. If you care about your daughter, you'll listen to what I have to say." She refilled Fanny's water glass from her pitcher.

"Oh, Martha . . . I've lost everything. Everything that's ever meant anything to me except little Mary Ellen, and I've done such a dreadful job of caring for her. If I take her . . . I'm afraid I'll destroy her life as well!"

"You said that already, though you probably don't remember it. Besides, that's nonsense—"

"But it's not, Martha! I know how you feel about Mary Ellen, and seeing how you take care of her, I . . . I hoped you would keep her until . . . well, I don't know. Until there's some sense of order back in my life."

"Order doesn't come from a bottle, Fanny. The drink will do nothing but destroy you—and Mary Ellen. If you really, *really* want a fruitful life, you have to stop it."

Fanny stared at the floor, no longer a handsome woman, her eyes dark and red, her hair tousled, skin pale. Martha felt for her, despite the fact that she brought it all on herself. "Dear, you're not the first person to be seduced by drink," Martha said. "You can overcome it, but it's going to take a stronger will than I'm seeing now. Now, as for Mary Ellen," she glanced at the little girl who had fallen asleep on one of the mattresses, "I know I can take proper care of her, just as I have been doing, but how will I support her if you lose your situation? I won't be able to manage without money from you."

"Oh, my! That's what I've been meaning to give you." Fanny reached into her tattered drawstring purse and withdrew an official-looking slip of paper. "This is my widow's relief ticket, Martha. I'm paid four dollars every two weeks on it, and it should serve to support Mary Ellen for as long as you require. I want you to take it." Fanny held it out and Martha took it from her.

"By giving this to me you're saying you'll be able to survive on your wages from the hotel. What happens if they let you go?"

"I have my situation at the St. Nicholas for the moment, Martha. If I do my best to stay out of Mr. Gilmour's path, I may be able to keep it for a long while."

"I . . . I know it's not my place, but Fanny . . . have you been indulging in liquor as a regular habit?"

The guilt returned to Fanny's face. She sighed and said, "I needed . . . well, something to keep mind from my hardships, Martha. Something to help me with the pain of losing Thomas until I was ready to face it myself. I'll put the liquor behind me now, I promise."

"See that you do, Fanny. I wouldn't want Mary Ellen to become an orphan." Fanny seemed to be thinking clearly enough to know that Mary Ellen was better off with Martha. With the relief ticket in her possession, she wouldn't have to rely on Fanny for payment. That was better security than she had with some of the other children.

Suddenly, Fanny reached out and hugged Martha tight. "Thank you, Martha. Mary Ellen loves you, and you're good to her. Thank you for loving her."

"No matter how much I love her, I couldn't do it without the money paid by this ticket. You just get back on your feet and come get her."

Fanny looked over and said, "Oh, my. Was she sleeping here the whole time?"

Martha nodded. Fanny appeared to be adequately recovered to allow her to hold the child now. Fanny lifted Mary Ellen from the mattress and hugged her tightly to her breast. Martha stood conspicuously close to her, prepared to catch the child if the woman had a fainting spell or started to drop her. When Fanny finally sat down, Martha relaxed.

Fanny sang the words, her voice a bit harsh, but the meaning sweet nonetheless:

> *There will come a handsome Prince*
> *on a grand horse white as snow.*
> *He shall gaze upon your grace*
> *and all his love bestow.*

"My mother used to sing that song to me," she said, tears glistening in her eyes. She kissed Mary Ellen softly on the cheek, then rocked her in her arms for nearly fifteen minutes before putting her back to bed. As she placed her on the mattress and covered her, she stroked her cheek and said, "I promise I'll overcome my hardships, Mary Ellen. We'll sleep under the same roof again soon."

Fanny reached to the back of her neck and unclasped a chain upon which a ring hung. She put it in Martha's hand, closing her fingers over it and squeezing them tight. "Keep this, Martha. If there comes a time you need money for Mary Ellen's care, I want you to sell it for whatever you can. It belonged to my mother, a gift she gave me before I left England."

Martha looked at it. "You'll get back on your feet, Fanny. I have faith."

"I hope so," Fanny said, walking toward the door. "I truly hope so."

5

It was nearly ten o' clock on a Wednesday night, and the pub was slower than usual. Terry Murphy wiped the splintered counter top as an Irishman named Joseph Gibbon sat at the bar and downed another whiskey. He rubbed a hand over his red stubble and ordered another.

Terry obliged. "There you are, lad. Drink up, now. You've got to help me make my rent payment."

"Aye, thanks," said Gibbon. "Whiskey's good for the soul." He looked at his reflection in the foggy mirror behind the bar and added, "Not so good for the eyes, though, aye, lad?"

"You had it right the first time," Terry said. "My business is to soothe the souls of men. The eyes are their own problem."

The door opened, and Fanny stepped into the pub.

"Well, I nearly forgot about the souls of women," Terry said. "Speaking of them, here's one of my favorites."

"Ah, women. Praise 'em," Gibbon said, turning to spy the stranger who had come in. His eyes followed Fanny as she walked in and chose the stool two down from Gibbon.

"Hello, milady," said Gibbon. "You cap the climax, that's a fact."

Her face drawn and sad, she managed only a slight smile at his comment. Terry removed a dirty glass from the bar and wiped the counter in front of her. "Joseph Gibbon, this is a good friend of mine, Fanny Wilson."

"I'm losing my touch, Terry," Gibbon said. "Usually women want to know what in the devil it means when I say they cap the climax."

Fanny looked directly at the Irishman. "That's exactly what I presumed."

Gibbon laughed. "What did you *presume*?"

"I presumed that you *usually* say such things—to women in particular." She turned to the bartender. "Terry, I'll have an Apple-Jack, please."

"Something's wrong with you," Terry said, as he got the brandy. "Time to tell me what it is before I get your drink."

Gibbon kept his eyes on Fanny.

"Get the drink," she said. "I was let go from the St. Nicholas today. Mr. Gilmour wanted something more than my situation called for and I had enough of it. I gave him a good kick where a man fears it most."

"I thought you had an ally in that other fellow . . . what was his name?" He put the snifter in front of her.

"Mr. Lindsey," Fanny said. "Yes, I thought I did, but he was transferred out of the St. Nicholas last week, and that was Mr. Gilmour's cue to have his way with me." She swirled the brandy around in the glass, then took a swallow.

"And you really kicked him there, eh?"

Smiling, Fanny nodded.

Terry clapped his hands. "Congratulations, darling! It felt good, didn't it? You're something special, I'll give you that. If you need to earn some money, perhaps I could come up with something for you to do here."

"That would be wonderful!" Fanny said. "I hadn't any idea what I would do."

"I'm sorry to interrupt you two, but I have to say that Fanny is just a dandy name. It's Frances, I presume?"

Fanny nodded. "Indeed it is."

"Well, Frances. Seeing as how you've got a fine Irish name, why don't you allow me to pay this kind man for your first drink of the evening."

"But I'm not Irish."

"I know, you're English. That doesn't matter in the least."

Fanny looked hesitant to accept his offer, but Gibbon wasn't about to give up. "Please, Frances. To celebrate the end of the war."

Fanny's face drooped as she turned toward the drink Terry placed in front of her. She picked it up and drank the glass empty. "There's nothing *about* the war I care to celebrate. Another, please Terry."

Gibbon eyed the empty glass, then glanced at Terry. "I'll get both of 'em, Terry. I'm ready for another whisky myself."

"Comin' up."

* * * * *

The night wore on and Terry occasionally glanced over at Fanny and Gibbon, who had moved to a small table in the corner an hour earlier. Just since their move, he'd delivered five glasses of straight Old Orchard whiskey and six Apple-Jacks to the table, and both of them were good and liquored.

Terry liked Joseph Gibbon well enough. He was a friendly man, and he drank enough to be a strong asset to the groggery. He came in later in the evening than Fanny usually did, but Terry was surprised the two had never crossed paths before now. It looked to him like they hit it off, by the way they were hunkered down talking. From what he saw, they might have even brushed lips a couple of times.

Around midnight, they stood to leave. Fanny had a good sized brick in her hat, but Gibbon helped her toward the door as Terry looked on. "You two gonna be all right?" he asked.

"Not only all right," he said, "we're gonna get married. That's what."

Terry's mouth fell open. "What's that you say, man?"

"She says I remind her of her first husband."

Terry laughed. "Good luck, man. I reckon you'll have a hard time finding a justice of the peace tonight, though. And by tomorrow the idea might lose some of its appeal to both of you."

"Aye, you could be right, and it might be a problem," slurred Joseph Gibbon, "if my brother-in-law wasn't in the marrying business. He's open all hours to his family. Oh, by the way, she'll no longer need that job you offered. I'll take care of this one from this day on."

Terry laughed aloud as the drunken couple swung open the door and disappeared into the darkness of the early New York morning.

* * * * *

June 1865

The war between brothers had played out its final hours. In March, the battle lines had broken and the Confederates began their retreat. On April 9th, Robert E. Lee surrendered his army to Grant, conceding defeat. Now it was June, and though some skirmish fighting at sea continued, the outcome of the war had already been decided.

Thousands of surviving infantry soldiers returned home to New York as huge crowds gathered at the Soldier's Relief Agency at the corner of 7th and 3rd Streets. Wounded soldiers and widowed wives filed in to collect money with which to support themselves and their families.

Among them, at the front of the line, was Martha Score, who held Mary Ellen in her arms and listened with disbelief as she received yet more bad news. Mary Ellen, whose mother had not been to visit her daughter in over two months, squirmed to be let down.

"I'm sorry, Madam. This ticket is no longer valid," said the one-armed officer behind the desk.

Martha shook her head. "That can't be, sir. You must be mistaken. This ticket is quite valid and has been paying me the sum of four dollars twice per month for some time now."

The tall, bearded man flipped the pages of a blue notebook on the counter and squinted his eyes at what was scribbled on the pages inside. "It says here you've married again. In April." He looked up. "Once you marry, the ticket no longer pays." He slammed the book closed. "If you married in April, you may be required to return a month's pay to us, Madam."

"I've not married, sir," Martha insisted.

He rolled his eyes impatiently and flipped the notebook open again. "Are you Fanny Wilson, wife of Corporal Thomas Wilson, now deceased?"

"No, I am not. I was given this ticket by Mrs. Wilson in order to care for her daughter, and I can guarantee you that she hasn't remarried—"

The officer interrupted. "Are you saying to me that you've been collecting government funds on a ticket belonging to someone else? Do you understand that is illegal? What is *your* name?"

The man's voice grew threatening and Martha was frightened. She glanced back and saw the line of people behind her—mostly widowed women—had grown quite long. Saying nothing, she turned and pushed her way quickly out of the building, rushing into the busy street. Martha walked with quick steps and didn't look back. If anyone pursued her, a glance in their direction may draw attention, and she would have enough trouble now without that.

God, what would she do? She now had only Mary Ellen and one other child in her care, for as the soldiers returned home, the need for her child care services had diminished. Two of the children's parents ceased payments to her, and never claimed their children. Martha did what she had to do; when she was absolutely sure they would not resume payments or pick them up, she took the children and their few belongings to the Department of Public Charities, telling them as much as she knew about their parents. Hopefully, the government agency would be able to find them. Otherwise, the poor children would end up in an almshouse.

Martha glanced behind her again, and now slowed to a walk. Nobody followed. She pictured her empty flat again, remembering when it bustled with the activities of children, and her purse always carried a few coins. As its mother took each child, Martha's financial concerns increased. Jason Shanahan's mother had told her she would be able to leave him with her only upon the condition that Martha accept half pay. She had agreed to the terms only because of the massive number of *baby farmers* in her neighborhood. These people were offering to care for children for much less than she, but their care was far inferior.

They would feed the children irregularly, and when meals were given, it would only be spoiled meat—if any at all—and stale bread. Some of these unfortunate children were even used in sweatshops to bring their keepers more money. Often, the care given the children amounted to nothing more than child slave labor. Martha would rather give up all of them than resort to that kind of inhuman treatment. At least in an almshouse the children would be well fed, and have some hope of being adopted by caring guardians.

When Martha reached her building, she climbed the first flight of stairs, looked behind her one last time, and knocked on the first door she came to. A man opened it. "Hello, Jack. I've come to fetch Jason."

"I'll get him for you, Martha." The man went inside, and Martha held Mary Ellen as she waited.

The front door downstairs flew open, and to Martha's surprise, Fanny Wilson stood in the doorway laughing hysterically. She could hardly stand up, and she was with a man in the same or worse condition. Jack returned to the door with the boy, but Martha pushed Mary Ellen inside and whispered, "Jack, please! You must take the children until I come back. Mary Ellen's mother is here, and she looks in a horrible state!"

"All right, Martha. They'll be here when you're ready for 'em." He took a quick glance downstairs. "You need any help?"

"I'll let you know if I do," she said. "Close the door, quickly!" The couple still hadn't noticed her, so Martha hurried up the stairs and into her apartment. Once inside, she paced back and forth, awaiting their arrival. What would she tell Fanny? She was obviously in no condition to take the child! And that man! He was as drunk as she was!

And then she knew what she would say. She had no choice.

Martha ran quickly around the apartment gathering up Mary Ellen's things and stuffing them beneath one of the mattresses. She smashed it down so it appeared normal and waited by the door as the racket in the hallway grew louder and louder. A few moments later, the loud knock came.

The door opened before she got to it. The couple fell face forward in a heap on her floor, and lay there giggling.

"Fanny! My God, where have you been?" Martha said.

Fanny looked up and smiled at Martha. "Well, I've remarried, for one thing," she slurred. "Martha, meet my husband . . . hmm, I can't think of his name right now, but you can ask him. He'll know." Fanny fell into another fit of laughter.

Martha had never seen anyone as drunk as the two in her apartment at that moment. "I searched for you, Fanny. I wanted to tell you . . . I have some terrible news to give you."

Fanny and her companion—or husband—climbed to their feet. He rested against the door frame and she rested against him. "Weeell, Martha what could be so awful? I've come to get my little Mary Ellen now. I want to introduce her to her new daddy."

"I need my shoes shined," the man bellowed. "Is she old enough to shine shoes?"

Fanny laughed and slapped him on the chest. "No, silly! She's just a little thing!"

Martha ignored them and walked into the kitchen. She would need to be convincing, and she was sure her expression would give her away if they could see her face. "Fanny, the typhus epidemic that swept through the city nearly two months ago . . . I—I don't know how to tell you this, but our little Mary Ellen was taken ill."

Forcing tears for Mary Ellen's sake, Martha sank into the lie she manufactured. As they rolled down her cheeks she turned toward Fanny, knowing she would be convincing now. "Mary Ellen died on the first day of May, Fanny . . . I tried so hard to reach you."

Fanny's lip trembled as she clasped her hands over her ears and screamed. She wailed until the man could take it no more.

"Shut up! For Christ's sake, Fanny, shut up!" He staggered to a mattress and fell down on top of it, rolling off onto the hard floor. "Stop that goddamned screaming, Fanny!"

Martha took Fanny in her arms and held her, shooting a disapproving glare at the drunken man. "I won't have you speaking to Mrs. Wilson that way, sir! Do you have any idea the pain she is feeling?"

"Let's get outta here," he said.

"Oh, God!" Fanny screamed. "What have I done? Why did I abandon my little girl?"

Holding her closer, Martha whispered, "God takes those He chooses and we have nothing to say about it. I . . . I tried to find you but you disappeared. I was afraid you were dead."

"I wish I was," she cried. "At least then I could . . . I could be with my daughter!"

Martha held Fanny for a long while, and after a quarter of an hour, the man who gave his name only as Joe insisted they leave.

Martha breathed a sigh of relief when they staggered out of her rooms and into the hallway. She closed the door behind them, sick from seeing Fanny mourn over Mary Ellen—even if the child was still alive. The pain Fanny felt was all too real, but it was her own fault. If only she could have stopped drinking.

Martha waited another half hour before going downstairs to get the children, just to be sure the couple had made their way out of the building. Jack opened the door looking haggard and relieved.

"I apologize for taking so long," Martha said. "Thank you for watching them. You don't know how much it means to me."

Jack Tyson gave her an odd look and smiled. "We *have* helped you with the kids before, Martha. There's no need to act like we saved your life." He laughed and closed the door, and Martha carried Mary Ellen with one arm, leading Jason by the hand up the stairs to her apartment. What Jack Tyson didn't know was he may have saved Mary Ellen's life by keeping her out of sight.

Once inside, Martha put Mary Ellen down. The toddler fell onto her bottom and started crying.

"Either you're tired or hungry," Martha said. "Hopefully your tired, since the food is running low." She unbuttoned and removed the little girl's light coat, then carried her to the mattress. She returned to the kitchen and dipped a bottle in the pail of water, then gave it to Mary Ellen. After a few moments of sucking, the child drifted off to sleep.

The relative warmth of spring had returned to New York City, and Martha was glad of it. The furnace downstairs remained in excellent working order through the winter, and had been kept well-stoked through the coldest months. The warmth drifted upward through the heat ducts fairly well, and Martha kept her own stove burning as much as she could afford. It became increasingly difficult to keep enough coal as temperatures dropped, for thieves were stealing it from the storage box each night. Not having to burn her stove would save Martha some money, and she could use all she could put her hands on.

Martha opened the drawer in the small bureau beside the kitchen table and removed the chain and ring Fanny had given her. Regretfully, she would have to sell them to feed Mary Ellen, not to mention herself. It would hurt to sell these things that belonged to Mary Ellen, for Martha realized the importance of having something—even only a small piece of jewelry—as a remembrance of those who loved you the most.

From her mother and father, she had nothing. According to all the records she could gather, her mother had been sent to an insane asylum when Martha was four and had died two years later from consumption. After her mother's death, her father had abandoned Martha and disappeared, and an overcrowded almshouse became her home for the next twelve years. Luckily, she had been a healthy six-year-old by that time, unlike the many sickly foundlings brought in from the streets each day. During those hard, lonely years, while she grew into a pretty young woman, she helped to care for the children, many of whom died soon after being rescued from the harsh, cold winters and brutally hot summers.

Martha put the chain around her neck so as not to lose it, knowing the few dollars she would collect from the sale of the items wouldn't last far beyond another month. Martha had no idea what she would do after the money was gone. With all the children to care for, she had not been to church for months, and maybe God needed to hear her prayers in a proper house of worship. She would take Mary Ellen and Jason on Sunday. She would have to be careful not to bump into Fanny.

Where her good fortune had begun to fail her, perhaps her God would not.

6

July 1865

Martha sat in the hot, stuffy office on Bond Street, holding Mary Ellen in her arms. The child was hungry and fidgety. The stale bread Martha had moistened with water to make it easier to eat was all gone. She had resorted to begging from the shopkeepers on the street, but they had seen their share of that. To give bread or money to Martha would encourage hoards of ragpickers to find their doorsteps, they claimed. Her neighbors, understanding of her situation, still had no way to help either. Many of them were in the same position, near starvation.

Fanny had never returned again, drunk or sober. She had believed Martha's story, and Mary Ellen's care had become Martha's sole financial responsibility.

To make matters worse, Mrs. Shanahan had removed Jason from Martha's care a week earlier. She surprised Martha with a visit, insisting Martha accept half of what was already half her usual pay, two dollars per month. Martha had grown angry then, telling the woman she could not even feed the child for that, much less be paid for her services as well. Mrs. Shanahan insisted she was under orders from her husband who was indulging in too much drink, and there was nothing she could do. There was no choice to be made. Martha refused. She had taken Jason that day, and with him, every last penny of Martha's income.

Mary Ellen's necklace and ring had only brought six dollars, and the money was already gone, spent on food not only for Mary Ellen, but for herself. It saddened and angered her to think she had sold the child's only remembrance of her mother, and for what? To be where she was now, doing what she was about to do.

"Uppy-down," said the sixteen-month-old. Mary Ellen didn't know which was up and which was down, so it was a word she developed to handle both needs. Martha put her down and she ran in circles around the tiny office of the Department of Public Charities and Corrections.

Martha smiled through her tears and watched her. Mary Ellen had lost many of her infant proportions; her legs were getting longer, baby fat disappearing. She was now very thin compared to just a couple of months ago. Martha worried it was for a lack of food. She fretted about it constantly, and it was another reason she was here.

Mary Ellen's hair was finally beginning to get longer—darker, too—and she just had to lay her fingers upon anything within reach. She had just stopped putting everything she found in her mouth, choosing to manipulate things with her hands instead.

As the door opened and the Superintendent of the Outdoor Poor, George Kellock stepped in, Martha wanted to scoop Mary Ellen up and run out of the office. But there was nowhere to run. She could no longer support the child properly. Martha would find a way to support herself, even if it meant prostitution. She would not expose Mary Ellen to that life, though. God would never forgive her that.

"Hello, Madam," Kellock said. "Please come into my office."

Though she'd met Mr. Kellock several times, he never seemed to remember her. A short man with a large mustache, spectacles and a nervous twitch in his left eye, Kellock made her feel insignificant and strangely uncomfortable.

"This child is in need of care I cannot provide her," Martha said, holding Mary Ellen's hand, keeping her from running around the modestly furnished office. "Her name is Mary Ellen, and her mother is nowhere to be found. Her father was killed in the war, a man named Wilson." Before long, she'd given him all the necessary information.

"Okay," he said, adjusting his spectacles, his left eye fluttering as if a mosquito plagued him. "Let me see if I have it all down correctly. Today is the seventh of July, and the child is . . . did you say sixteen or eighteen months?"

Martha shrugged. "Somewhere between there, I believe, sir."

He looked at Mary Ellen, who was pulling a paper from his desk. Martha took it and placed it back in the pile. "She's a good size," Kellock said. "I'll just put eighteen. Okay, you say her name is Mary Ellen Wilson. You've cared for her since May of '64, having received eight dollars per month until around three weeks ago. You've no idea where her mother is?"

"No, sir. I do not," she said. "Mrs. Wilson simply stopped payment and never returned for her."

"Anything else you know about the mother?"

"Just that her first name was Frances, and . . . well, I believe she may have died. A mutual acquaintance that I did not know very well said she heard of Mrs. Wilson's passing. I realize it's only hearsay, but . . . for one reason I tend to believe it; she loved this child dearly, and I can't imagine her leaving unless something became of her . . . you know what I mean."

Kellock nodded. "Do you know this person's whereabouts? Perhaps—"

Martha shook her head. "No, she's since moved away, and I've no idea where."

"Well, that leads us nowhere, I'm afraid," Kellock said. "I'll simply put down that the whereabouts of the parents of the child are unknown and there are no known relatives."

Martha nodded. At least she planted the thought in Kellock's mind, and they might not try to find Fanny. A woman in her condition could do the child no good whatever.

"Okay, then," Kellock said. "You're at 235 Mulberry, correct?"

Martha nodded and stood from her chair.

"There we are." He looked up. "I suppose that's all we need from you, Mrs. Score."

Martha cried as she took Mary Ellen's hand. She could have done nothing to stop the tears even if she wanted to. "What will you do with her?" she asked.

"She'll be checked by a doctor to make sure she's well," Kellock said. "If she is, she'll be sent to an almshouse—one capable of accommodating children, of course—and cared for until we can locate Mrs. Wilson or another suitable guardian."

"Mr. Kellock, I wonder if . . . I can have a moment alone to say good bye to Mary Ellen?" Her voice wavered.

He nodded. "I see no reason why not. Take all the time you need, Mrs. Score." He left the office and closed the door.

Martha knelt down and pulled Mary Ellen toward her. "Mama!" she said. Martha's tears began anew. "Yes, child. I'm your mother. In my heart I'm your mother."

"Mama-mama-mama"

Martha held her close, feeling the child's warmth. Mary Ellen wrapped her little arms around Martha's neck and mimicked her by holding on tight. It felt wonderful to be hugged by her, even if the toddler didn't know what it meant. "You're a beautiful, strong girl, Mary Ellen. Perhaps your mother will straighten out her pitiful life and come back for you someday." She placed her hands on Mary Ellen's cheeks and gave her a soft kiss on the lips.

The door opened, and one of Kellock's assistants came in. "Are you finished Mrs. Score?"

She nodded. The woman took Mary Ellen by the hand and led her away, and the little girl didn't look back. It was just as well. Martha watched her until she disappeared through the door at the end of the hall. Martha sobbed heavily now, and the receptionist at the front desk shifted in her chair, probably embarrassed to be a witness to her grief.

* * * * *

October 1865

John Connor, Jr. walked briskly along Fifth Street on his way to work. He was near completing his third year as a carpenter's apprentice and had only one more year to go before he could call himself a full-fledged carpenter and write his own ticket. He could do any of the work now, but Mr. Lewis, his crotchety old boss, insisted he wasn't a quarter as good as he thought he was.

It was hogwash and John knew it, yet he had little choice. The rules of apprenticeships, designed to maintain standards, were nearly chiseled in stone. He enjoyed his work, and he was close enough to the end of his apprenticeship that the distant glimmering light through the trees kept him pushing ahead.

The autumn morning was quite cold, but the nineteen-year-old was bundled up and warm. He whistled a perky tune, the steam from his music drifting behind him as he made his way down the sidewalk toward Mr. Lewis's house. Up ahead, he saw a woman wearing somewhat ragged clothing sitting on a public bench. As he passed her he nodded and said hello, but after taking six or eight more steps, he stopped.

Did he know her? There was something about her that looked so familiar. John stopped and turned around. He squinted his eyes and looked more carefully. Could it be? He walked toward her, and as he approached her again, he said, "Fanny? Fanny Connor?"

The woman lifted her head and looked at him. It was she! The blank expression in her eyes told John she had no idea who he was. Why should she? Why, she had not seen him for nearly two years, and he was only seventeen years old then! A mere boy! His hair was much shorter then, as his father had insisted, and not only was it longer now, he was beginning to grow a mustache and beard. God, he was nineteen, and Fanny was—what . . . twenty-five? He took off his hat and said, "Fanny, it's me, Johnny!"

"She squinted her eyes and said, "Cousin Johnny! It's been . . . well, it's been forever, hasn't it?"

"Not that long. Remember, I saw you for a few moments when you first had your baby, near 4th Street."

"Oh, yes. I'd almost forgotten all about that," she said, her eyes becoming distant again.

He took her in his arms and hugged her. A faint, yet pungent scent met his nostrils and he pulled away. "Fanny, are you okay? Your clothes look—well, they don't look near warm enough."

She shook her head. "I'm not really that well, cousin. Not really, but I do have a better overcoat at home. I suppose I misjudged the weather today."

"Well, cousin, when I last saw you your baby was brand new and your husband was off fighting for the victorious Union Army! Tell me, how is Mary Ellen? I'll never forget *her* name. And how is your husband faring?"

John suddenly realized he wasn't giving her time to answer his questions.

Fanny's head drooped and her hands fell from his shoulders. "Thomas was killed in the war, Johnny. I found out just days after we saw one another."

John felt terrible. He knew she looked ragged, but somehow hardship didn't enter his mind as a reason. Damn he was stupid sometimes! "Gosh, I'm so sorry, Fanny. I should have been more thoughtful than to assume—"

"No, Johnny. It's all right. I've remarried, just recently. This year, in fact. My husband's name is Joseph Gibbon. He's an Irishman, just as Thomas was. He's . . . he's a decent man, but . . . well, you know. I still miss Thomas. I always will, I imagine."

"I'm sure." John hesitated a moment, then asked, "How *is* your daughter? She was just a sprout when I last saw her."

"Dead," Fanny said. Something flashed in her eyes, but it was so momentary, John wasn't sure what it was. Still, her bland response told him the child's death had been dealt with, or at least, the pain suppressed.

He was shocked nonetheless. "What in God's name happened? My God, Fanny! She was just a little infant!"

Fanny took his hands in hers. When she drew close to him he finally identified the smell as stale alcohol, and he could smell putrid tobacco smoke in her hair. When she spoke, he had to fight the urge to pull away from her, her breath so disgusted him.

"I put her out to nurse with a woman so I could have the time to work. I wasn't able care for her and keep a situation as well."

To John's relief, she let go of him and stepped away.

"She died there, Johnny. My little girl died in some strange woman's home, her mother nowhere near to hear her cries, to soothe her, and pray to God to make a place for her in his Kingdom. I'm so ashamed, Johnny. I miss her so much. So much of it was my fault . . . "

John could feel the pain in each word she spoke, and the news of her child's death stung his heart. He needed to change the subject. "Father died last year, in case you hadn't heard. The doctor said his heart gave up on him."

"I'm so sorry, Johnny."

Johnny shrugged. "I know he mistreated you, Fanny, leaving you by yourself when we got off the ship. I wish there was something I could've done."

71

Fanny just stared at him, her eyes bloodshot and tired-looking. Johnny wondered just how much the events of one day could affect one's life down the road. If his father hadn't abandoned her all those years ago, would she have a good life today? He excused the thought. It was, after all, pointless, and he was certainly in no financial condition to help her, though he was sure she needed more help than money alone.

"You were twelve years old, Johnny. I was eighteen and another mouth to feed. Your father did what he thought was right."

John nodded and shrugged his shoulders. "I . . . I have to go, Fanny," he said. "My boss doesn't like it when I'm late. Try to remember, I live on East 11th Street, number 401. Come see me and my wife sometime." He turned to leave, then added, "You took care of me on the ship, Fanny, and when father left you at Castle Garden I cried for days. I never did let him forget that."

"You should have let him forget, John," she said. "There's no sense in being reminded of your mistakes. I know all too well you never forget the decisions you know in your heart were wrong." Dirty tears ran down her cheeks.

Against his better judgment, John leaned over and gave Fanny one last hug. To his relief, she did not cling to him. "Come see me," he called as he released her and hurried down the sidewalk, leaving Fanny behind. John looked back once more to see Fanny wave and turn slowly away. In his heart, he knew she had no one waiting for her to return home.

* * * * *

Just a few streets over from Martha Score's tenement building in Mulberry Bend, Tom and Mary McCormick watched as the doctor listened to their only remaining child's chest for a heartbeat. Tom knew from the physician's expression that there was none.

His eyes met theirs, his face grim. "I'm sorry," he said quietly. "Maggie's passed on."

Four-year-old Margaret McCormick had suffered for the last nine hours, and Mary and Tom had both known from experience that it was only a matter of time. From what they knew of other children in the building, it didn't take very long for the fever to take its victims.

Tom, a butcher by trade, shook his head and walked away. Maggie's body was already swelling and it disgusted him, just as a rotten piece of meat would turn his stomach. What lay there on the bed, bloating with each passing second, was no longer his daughter, but a testimony to the weakness of the blood that had coursed through all their children's veins. Three children, three corpses.

Tom sank into a dirty chair, a handkerchief pressed against his nose, and said nothing. Mary turned away from Maggie's body too, but Tom noticed she had no tears to shed for their last daughter. She wept when Avery died, but not for Helen, and now, not for Maggie, either. He wondered in his heart if she ever loved any of them.

Avery, his only son, had been seven at the time of his death last year. Mary always insisted he was a disobedient child, although Tom had seen no proof of it—his mischief was no different than what Tom himself made as a child. Avery had been a good, strong boy, and his sickness had taken Tom completely by surprise. He still wasn't past the sorrow and now had two more children to grieve over.

Six months after Avery, when Helen fell sick, Tom hadn't realized the extent of her illness. After all, children became ill. It was part of life. His only boy had died, and that demanded all of his sorrow. Three days before Helen's death, he finally realized that she wasn't suffering from a chill or any other mild sickness. She had the fever. A different type than the one that took Avery, but clearly the doctor was at a loss to cure her. The many bleedings he administered frightened the child, but in the end, did nothing to save her.

Following Helen's death, Tom would often pick up little Maggie and hold her in his arms for hours at a time. She would try to wriggle away, but he held tight in his sorrow, and she would eventually fall asleep. At four years of age, she wasn't sure what happened to her big brother and sister, but she often asked about them, wondering when they would come home. The innocence in her bright, blue eyes made his heart ache, and as he brushed the golden locks off her forehead and looked into them, he strove to see some sign that she was stronger; that she would survive where his other children had not.

It was not to be. God had taken her as well.

It wasn't only *his* children God wanted. Diseases swept through the tenements with regularity, taking a woman here, a man there, always a few children. Cholera had besieged the crowded cities hard at times, only to relent unexpectedly, fading back into some dark, foul place until it surfaced again. Tom and Mary called it "the fever" like everyone else, but there were several types that all led to the same horrible result. Consumption, typhus, diphtheria, scarlet fever, and cholera each left nothing but emptiness and sorrow in their paths, providing near certain death, with varying levels of suffering beforehand.

Tom's life, once so satisfying in spite of the hardships he and his family faced, was now meaningless. No children, and a wife he didn't trust. How would he go on?

Tom left his deep thoughts behind as the doctor departed.

"I'll send my apprentice to come pick up Maggie's body," he said. "Mr. Carter shall get her arranged for burial, and I'll be in touch."

Tom didn't acknowledge him as he pulled a blanket over Maggie's body and left the room.

Standing there, consumed by grief, a strange thought struck him. Though he carried the burden of knowing all his own children had died and the knowledge that his wife was a heartless woman, he already knew how he would get another child. After all, there were countless orphans in a city the size of New York.

7

December 1865
Five Months Later

The building that served as Mary Ellen's home stood in the dead center of a narrow, two-and-one-half-mile strip of land in the East River called Blackwell's Island, isolated and separated from the shores of New York proper by three hundred yards of deep, flowing current. The island and its several government institutions served as home to many of New York's criminally insane and diseased. It was a home for those who had none, and for those who had lost their privilege to live among law-abiding citizens. For many sick young foundlings, the almshouse on Blackwell's Island—as well tended and clean as it was—was a place to die.

On the first floor in the west wing of the almshouse, Abigail Quigley performed her weekly duties, which currently included bathing a two-year-old named Mary Ellen. Up until a month ago, Abby had been an inmate of the almshouse, staying there because she was as hungry and homeless as the children she cared for. She had plenty of experience in raising children, and had worked there for a place to stay. Now, with the recent changes in the way the

75

almshouse was run, she was a full matron on the staff, paid for her work with a small cottage off the main building and enough money for food and very meager savings.

The work was hard, though. Every day children died and the majority of inmates who cared for them—up until three months ago—were untrained and treated the infants with an indifference that appalled Abby. The foundlings brought in were often very sick, and the doctors on staff could do little for them. Many children were simply put in a separate area for the incurable. These horrible cases frightened Abby, but they also made her strive to learn how to better help the children. And learn she did.

Still, no matter how much she gave, no matter how fast Abby learned, most of the children who were brought in would die within a year. Things had improved, though. Since the inmate care had been discontinued and the most qualified of them were hired on as matrons, the death percentage had dropped dramatically. The current rate was now only seventy-five percent. Three out of every four children died, and compared to a year prior, that was a vast improvement.

For this reason, Abby vowed never to become too attached to the children. They transmitted disease to one another like wildfire, and it was impossible to tell when a seemingly healthy little boy would be found lying cold in his bed in the morning. It was better not to think about such things, for little could be done about it.

Abby fluffed the little girl's hair with a towel, then dried her neck and back.

"Don't tickle, Abby!" Mary Ellen said, laughing as Abby wrapped the towel around her bony little shoulders.

"Oh, nonsense. Everything tickles you," Abby shot back.

Mary Ellen laughed again, then took the towel from her shoulders and wrapped it around Abby.

"I'm not wet, Mary Ellen. You only need a towel when you're wet."

"You wet."

"Nope. Dry as a bone."

Mary Ellen reached down into the tub of water and splashed it on Abby. "You wet!" She ran across the room, laughing.

"Mary Ellen!" Abby dabbed at the water on her white uniform and chased the child down with the towel. Always good-natured, Mary Ellen was a favorite of Abby's since she first arrived.

"Gween," Mary Ellen said, pointing to the wall.

"Yes, it is green," Abby said. "Wouldn't we like to paint it a pretty blue, Mary Ellen?"

"Boo," Mary Ellen said. "Booboobooboo."

Abby opened the door and carried her through the spotless hall, despising the institutional green paint to which Mary Ellen had pointed. It *was* depressing, and Abby would have preferred white any day of the week. At least white would provide a brightening effect—the green just reflected on everyone's faces, making them appear sickly.

"Land sakes, Mary Ellen. You almost made me forget I have to see Mr. Kellock while he's here."

"Down, Abby."

"No, you stay here in my arms until we see Mr. Kellock. I need to get some records from him on Jenny Thress."

As Abby entered the office, she found George Kellock in a meeting with a man whom she had never seen before. When she spoke, the stranger did not turn to look at her.

"Excuse me, Mr. Kellock. I didn't realize you were busy."

"I'll just be a moment, Mrs. Quigley. We're finishing up here now."

"I'll return in a bit then," Abby said, leaving the office. She carried Mary Ellen halfway down the hall where a small playpen was set up and placed her inside. Her little petticoat and dress were folded up there, and Abby put them on her.

"There," she said. "Nice and clean and dry." Abby heard the door close at the end of the hall, and saw the man leaving. "I'll be back in a moment, Mary Ellen. You play until I come back."

As she walked toward the office, she scrutinized the man coming down the hall toward her. He looked like a working class man, dressed in old but clean clothing, gallowses, and worn boots. Abby wondered why he was meeting with Mr. Kellock. As they passed one another, he tipped a threadbare bowler hat that looked completely out of place with the rest of his clothing. He had probably salvaged it from the waste bin of some upper class gentleman. She nodded, then continued toward Kellock's office.

* * * * *

Tom McCormick thought the meeting with Kellock went well. After a few moments of feeling each other out, the superintendent indicated offhandedly that for a small fee he could arrange for Tom to get a child with a minimum of trouble. That was when Tom decided to confide in him.

"My three children died of one fever or another, Mr. Kellock. I'd like to have a child in our home to fill the space left behind."

"I see," he had replied. "It must've been hard on you."

"For my wife 'n me. Hard for both of us, but I know my wife wouldn't let another child in our house unless there was a good reason."

"What do you mean, Mr. McCormick?"

"I mean to tell her the child's mine by another woman. If it's my own blood, she can't deny me."

Kellock had told him there would be no problem; that whatever he did was his own business. That was when they'd shaken hands on the agreement. The only thing left was to choose a child.

As Tom walked down the hallway, he saw a little girl in a playpen. What a stroke of luck! There was no reason not to start his search immediately. He slowed and turned to watch the petite woman he'd passed, giving her time to reach her destination. She disappeared into Kellock's office and Tom McCormick walked faster until he reached the playpen.

Kneeling down, he said, "Hello there, little girl."

She stood up and smiled, a worn rag doll in her hands. She held it over the edge of the rail and dropped it outside the playpen. "Oops," she said. "Dolly back!"

McCormick picked it up and shook it at her playfully. She flashed a big smile, took the doll from him, then dropped onto her bottom again. McCormick reached down and gave her a tickle. She laughed, and her little voice instantly reminded him of Maggie when she'd been a toddler.

He glanced down the hall again, making sure the woman had not yet left Kellock's office, and folded back the collar of the little girl's dress and squinted his eyes. Sewed into the collar of the dress was the number 352, and below it was the child's name.

78

Mary Ellen Wilson.

Perfect! So cute and good-natured. She was almost everything Maggie had been—except his daughter, of course, but only he and Kellock would know that. Mary hadn't given him any strong children, a fact she couldn't deny. They were all in the grave. He would tell her Mary Ellen was one of three he fathered with another woman.

Tom worked out the details on the way back home. He would tell Mary the child's mother was a no-good woman who was feebleminded and he had only very recently discovered she abandoned his three children. Tom could tell her this Wilson woman was now somewhere in an insane asylum, and he simply never saw the need to tell her of his relationship with her until now. On his next visit, he would give Kellock the name of his youngest daughter, and Kellock would act very surprised at Tom McCormick's good fortune to have stumbled onto the correct institution.

* * * * *

Wearing a long, black overcoat and a top hat, Henry Bergh walked slowly down Broadway. He strolled along, carrying a fashionable black cane with a brass handle, touching it to the ground just in front of his right foot as he walked. His long face turning from side to side, Bergh twisted his long mustache between his fingers and scanned the busy New York City streets.

He was on unofficial patrol—for now.

Bergh felt refreshed and excited about the days and months to come, still pondering the way things came about—when you least expected them.

Just weeks earlier, Bergh had been serving as Legation Secretary at the Court of Alexander II of Russia. Though he had been an outstanding cabinet member, appointed by President Lincoln himself and highly regarded by the Russians, he would be forced to step down for almost the same reasons. How ironic that his creditable service and acceptance by the Russians would end his career in government politics.

The man he'd served under, Cassius Marcellus Clay, an ostentatious man, had quite a streak of jealousy. When Clay realized that Bergh threatened to grow more popular with the Russians than he, his campaign to put an end to it began. The man mistreated not only Bergh, but all of his underlings. He embarrassed them in front of dignitaries, concocted lies about their private activities, and attempted to ruin their reputations. The moment Bergh recognized Clay's intentions, he resigned rather than be trounced by the shallow, idiotic man.

Upon leaving Russia, Bergh traveled to London, where he attempted to maneuver a new appointment with no success. With President Lincoln dead, his appeals fell upon deaf ears as the nation scrambled to regroup. Fortunately, his trip to London had served another purpose, and it was that purpose which now raised his spirits and occupied his mind. He had an idea that could give him the meaningful position he longed for. An idea that would allow him to defend and speak for millions of the abused and tormented who could not speak for themselves; animals who suffered abuses at the hands of man.

He first became interested in the welfare of animals in Russia, when he'd been riding along the cobblestone streets of St. Petersburg, and saw a horse struggling to pull a heavy cart up an incline. The horse labored, straining against the load, then finally fell to its knees. The horse's master screamed at it, beating it mercilessly as it lay there helpless in the street.

Bergh was enraged. He stopped his carriage and, in full uniform, approached the man to intervene. With threats of prison, he put a halt to the offensive display of cruelty. He had not felt so good about an act since becoming legation secretary. "I've finally found a way to utilize this gold lace," he told a friend later that evening, referring to his decorated uniform. It was shortly after that experience that he turned in his resignation—and his uniform—to Clay.

In London, frustrated by the delays and obstructions he faced while his contacts in the U.S. tried to arrange another appointment, Bergh arranged to be introduced to the Earl of Harrowsby. The earl was the president of the Royal Society for the Prevention of Cruelty to Animals, an organization in its forty-first year. Bergh spent nearly three weeks with the earl, learning all he could of the services rendered by the RSPCA. It struck him immediately that the United States had no similar organization that he knew of. After his visit with the earl, Bergh decided he would form such an institution at home, and suddenly, he was anxious to return to America and begin the organization's charter.

It had been quite a revelation, and his wife stood by the decision from the start. Removing his top hat and smoothing his hair back, Bergh closed his eyes for a moment and enjoyed the light breeze that touched his face. Then a sound made his teeth grind together and his muscles stiffen.

Just half a block away, on the corner of Broadway and Chambers, a teamster beat a tired, sweat-soaked horse, cursing each time he lashed the animal. Bergh sped up, approaching the teamster with a quick step. Standing well over six feet, Bergh looked down at the cruel man.

"I implore you sir, stop beating your horse this instant!"

The man looked up at him with disbelief on his puffy, red face. "I'll beat my own damned horse if I care to," he snapped. "To the devil with you!"

As the teamster raised his crop again, Bergh seized his wrist in midair. "I suggest you study my face carefully, sir," he said. "You shall see it again, and for you it will be too soon."

* * * * *

Etta Angell Wheeler, wearing a thick, woolen scarf and heavy frock coat, walked to St. Luke's Mission, where she would receive the necessary goods to care for her charges. Her church was a generous organization, and Etta was happy to devote her life to its cause. Many of its poorer parishioners could barely afford to live, even in their tenement homes.

Etta cared for those who lived in the tenements between West 38th Street and West 42nd Street. Several members of her church lived in the dilapidated dwellings there, stacked together like dingy, block-shaped mountains. Even on the sunniest days of summer, they blocked out the kiss of the sun on the sidewalks, and made a gloomy place even less friendly.

Etta tried to help those who were not members of the church, though there were barely enough supplies to go to her parishioners. Still, she did what she could for each person she found to be in need. As charitable as St. Luke's was, Pastor Jameson would not approve of her offering church services to nonmembers. He had told her a hundred times before, there was no way to give to them all and still make a significant difference in anyone's life.

After gathering her supplies at the mission, Etta hurried—as best she could with the numerous bags to carry—to West 41st Street. Mondays and Tuesdays she concentrated her efforts here, for the number of needy within the area required as much time as she could afford them. On Wednesdays she visited the tenement rooms on 39th Street. 40th Street, another very crowded area that required two days of attention, was attended to the remaining two days of her week's work.

Etta not only supplied packages of bread and some meat when possible, she also shopped for those unable to leave their homes. Some were sick; others were without adequate clothing to withstand the subzero temperatures of New York City winters. Margaret Bingham's building at 325 West 41st Street was always her first stop, for several of St. Luke's parishioners boarded there. Mary Litzbeney, a woman with whom Etta had become close friends over the years, lived in the building. Mary was better off than many of her neighbors, but Etta always stopped in to see her after attending to her regular charges.

Etta made her way up the dangerous staircase, eager to get started but not so eager to break her leg in a rotted floorboard. Lillian Cane, who lived on the second level, was distraught and near penniless. She was a widow of the war with three children, all of whom were too young to earn the family any income. All she had was her widow's pension to keep the roof over her head, and it was hardly adequate.

Etta heard a child crying as she approached the apartment. She knocked on the door twice, then turned the knob. Her heart sank as she looked inside.

Curled up in the corner was the three-year-old, William. Etta could see, without closer examination, that he was dead. She caught her breath and instinctively removed a handkerchief from her handbag and held it over her mouth. Little William had been such a playful child, always happy and good-natured, even living in such miserable poverty. The little boy never knew any different life, so he was as content as a child living in a mansion—maybe more so. Etta wiped away her tears with the handkerchief before stepping into the room. She would have to appear very strong for this family today, no matter how much pain she felt in her heart.

Lillian sat in a rocking chair in the opposite corner of the room. Her arms were wrapped around her chest as though trying to squeeze the pain from her body, her eyes fixed on Billy's body. Her bare feet pushed off the floor, keeping the chair rocking steadily, and as her feet hit the floor, they made an eerie *thump . . . thump . . . thump.* The hollow sound gave Etta a horrible chill, and that feeling was reinforced by the blank look on Lillian Cane's sunken face. There was nothing in her eyes but the cold emptiness of lunacy.

The oldest child, Allison, began to wail in agony as soon as Etta entered the room, and Bruce, barely two years old, stood next to Lillian's chair, already sobbing. It was his soulful weeping that Etta had heard from the hallway. Bruce wanted his mother— he needed food. But most of all, he needed someone to hold him and tell him everything would be all right.

Etta could feed him, but whether his mother could be brought back to him remained to be seen. "Come here, children," Etta said. "Hurry to me." Allison ran to her, hugging her so tight she couldn't breathe. She had to walk over and take Bruce's hand. "There, there. Hush, now. It'll be okay."

The soft words comforted the children, but their lives would never be the same again. Lillian Cane, in the most likely circumstance, would be put in an institution. It wouldn't be the first time Etta saw such things happen.

She took both children to Mary Litzbeney's apartment and asked her to care for them until the pastor sent the proper authorities down to fetch them. Mary readily agreed. Afterward, she went back upstairs to see Billy.

With her handkerchief over her mouth, she knelt down to look at the child. The caked vomit next to his body and the drawn, puckered skin on his hands told Etta that cholera had taken him. Contracted by dirt and filth entering the digestive tract, Billy could have gotten it any number of ways. Unwashed hands, raw or unwashed vegetables, sewage-contaminated water. Etta had seen all of these. Billy had probably been perfectly all right last night, and when the family awakened this morning he had been dead. Death for cholera victims came swiftly.

Etta took a thin blanket from the mattress and put it over the boy's body. She glanced at Lillian again but she still rocked back and forth in her chair, blind to all but her inner nightmares.

Pastor Jameson would need to know right away. He would make the proper arrangements to have young Billy's body taken away. Lillian's only relatives lived somewhere in New Jersey, but as far as Etta knew, they never saw one another. Etta placed her hand on Lillian's and closed her eyes in prayer. When she finished, Etta pulled away, tears rolling down her cheeks. Lillian's feet pushed. The chair rocked.

Thump . . . thump . . . thump . . .

83

Etta stood to leave, her heart heavy with sorrow. Lillian's children needed attention first. If it was God's intention that Etta make a difference in the lives of the poor, then these unfortunate children should have a great many years of life ahead of them. Hopefully, thought Etta, it would be with their mother.

* * * * *

The almshouse on Blackwell's Island was a four story, rectangular building that ran north to south, as did the island itself. The main halls on each level ran lengthwise with the structure, and on each level just off the main halls were small infirmaries that accommodated five beds each. Three doctors shared the work in shifts, staying very busy most of the time.

The entire first floor comprised the children's wing. Located in the upper cross were the main offices, including George Kellock's office, which he used when he visited the almshouse. Most of his time was spent in the city, handling the enormous number of children being brought in daily.

Abby usually spent her time with several children in the small playground outside the children's wing. But today, as most days, was bitterly cold, and the counselors and children were forced to spend their time indoors for several more weeks until spring returned to the city.

To make room, they had joined three rooms together, and the large space served the purpose well. There were two fireplaces for immediate warming, and the ducts along the floor allowed the heat from the basement to drift upward and heat the rooms.

Mary Ellen played quietly in the corner of the large room, watching the other children with intense curiosity. Abby could tell by her face and expressions that she liked to be near them, she just wasn't quite ready to play *with* them. Mary Ellen would start to join in within a few months, and from then on it would be impossible to tear her away.

Several children were down for naps, a necessity since the playroom would never allow them all space to frolic. Maximum capacity in the children's wing was seventy, but there were now well over one hundred fifty children staying in the rooms at the almshouse, with more being brought in each day. Triple capacity of the almshouse was not unusual, especially in the children's wing.

84

She looked away from the children when she heard footsteps in the hall. The strange man in the bowler hat stood in the doorway, watching the children. A strange smile resided on his lips, and Abby could not help but notice he wore the exact same suit of clothes he wore when she had first seen him. "May I help you sir?" Abby asked, her eyes narrow.

He tipped his hat and said, "No thank you, madam. I'm just enjoying the lightheartedness of childhood for a few moments before seeing Mr. Kellock. My name is McCormick."

"Yes," she said. "I remember you. Would you like for me to announce your arrival to Superintendent Kellock?"

He smiled and winked at her. "I'm expected at ten o'clock this morning. Just passing a few moments before going to his office. Good day." He disappeared from the doorway.

Abigail Quigley would not deny her own nosiness. In her opinion, it was a necessary trait when working with children, some of whom could be quite mischievous. She peered around the corner and watched McCormick's progression toward Kellock's office. He would have had to have an appointment to see him, as the superintendent was only on the island two days a week.

At the end of the hall, McCormick stopped, straightened his hat, and rapped on George Kellock's office door. A moment later he disappeared inside.

Abby didn't hear the door close. Perhaps she could tiptoe quietly down the hall and pick up a word or two of their conversation. If they came out, she could simply pretend she was coming to see Mr. Kellock. She leaned her head inside the nursery. "Lucy, I'll be back in two shakes of a lamb's tail. I'm going down the hall to see Mr. Kellock."

"Take your time," said Lucy. "These ones are winding down now."

After stepping into the hall, Abby slipped off her white shoes and carried them in her hand as she tiptoed her way to Kellock's door. God, she thought. If anyone sees me doing this they'll think I've completely lost my mind. She glanced back once, saw the hallway behind her was empty, then continued on.

8

Tom McCormick sat at Kellock's desk, waiting patiently as Kellock finished up some paperwork he had been working on. "You looked a bit overworked, Mr. Kellock. Must be a lot of responsibility with so many children to concern yourself with."

"It has its share, sir." Kellock looked hard at his papers, signing here, initialing there.

"I only have the butcher shop, and that's enough to drive a man mad, trying to keep good workers tending things. Turn your back and they steal your meat just like that."

Kellock dropped his pen. "We have good people employed here, Mr. McCormick. And you may think we have a lot of children here, but if I told you we have four times as many as you've seen, and twice again that many adults, what would you say to that?"

"Why, I'd say you've got a task on your hands, superintendent. How about if I make it one child easier on you."

Kellock laughed. "I'd welcome that relief. So would the children, for that matter. If they don't die of disease, they'll be cared for by the city of New York until they're adults." Kellock shook his head and stared at McCormick, his bushy eyebrows furrowed, then said in a low voice, "Did you consider my proposal?"

"What proposal were you speaking of, Mr. Kellock?"

Kellock leaned back in his chair and cleared his throat. His spectacles seemed to fog up for a moment, and he rubbed his hand lightly over his slicked, gray hair. "Well, Mr. McCormick. I believe I mentioned to you at our last meeting that there are certain fees and the like which, if taken care of in advance, can expedite the indenture process. I don't believe I gave you a figure, however."

McCormick raised his eyebrows. "I *am* a butcher, Mr. Kellock, on a moderate income. I'm afraid if the fee is too high I may have to wait for the progress of bureaucracy."

"Bureaucracy takes its time, doesn't it?" smiled Kellock. "I do try to tailor the fee to the businessman—if that makes it any easier for you."

"Excellent," said McCormick. "What's next?"

"You need to choose a child. After that—"

"—I've already chosen one."

Kellock stopped. "Really? Very well, write the name down here." He slid a piece of paper across the desk.

"Her name is Mary Ellen Wilson." He wrote it and slid the paper back to Kellock.

"Okay, let me do something here."

As McCormick watched, Kellock opened a drawer marked 'W-Z' in a cabinet behind his desk. He removed several files. After looking at them carefully, he wrote down two more names beside that of Mary Ellen.

"These are your children's names," Kellock said. "Of course, only one of them can be found here."

"What's the purpose of that?" McCormick asked.

"Makes it look like you have a right to the child as her father," he said. "You had three children you were trying to find. Jeremy Wilson, four years old, Rebecca Wilson, six years old, and Mary Ellen Wilson, one-and-a-half. The odds were against you finding all of them, but one of them, we'll that's possible, even probable, to a degree. That's how I speed up the process."

"I see. If it's my child, there are no delays."

"Exactly." He slid a paper across the desk with a figure written on it.

McCormick looked at it, took Kellock's pen, marked through it, and wrote a revised figure. "How's this as a compromise?"

"Acceptable, Mr. McCormick. Now, shall I process this, or would you have me tear these papers up and we can part company?"

McCormick stood and held out his hand. "I guess it's my lucky day, Mr. Kellock! I've found my Mary Ellen!"

* * * * *

The meeting was coming to a close. Abby hurried away from the office and shuffled shoeless down the hall, feeling the need to return to Mary Ellen immediately.

Much of what she heard was muffled. The door was partially closed and the men spoke in low voices, but she did hear enough to understand that this man was probably Mary Ellen's father.

If it were so, then shouldn't Abby be happy? Such a sour response made no sense, and neither did Abby's sense of panic. If the man was her father, then Mary Ellen belonged with him, didn't she? Absolutely. Then why did this suspicion sit in her stomach like a stone?

One thing she did hear clearly was Kellock's talk of "tailoring fees", and Abby recognized it for what it was; a request for a bribe. There were only small, incidental fees associated with adopting one of these children. Besides, if Mary Ellen was his child, there would be only minimal charges to reimburse a percentage of the department's expenses.

And where was Mary Ellen's mother?

Abby couldn't fight the feeling that George Kellock, a man she had always respected, was selling children from the almshouse. But if that were happening, surely someone would have discovered it by now. Perhaps Mr. Kellock was just slackening the rules a bit to allow the children to find homes. Even if it were true she could tell no one, for suspicions were all she had. Her job would be at risk. Whatever Mr. Kellock was doing, it would never be found out unless he revealed it himself.

And as for her suspicions about McCormick, they would have to remain just that.

Reaching the nursery, Abby glanced back once more and saw McCormick leaving Mr. Kellock's office. Not wanting to be conspicuous, she hurried into the room to find Mary Ellen asleep on a mat amidst the noise and chatter of the other children. Abby looked after some of the others, fetched toys for them, disciplined two rambunctious boys, and then sat on the floor beside Mary Ellen. She lifted the child's little head and rested it on her lap. When she looked up, Mr. Kellock and the man who claimed to be Mary Ellen's father were in the doorway of the nursery, looking in her direction.

She doesn't look a thing like him, Abby thought. Not a whit.

* * * * *

On New Year's Day, Tom McCormick invited two of his laborers home from the butcher shop and offered them warm lager for their efforts. This occasion was the holiday, but he offered them beer every week as it seemed to encourage loyalty among them. Where there was loyalty, there was a hesitation to steal, and stealing could ruin his business. He could not be there each and every hour of every day, and needed to have men he could trust working with him.

"What's with this place, boss? You own your own butcher shop and you can't get better rooms than this?"

Tom shook his head. Gilby, his best meat cutter, always said stupid things when he was drunk. "If Mary would keep the place clean it might not be so bad," Tom said. "She does little else, that I can tell you."

"You might find out just how little I *can* do if you don't watch your words, husband."

McCormick ignored his wife. "Besides, Gil. If I get a better place it'll cost me more money, and I'll have to pay you lower wages to keep it. How would you like that?" Tom grunted and trotted off to the bedroom.

"Go down to the privy, Tom!" called Mary. A groan came from the room.

Otto Parkhurst, another of Tom's employees, laughed at this. "A man gets tired, Mary. He works hard all day, and the chamber pot's more convenient."

Mary, who sat on the floor with the men having a lager of her own, put a hand on Otto's leg. He had worked with Tom only a couple of months, and was a good looking young German man with blond hair and blue eyes. "You're the strong one, aren't you Otto?" asked Mary in a low voice, her hand caressing his muscular thigh. She faced the bedroom so she could see if Tom returned. "Maybe you'll come up and visit me sometime when Tom is working the store alone."

"Why not, Otto," Gilby said. "I did." He sat across from them, his full jowls bouncing as he laughed. "I ain't much in the looks department, but she's still an almighty friendly lady, she is."

"Don't be an ass and give away my secrets, Gilby," Mary said. "Besides, why shouldn't I be friendly? My husband is, from what you men've told me."

"I heard he's got some kids even he don't know about," said Otto.

"Yeah," said Gilby. "Ol' Tom's got his share of kids runnin' around. No need to go crazy about it."

Mary shook her head. "I don't care if he has ten or twenty. Let him have a hundred!" She laughed and finished her glass of ale.

Tom came back into the room. "Piss pot's full up," he said. "Better go drain it, wife."

She laughed at him. "You're so drunk there's probably more on the floor."

The men laughed too, and Tom poured himself another beer. "What were you talking about in here? I heard a mighty lot of chatter."

Otto winked at Mary and Gilby said, "Just talking about you, Tom. How come this wife of yours ain't carrying a belly on her like all those other women you were with?"

"Mary's through with having babies, that's why," he replied. "We had three of 'em and now we're down to none." He paused, then said, "But we're going to pick up my little girl tomorrow."

Mary glared at him, her smile gone. "What are you talking about?" She poured herself another lager. She was feeling drunk, and the more she drank the less she cared what Tom said about her condition.

"Easy on the lager, woman. You get slobbering drunk and I may not be able to control these boys." Tom flicked her breast with his fingers.

Otto ignored it and took another swig of beer.

Gilby looked at Mary and licked his lips in a lewd gesture.

Mary smiled at him and said, "Control them or don't. I don't care a whit. Where's the mother of this little child of yours?"

"Don't know. Don't really care. All I know is she dumped the child and now I'm going to take her. Just feel lucky I don't bring 'em all home, Mary. That sure would keep you busy, wouldn't it?"

Mary didn't like this game, and Tom was lying, plain and simple. It was the first time he'd spoken of having any children besides the ones they'd had together. "How many do you say you have, Tom?"

"I told you before, Mary," Gilby interrupted. "Tom's got lots of 'em around. He's a regular ladies' man!"

Tom jumped to his feet, the muscles in his jaw suddenly tense and pronounced. "Three!" he shouted. "I got three kids. Now you get out of here, Gilby! You too, Otto. I gotta talk to the wife. I'll see you two at the shop tomorrow morning."

Gilby stood, then staggered into the wall, knocking a framed photograph to the floor. The glass shards scattered over the faded wood floor like tiny razors. In the picture, Tom's frowning father, standing outside the butcher shop a decade earlier, stared upward through the shattered glass.

Gilby stared in disbelief. "Now I'm real sorry about that, Tom."

"You'll pay for the frame out of your earnings, Gil. Now get out of here, you drunk." He shoved him toward the door.

Mary climbed to her feet and flashed Tom a dirty look.

"I'll show these gentlemen down the stairs," she said, her words slurred. "They're your workers, and they should be treated better than that." She started out the door, then turned back. "Why don't you go empty your piss pot yourself, 'cause I might decide to walk with them all the way home. Don't bother waiting."

"Go on," he said. "Makes no difference to me."

"Happy New Year!" she said, slamming the door behind her.

* * * * *

The next day, as Mary and Tom waited for the ferry to pick them up at 69th Street, Tom remained silent. He had always played the part of the indifferent husband quite well, and he noticed Mary played her part equally well. She had come home well after eleven o' clock the previous night, and he suspected she had gone to Joseph and Gilby's apartment. What exactly she did there, he was sure he *didn't* want to know. Gilby hadn't shown up for work

91

that morning, but a groggy-eyed Otto did, and he agreed to tend the shop himself for a few hours while Tom ran an errand.

The ferry glided up and landed at the dock, and Tom and Mary waited for the few passengers to disembark before stepping on. They stood against the rail in silence for half the trip, then as Blackwell's Island grew larger, Tom spoke.

"She's at the almshouse. The director, Kellock, may ask you about a doctor. You just tell him we have a family doctor who can verify my relationship to the child. Use my doctor's name, Dr. McLaughlin. You'll just answer the man's questions and offer nothing. I'll do the dealing."

"Dealing? What in the devil do you have to deal for? She's your daughter, ain't she?"

"See? That's why you should be quiet," he said. "Mary, I got three kids. I only know where one of 'em is, and she's nearly two years old. We've lost all our children, and this one's lost her mother, who was a no good woman to begin with." He stared at the island for a moment, then continued. "It looks like it's a perfect match, wouldn't you say?"

"If she was ten, it might be perfect," Mary said. "Then, at least, she could help with the house cleaning. As it is, she's not only the daughter of a whore, she's going to be a burden to me."

"She'll be a help to you later," he said as the ferry reached the dock of Blackwell's Island. "If she lives long enough."

Mary said nothing more until they were inside Kellock's office.

* * * * *

George Kellock, wearing a dark gray suit and a matching necktie, greeted the McCormicks and got them comfortably seated in the chairs in front of his desk. After some small talk of the weather and discussion of Mary Ellen, Kellock grew impatient as he waited for McCormick to give him the agreed upon fee to expedite the process.

"In this procedure there are always delays to be experienced, and of course there will be some officers of the State coming by your home to inspect your living conditions. They'll also want to see your business ledgers to verify you can support the child," Kellock said.

"I'm familiar with the necessary inspections, Mr. Kellock, but perhaps this prepayment might allow us to take Mary Ellen home today."

Kellock grinned. As Tom McCormick slid the plain, white envelope onto the desk, Kellock flashed McCormick's wife a big smile and said, "Mrs. McCormick, do you have anything to add that might convince this office you can support and care for this child?" He plucked the envelope from the desk and slid it into his breast pocket.

"Yes, sir, I do," Mary said, her eyes narrowing. "I'd like to add that I watched you slip that white envelope full of money in your pocket there, and that means you're selling us this child. I'd also like to add that we probably aren't the first two folks who walked in here and gave you a packet of money for a child." She glared at him, then added, "Now, do we get her today or not?"

Kellock's chest tightened and he stuttered, "I . . . I can return the fee if you like and say good day to both of you," he said, his brow twitching.

"Nonsense! You have our money, now give us the child my husband wants. And hurry, because I want out of this stinking place."

The confrontation was utterly unexpected. It was easier to agree and finish this thing than have an embarrassing scene in his office. Besides, someone might hear Mrs. McCormick if she became any more belligerent. "Yes," Kellock replied softly, trying to calm her. "I believe I can arrange for you to take her with you within the hour."

Tom McCormick stared at his wife in disbelief as Kellock rose slowly from his desk and exited the room.

* * * * *

Abigail Quigley knocked on the door of Kellock's office, didn't wait for an answer, and stormed in.

Kellock looked up, surprise on his face. "Mrs. Quigley. What can I do for—"

"*You* can shut your mouth, Mr. Kellock. I have something to say and you'd better listen to me, and listen good."

"I beg your par—"

"You'll beg me to keep my mouth shut!" Abby walked around to his side of the desk and stood over him. "I was told to prepare Mary Ellen Wilson for indenture just over an hour ago, and now Lucy tells me they've already taken her!"

"All the details were attended to," he snapped, standing from his chair. "What *is* your point, Mrs. Quigley?"

"My point is, Mr. Kellock, that I was outside your office door Monday last when you suggested Mr. McCormick pay you a 'fee'. I heard you tell him you would insure a speedy process. I heard it *all*, Mr. Kellock."

George Kellock took a step back. "What you think you heard is none of your concern, Mrs. Quigley." He leaned on the desk and Abby noticed his hands were shaking.

"Oh, I know what I heard," Abby said. "How could you? You sent this child off with no proof, no evidence that these people can properly care for Mary Ellen! She is a person, Mr. Kellock! Do you hear me? Not something to be sold, but a person!"

"Now, now, calm down," he pleaded. He stepped around her and closed the door to his office. "What do you want?" he asked, turning toward her.

"What do I want? I want the child to be taken care of, that's what I *want*, Mr. Kellock. I believe it's more than you ever considered. Have you drawn up the indenture papers yet?"

He shook his head. "No time. They wanted the child immediately."

"Yes, and you already have the money, I presume." She thought for a moment, and Kellock remained silent. "Then I shall have provisions for you to add to the contract. Provisions that will guarantee Mary Ellen is well cared for. In other words, I would like a supervised indenture arranged."

"Supervised?"

"Yes. Put directly into the contract that the McCormicks must bring the child to you for inspection once each year—a written report will not do. There are other things I would like added as well. There shall be provisions for her education, religious and otherwise. For adequate clothing to be supplied, and anything else I can think of. These items will be verified when she is brought in each year. If you do that, I'll keep my silence—unless my conscience won't allow it."

Kellock objected. "Once every two years is the standard—"

Abby raised her hand. "I said once each year. I will leave you now to

94

draw up the papers. And remember, Mr. Kellock. I'm sure it wouldn't be too difficult to find others who've paid for children in the past." She turned to leave, then stopped. Abby rested both hands on the desk and looked Kellock directly in the eyes. "While I've got you here," she said, "I've been meaning to request an increase in salary. A decent increase. You *will* see to that, won't you?"

She left the office without waiting for a reply.

9

February 1866

Bergh wiped the beads of sweat from his forehead and looked out over the gathering crowd at Clinton Hall. He smoothed the pages of his speech though they weren't out of order. Even the murmur of the crowd was unnerving at this point. It was do or die now, the most important presentation of his life.

Bergh had put all the pieces together very quickly. With his knowledge of government procedures and past dealings with prominent political figures in high places, knowing how to present a convincing case came naturally to him. The first American chapter of the Society for the Prevention of Cruelty to Animals was the prize tonight, one he wanted so badly he could taste it.

The gathering was small, and absent were some of the dignitaries Bergh had hoped to see, but many influential men were in attendance. Bergh hoped the raging storm outside had more to do with it than the proposed subject matter. Either way, the gentlemen here would decide the fate of the charter.

It was all a question of morality—a question of what was right and wrong. Was it moral to beat a dumb animal, be it a horse, dog, or other creature, for any reason? The labors of the horse moved this country forward through each and every day, and the dog was a faithful friend to man. The abuses on these creatures had to end.

"Welcome," Bergh said, and the room fell into relative silence. "I thank you, gentlemen, for coming here tonight, despite the foul weather," he said. "What I have to propose to you tonight is of the utmost urgency and will be undertaken with the most sincere dedication, if supported and approved by your numbers. Prepare yourselves, for I am going to present to you many statistics relating to the cruelties practiced upon animals." Bergh paused for effect, adding, "Much of it is not pleasant, nor is it intended to be. It is my hope that it alarms you as much as it does me."

Over the next hour, Bergh explained how in London and other cities of Great Britain and Ireland, a society existed that protected the rights of animals. He expressed his interest in founding a kindred society in America. He delved back into history, noting what had happened to animals and humans in the Roman arena, the tortures of the Spanish bull rings, and many other violations of morality.

Well into his speech, and far past the nervousness, the fifty-three- year-old Bergh spoke of the atrocities he witnessed daily in New York City where street railway and omnibus companies abused their horses mercilessly. He recounted the many times he witnessed animals being taken for slaughter stacked upon one another in open carts like sacks of flour, their legs bound together. He told of seeing children break down into tears as these carts passed them by.

"Do these little children see that which we do not?" He asked, pounding the podium. "That it is cruelty to transport living, breathing animals in this manner? Do they not deserve a quick, painless slaughter for feeding our families?" Nods came from the men seated before Bergh. His words were received well.

"Gentlemen," he concluded, "this is a matter purely of conscience. It has no perplexing side issues. Politics has no more to do with it than astronomy, or the use of globes. No, it is a moral question in all its aspects. It addresses itself to that quality in our nature that cannot be disregarded by any people with safety to their own dearest interests. It is a solemn recognition of that greatest attribute of the Almighty Ruler of the universe, *mercy*, which if suspended in our own case but for a single instant, would overwhelm and destroy us."

He nodded, thanked the audience, and gathered up his papers, throwing a wave toward the crowd. The applause was deafening as he stepped down from the stage. Only time would tell whether his appeal was successful, but several men approached him afterward with outstretched hands, many promising moral and financial support for the society.

Bergh's hopes soared.

* * * * *

"You should never have let them remove her from the almshouse without signing the proper documents in the first place, Mr. Kellock," Mrs. Quigley said. "If I were to read the statutes applying to the indenture process, I believe I could locate the precise decree to confirm your violation of the process." She sighed. "I suppose it is yet another of the laws you rewrite for yourself."

"That was last month, Mrs. Quigley! All has been signed and done, so will you simply let me be?"

Kellock was sick of Abigail Quigley, but wary, too. Since he had approved the adoption of the Wilson child to the McCormick's, she had made his life miserable. She had gotten the increase in salary. What else did she want? He would ask her now, damn the consequences. "Exactly how long do you intend to threaten my position here, Mrs. Quigley? Have I not done everything you requested?"

She smiled, and George Kellock realized he was also sick of that smug smile. "Yes, Mr. Kellock. You have, but I remind you that it is not from the goodness of your heart that you do it. It's only to save yourself."

"Here is what they signed, just as you wanted it." He gave her the original agreement he penned two weeks after the McCormicks took the child:

This indenture witnesseth: that Mary Ellen Wilson, aged one year and six months hath put herself and by these presents and with the consent and approbation of the Commissioners of Public Charities and Correction of the City of New York doth voluntarily and of her own free will and accord

98

put herself to adopt to Thomas McCormick, butcher, and Mary his wife, residing at 866 Third Avenue in the City of New York, and after the manner of an adopted child to serve from the day of the date hereof for and during the full end and term of sixteen years and six months next ensuing. During all of which time the said child her parent faithfully shall serve, his secrets keep, his lawful commands everywhere readily obey; she shall do no damage to her said parents nor see it done by others without preventing the same so far as she lawfully may, and give notice thereof to her said parent; she shall not waste her said master's goods nor lend unlawfully to any; she shall not absent herself day nor night from her said parent's service without his leave nor frequent ale houses, taverns, not play houses and in all things behave herself as a faithful child ought to during the said term; and the said parent shall use the utmost of his endeavor to teach or cause to be taught or instructed the said child in the trade and mystery of housekeeping and plain sewing, and procure and provide for her sufficient meat, drink, apparel, mending, lodging and washing fitting for an adopted child and cause her to be instructed in reading, writing, and arithmetic during the said term; and at the expiration thereof shall give a new Bible to the said child and a suit of new clothing in addition to her old ones in wear, and shall furnish to her at all times when necessary or proper medical assistance and attendance and nursing, and at all proper times the utensils and articles required for keeping her healthy and cleanly.

Special. To report to the said Commissioners of Public Charities and Correction once in each year the character and condition of said girl. And for the due performance of all and singular the covenants and agreements aforesaid the said parties bind themselves unto each other firmly by these presents.

Mrs. Quigley finished reading the contract and smiled. "Just as I specified, Mr. Kellock, except the indenture is incorrect. Anyone could see the Wilson child is somewhere around two years old, not eighteen months. Besides, how can, as the document reads, a mere child 'voluntarily and of her own free will, offer herself to adopt'?"

Kellock fumed, and spoke through gritted teeth. "The wording shall remain, Mrs. Quigley. It is strictly according to our procedures. In the case of her age you may be correct. I didn't bother referring to the original paper from when she was brought here, and Mr. McCormick told me she was under two years. What difference does that make?"

"If the home is not a good one, Mr. Kellock, it makes an enormous difference. It requires her to remain there six months longer than is necessary."

Kellock shook his head and said nothing. It was pointless anyway. The woman would simply say her piece, and if he was lucky, she would leave.

"I wish to be informed before each yearly visit," Quigley added. "If possible, I want to see her when she's brought in. Besides that addition, every other provision I requested is there and meets with my approval."

Her *approval*. She was just a goddamned nurse. Not even that. She used to be a goddamned inmate. He nodded. "I'm so happy it meets your approval, Mrs. Quigley. Now, may I return to my duties, or will there be anything else?"

"Nothing now, Mr. Kellock. I'll be sure to let you know."

* * * * *

Etta Wheeler spent many hours with Lillian Cane, and she gained ground each day. Two months ago, just after Billy's death, Etta wouldn't have given her a chance, but Lillian soon overcame her stupor. Her heart was bruised and battered over her family's loss, but with Etta's help and prayers, Lillian realized she had two more children who needed her. Of course Lillian would have to live in an almshouse for the present, but the children would be placed in the same facility, and she could see them every day.

Lillian's case was only a single example of why Etta reaped such warm satisfaction from her work with the church. If she hadn't arrived that day, God only knows what would have become of Lillian and her family. It was rewarding despite the plain truth that Lillian would probably never be more than another number in New York City's welfare system. Still, Lillian had proved her wrong before, and Etta welcomed it to happen again. Even if she never accomplished anything beyond mothering her children, perhaps they would grow up to do great things someday. That alone was enough to make it all worthwhile to Etta.

On a brisk, Thursday evening, Etta stopped by the church to pick up her sweater. She was surprised when Pastor Jameson called her aside to speak with her.

"Etta, I hope what I have to tell you doesn't upset you, but I've given it a lot of thought, and I simply don't see any other alternative."

"What is it, Pastor?" she asked, concerned.

"I've decided to adjust your route so you'll better serve those in need," he said. "You'll be serving our parishioners living in the buildings on 47th through 53rd Streets from now on."

Etta protested, but the pastor interrupted her. "Now, Etta. I realize it's a larger area, but you're younger than many of our caseworkers. You've more energy than three of them combined."

"But I've come to know many of my families so well," she said. "They'll miss me, I'm sure. Some of them . . . well, some of them may feel abandoned."

"They'd be foolish not to miss you, Etta. You've been wonderful to them. You can go by and tell them of the change so they know they aren't abandoned"

He smiled, and she found it hard to argue with him, for he *was* a well-intentioned man.

"You know the neighborhood I'm putting you in, Etta. It's closer to your home, and overall, there are fewer buildings. It should be as easy for you to cover as the other route, and since your home is closer, you should be able to spend more time assisting people before you leave for the day. I'll see that the families you're tending to now are taken care of. Don't have concerns over that."

There was no reason to worry, as long as she was doing God's work. "I'll still be doing what I love, Pastor Jameson. I'm sure everything will work out just fine."

"I know it will, and God bless you, Etta. You know how much you mean to the church."

Etta would visit the old neighborhood on occasion, just to make sure all was well. The more she thought of it, the more exciting a new neighborhood would be. New faces, new challenges. Nearly everything that had happened to her in the past turned out to be for the best, and that was something she would have to remember.

* * * * *

The results of his appeal were better than expected, and though Bergh was apprehensive, he couldn't deny his excitement. Promises of support came from John Dix, a well known soldier and cabinet officer; the publishing Harper brothers; from James Lenox, inventor and book collector; from Mayor Hoffman; from Peter Cooper, a manufacturer, inventor, and philanthropist; from Henry Clews, the banker, and a host of other influential men. It was overwhelming!

Bergh knew he would meet his opposition from others, though. Men— and perhaps women—who would fight his cause and accuse him of taking their rights away. That didn't trouble him, though. Henry Bergh welcomed adversity.

In 1843, after the death of his father, he and Christian Bergh's other children inherited the shipyard, which was soon converted to a coal yard. But the operation was run by qualified foremen, and overseeing the business was hardly as satisfying as he had believed it would be as a young man. Rather than busy himself with the family business, he and Matilda traveled abroad for the next fifteen years, returning to New York several times, but only for short stays before taking off again.

Still, through all this, Bergh always had the feeling he simply wasn't *doing* anything of great importance, and that bothered him immensely. Something in his heart told him he needed to search until the empty place in his gut was filled, and his society felt right, no matter how difficult it would be.

Since studying the history of the RSPCA in London, his heightened awareness of the problem made it seem to him that the abuse of animals was everywhere. Since his return, he had seen it on the streets of New York everyday, in various levels of severity. He silently blanketed the city during the evenings, locating the arenas of animal torture he would visit when the law was by his side.

One rainy evening, he visited a place called Kit Burn's Sportsmen's Hall on Water Street, where regularly, bulldogs were thrown into a ring and made to fight angry black bears. The dog and rat ring was a regular attraction here, too, and when the show was over, Mr. Burn's son-in-law would bite the head off a live rat for a mere glass of lager. The entire atmosphere disgusted Bergh, and he despised the men who stood beside him cheering. It would not be long before he would return—representing the American Society for the Prevention of Cruelty to Animals—and work to shut the operation down.

Bergh circulated a paper outlining the objectives of the proposed society, and it was immediately endorsed by Horace Greeley, the founder of the *New York Tribune*, and by William Cullen Bryant, who headed the *Evening Post*. With these names behind him, Bergh wasted no time. A leading New York attorney, James T. Brady, drew up its charter, and grasping the official application in his hands, Bergh was eager with anticipation as he headed off to Albany.

Finally there would be an actual law to support this just cause—and a private society with a great deal of public influence.

* * * * *

Tom McCormick was happy to have a child again, but Mary wasn't pleased at all. Each time she laid eyes on the child, Mary despised her more. She was a living mistake created from her husband's lies and carelessness.

To Tom, Mary Ellen was proof that his blood was strong, and hers weak, for his child had lived while those made from her had died. Maybe he would soon find out it wasn't so.

Not that she cared so much about what Tom did or where he spent his time. Mary had secrets of her own, and she liked it that way. No, that wasn't the trouble. The trouble begins when a man's mistakes are brought into his woman's home. How would Tom like it if she came home carrying another man's child within her someday? Not very much. He wouldn't like that at all.

Mary looked at the little girl Tom called Mary Ellen. Not a handsome child, really. Her hair grew too high on her forehead and wasn't very thick. Her eyes were an uninteresting brown. She remembered how beautiful her own children had been. "I will spend no money on you, that is a certainty," she said to the child. "Unless your father brings you something to wear, that dress will just have to do."

"Abby," said, Mary Ellen. "Want Abby!" She fell to her bottom and sobbed.

Mary Ellen sat on the floor wearing the dress she had on when they picked her up. Just a little more than a month ago, it had been quite pretty. Now it was filthy, for Mary never washed the child or her clothes. She'd spent most of her time trying to teach Mary Ellen to use the chamber pot so she wouldn't have to change her underthings. It wasn't coming along very well.

Mary left Mary Ellen to crawl about on the floor most of the day. When the child got tired she would cry, eventually falling asleep on the grimy wood slats.

"I have to go out for a bit, and you've been getting into too many things around here." Mary looked around the apartment, then an idea came to her. "Come here, you."

She bent and scooped Mary Ellen into her arms. She carried her to the small closet and opened the door. "This is a perfect place for you to stay out of trouble," Mary said. "In you go."

Mary smiled at the child as she closed the door to her cries of terror, encasing her in darkness. The child surely wouldn't bother the neighbors now, nor would she tinker with things she shouldn't.

Mary left the apartment and visited a man named Francis Connolly, a former employee of the butcher shop. He had taken an apprenticeship as a mason while working for Tom, and after missing work several times he was eventually fired. He was a good looking man, and Mary took to him immediately. Since his departure from the butcher shop he had taken an apartment just one block over, on Lexington Street—a quick walk from Mary and Tom's apartment. Today, she spent over two hours there, drinking ale and playing wife.

When she returned home, Tom sat in a rocking chair holding the sleeping child. "Damn you," he said, angrily. "Why the hell did you put this child in that closet?"

"She meddles with everything. I warned you, I'll not have her in my house breaking things." Mary was smug. She walked to Tom's chair and removed her hat. "I have to keep my home proper for my man."

Tom stood and put Mary Ellen on the cushion of the chair where she curled up and slept. Without warning, Tom pulled back his arm and slapped Mary across the cheek with all his might. She tumbled backwards against the wall, and the photograph of Tom's father in front of the butcher shop came toppling down on her head, the newly replaced glass shattering again. She held her hands to her face and moaned in agony.

Tom took slow, deliberate steps toward her, and she cowered at his approach. When he spoke his voice quivered like a man balancing on the edge of control. "If . . . I ever come home to find this child locked in a closet or anything like it, I'll beat you until you're standing on the doorstep of death, you understand me?"

Mary said nothing. She sat there on the floor, strangely aware of the moisture soaking through her dress, all that remained of the time spent with Francis Connolly. The utter absurdity of her mind's focus made her laugh, despite the stinging of her face. She slipped into a hysteric giggling fit as Tom stood gawking over her. She looked at the anger on his face and the laughter increased until her eyes squirted tears and she felt as though she had slipped into lunacy. Surprisingly, *it felt good*!

"Stop it!" shouted Tom, and he landed a worn calf-skin boot against her splayed leg.

The pain was intense, but Mary's laughter became an anesthetic. She rolled onto her side, bellowing even harder despite the fact that she would be showing off an array of bruises the next day. Her belly now hurt from laughing so hard. She wished Tom would leave her so she could stop. Somehow, as long as he stood in front of her, his face as red as a tomato, she could not escape her fit.

Eventually he stormed off, taking Mary Ellen with him. After he left, Mary limped to the basin of water, where she rinsed away the evidence of her earlier infidelity with Francis. The child was already becoming a problem, just as Mary feared she would. If Tom was going to act like that each time she disciplined or tried to gain a bit of freedom from her, it would be a hard road to hoe. She would have to think of some way to arrange things better. It was just sour luck that her husband left work early today.

She would find a way to live her own life, even with this child of the devil. Mary McCormick was a resourceful woman, and she *would* find a way.

10

April 1866
Two Months Later

Thirteen. That was her tolerance limit. It was how many times Mary's thoughts drifted to her little boarder before deciding she must get out of bed and make her pay for distracting her night's rest. The bruises from the beating she had received on Mary Ellen's behalf had faded, but the memory had not, nor would it for some time. Maybe never. The child's very presence made Mary's life miserable, and she deserved to know it. She *would* know it as long as she lived under Mary McCormick's roof.

Mary slipped out of the small, lumpy bed and shuffled her bare feet across the floor to the front room. With each step she took, her anger grew. She was tired and should be sleeping. Still, her mind went repeatedly to the little girl who had captured her husband's loyalty and affection.

Mary hadn't even realized she cared where Tom's affections were directed until Mary Ellen had become, more than she, the object of them. Tom's extramarital affairs were unseen, and therefore unimportant and inconsequential, save for the existence of the child—somewhat more than a minor conse-

107

quence. The affection he gave this child was blatant and obvious. Worse, it just plain irritated her.

Mary stood over the child, her hands clenched. The girl slept on a tiny mattress placed beneath the front window, one Tom had bought at a second hand store. Mary complained to Tom that the mattress was a waste of money when there were plenty of blankets she could sleep on, but he had insisted, and even tried to put the mattress just outside their bedroom. Oh, how Mary had protested! She *would not* share any part of her bedroom with her husband's mistress' daughter. Never! She made that point very clear to him, and he eventually forgot about the idea. It was but one victory for Mary. She would have to stand firm from now on if she were to keep control of her house. The visitor would learn who was boss.

Mary stood there growing angrier as Mary Ellen slept in the darkness, enjoying a quiet peace Mary did not have in her heart. She leaned down and lifted the child from the mattress; she didn't awaken.

Carrying her to the rocking chair, Mary sat down and rocked back and forth, the child's head resting on her shoulder. Mary Ellen released a little sigh and for one brief moment, Mary realized that if the girl had been her daughter, she might have thought, *how precious, this little child.*

But she wasn't her child. Mary stroked the child's leg. So soft, a child's skin. Like silk. She pinched the tender skin between her thumb and forefinger. She pressed her fingers together hard, smiling as she did so.

Mary Ellen awoke from her heavy sleep, tears already streaming from her tired eyes. As she struggled, Mary pinched her harder, twisting her fingers now, and her jagged, bitten fingernails dug into the little girl's leg. Mary Ellen tried to push away, but Mary held on tight, holding the little girl to her breast.

Her fingers slipped away as Mary Ellen wiggled, but she got another grip in the middle of Mary Ellen's back and squeezed again. Hard. As she pinched and held her tightly with one hand, Mary's other hand found and viciously pinched the little girl's arm. "There, there," she said. "Hush, now."

Mary Ellen screamed in pain as she struggled to get away, but Mary McCormick had a smile on her face, a distance in her eyes. She was—as the gangs of youths who roamed the streets of New York City declared—defending her territory. It was her right. She kept her eyes on the bedroom as she tortured the little girl who had invaded her home.

She heard a grunt from the darkness beyond the bedroom door, and a moment later Tom staggered out in a half-sleep and said, "What the hell's going on here? What are you doing to her?" His voice was angry.

"I don't know what's wrong with her," Mary said, feigning concern. "She was crying and since you didn't get up, I came to see to her. I suppose she had a bad dream." She released her grip on the child when Tom walked in, and now stroked her back as though trying to comfort her. Mary Ellen struggled, though, and Mary released her. The little girl tumbled to the floor and wailed as she lay there, writhing in pain.

Tom bent down and picked up the sobbing child. "C'mon girl. Let's put you back to bed. It's all right, now." Mary Ellen's tears flowed, and Mary watched as Tom carried her to the mattress. He whispered to her, kissed her puffy red cheek and stroked her hair.

Mary turned away and left the room. She felt better. Now, perhaps, she could get some sleep.

* * * * *

It was an unseasonably warm evening for the month of April in New York City. Henry Bergh stood at the intersection of Twenty-third Street and Fifth Avenue, watching a snarl of omnibuses, carts, and drays attempt to make their way to their varied destinations. As usual, it was more of a tangle than a flow, and watching the scene, Bergh realized he had his work cut out for him.

Indeed, earlier that afternoon, the nineteenth of April, 1866, the New York legislature passed the bill protecting animals. It punished an act, or omission of an act, that caused unjustifiable pain to any horse, mule, cow, cattle, sheep, or other animal. Not only that, the Attorney General for the State of New York and the District Attorney for New York City gave Henry Bergh's ASPCA the responsibility of representing them in any and all cases involving the law for the protection of animals. It was exactly what Bergh had hoped for.

Amidst the tangle of traffic, Bergh spotted an overloaded butcher cart. Stacked on their sides in the wagon were no fewer than eight calves, all strapped together with thick rope which burned into their skin as they swayed from side to side. One of the pitiful animals' heads was hanging over the side of the cart and had been crushed by a passing vehicle. A spatter of gore now decorated the rails of the cart and a rain of crimson droplets dotted the avenue as the cart made its slow progress toward the butcher shop.

Bergh nearly fell ill when he spotted it. As the cart labeled *McCormick's Fresh Meats* lumbered by, he called to the driver, "Are you the proprietor of McCormick's?"

The man nodded. "What of it?"

"The way you transport your animals, Mr. McCormick, is inhumane and unacceptable. I shall address my issue with you at a later date." McCormick glanced curiously back at his full cart as though he had never considered his methods of transporting stock to be inhumane, or indeed, anything out of the ordinary. He threw an arm up and snapped the reins, ignoring Bergh's warning.

Bergh let him go. He could find McCormick's shop later, and right now he had his eye on a teamster who was beating his fatigued workhorse with a leather whip. The horse was lathered from head to tail, and looked ready to collapse under the cutting sting of the whip.

"My friend," called Bergh. "you can't do that anymore."

He looked up at Bergh. "Can't beat my own horse? The devil I can't," he said, raising the whip even higher, and planting a boot in the horse's rib cage as well. The horse labored to breathe and foam dripped from its mouth in steady, frothy rivulets.

Bergh, now with the law behind him, remained calm. He approached the teamster. "You are not aware, probably, that you are breaking the law, but you are," Bergh said. "I have the new statute here, in my pocket, and it states that the horse is yours only to treat kindly. I could have you arrested."

The man had stopped and now stared at Bergh, his mouth hanging open.

"I only want to inform you what a risk you run."

"Go to hell," the teamster cursed. "You're mad!"

Roughly one hour after their initial exchange, the man became the American Society for the Prevention of Cruelty to Animals' first arrest—after Bergh convinced the policeman he approached that it was truly a law. To convince him, he showed him the statute and implored him to seek out a higher authority who would recognize it for what it was.

The next day, Bergh found a modest office in an upstairs room at Fourth Street and Broadway, a simple, unimpressive room, with a carpet, half a dozen chairs, and a table. From there, he could stand at the window and witness for himself daily violations of the ordinance he fought to enact. Soon, he hoped, he would be able to stand at that window, or some other, and see not one cruelty imposed upon a defenseless animal.

Over the next weeks, prestigious members of the New York professional community needed to be secured as financial supporters, board members, and officers for the society. When this task was complete, the society could get on with the work it was made to do.

It was the beginning of what Bergh knew in his heart would be his life's work.

* * * * *

August 1866
Four Months Later

Mary McCormick was truly frightened for the first time since the riots in 1863 had lit her entire neighborhood ablaze. This time it wasn't fire.

Doctor McLaughlin twisted his gray handlebar mustache between his fingers as he sat by her husband's bedside. "He's in advanced stages, Mary," the doctor whispered.

"I can't talk to you now, doctor," Mary said. "I'm too . . . I'm scared out of my mind and I don't want to talk right now." But it wasn't her fear of Tom's death that frightened her. Talking meant she would have to breathe the air in the room.

Tom McCormick's face showed the effects of massive dehydration; his normally sharp features had become pinched, and his once tanned face had turned a pale blue. All of his extremities had turned dark before Mary's eyes, and as ashamed as she was for being more fearful of dying than of her husband's departure, she was unable to help herself. A good wife would be right by her husband's side comforting him in his hour of death, not cowering from his illness. But a powerful fear of death gripped Mary. She pressed against the wall farthest from where Mary Ellen and Dr. McLaughlin sat over her husband, watching in silent dread as the little girl touched him and whimpered.

Tom loved Mary Ellen, Mary knew, and that only made Mary hate her

111

more. It seemed the youngster knew he was the only one who cared for her, but that didn't really surprise Mary. Never good at hiding her true feelings, she couldn't pretend to love the child and didn't bother to try.

Mary slid along the wall and dropped into the rocking chair. The door was so close . . . how she wanted to bolt and run outside where the air was clean and pure! Let Mary Ellen touch his wrinkled skin and become ill, not her. She was nothing more than a poor substitute for their own children, Maggie, Avery, and Helen. Tom had loved them so much it tore him apart to watch them die, one by one. *And he had blamed her.*

When she was fifteen years old, Mary had run away from a home where her mother's man friends would have their way with her. Her mother had known about it but did nothing, so she had ended up here, in New York City, having known since her teens that she would never love any man. But she wasn't stupid; it was clear she would need them eventually. After all, they ran the world and they had the means to keep her alive.

If she had to sleep with them, she would take as much pleasure as she could from it, and she learned much about it over the years, from her husband and scores of others. It wasn't their companionship she wanted. It was the satisfaction of taking from them what she had given unwillingly as an adolescent girl. She no longer cried, as she had then. Now, she laughed. It wasn't them who *gave* her pleasure. Mary took it. She *stole* it.

Dr. McLaughlin stood, bringing Mary back to the present as he brushed the wrinkles from the legs of his pants, then turned toward her, his face solemn. The wrinkles had creased his face over the years, and Mary thought it was amazing he was still alive, being exposed to so much disease and death for years upon years. How did doctors stay well? Maybe they were angels, hallowed, impervious to the ravages of plague.

"I presume you're aware, Mary," said the doctor, "that he is going to pass on soon."

Mary nodded.

"I . . . recommend that you keep Mary Ellen away from him, I'm afraid," he added. "Children are especially apt to contract this type of asthmatic cholera."

"Mary Ellen! Come here, now!"

Mary Ellen looked at her, her eyes huge with fear.

"Now, I said!"

The child moved slowly toward her and Mary put up her hands. "Don't touch me!" she screamed, pointing to the other room. "Go in there and don't come out until I tell you."

McLaughlin looked at her in shock. "She's frightened, Mrs. McCormick. Understandably so, I should say."

"She isn't a very obedient child, though I don't expect you to know such things."

Mary Ellen's cries could be heard from the other room.

"Well," said the doctor, "you've lost enough children, Mary. I don't want to see you lose another." He stepped toward the door, opened it, and took one glance back at Tom. "Send a messenger when the time comes. There's nothing more I can do for him." He stepped out, closing the door behind him.

Mary let out her breath, fearing she was already ill. Moving around her husband, she looked out the window toward the alley below. She saw Dr. McLaughlin walking away, and waited another ten minutes before taking her shawl and hat from the table.

Mary left the flat and locked the door behind her. Francis Connolly would need to know what was happening. Whether Tom died in an hour or a week, she needed to secure her future.

* * * * *

After the door closed, Mary Ellen waited until she was sure Mama was long gone before creeping out to see her daddy again. She looked through the door and saw him still there, lying on her little mattress in the front of the house.

She went to him and knelt beside him, resting her head on his shoulder. He was asleep, so he didn't stroke her hair, but he was there and that made her feel safe. She hummed to herself, thinking about her story books and hoping things would someday be like Timmy's life, the little boy in the stories who had a doggy, a sister, and a lot of little playmates. Mary Ellen knew his name was Timmy because Papa had told her so.

As she lay there dreaming, she didn't notice Papa's chest stop rising and falling. Mary Ellen drifted off to sleep a few moments later, never once worrying about who would protect her from that moment forward.

* * * * *

Bergh read the anonymous note once more. Whoever wrote it seemed to have a good deal of knowledge. Too much to ignore. He checked his pocket watch. It was just after three in the afternoon. "Mr. Evans," he said, "let's head down to the docks. We can round up some more agents on the way."

"What's happening, Mr. Bergh?" Alonzo Evans asked, one of his best young ASPCA officers.

"We," Bergh said, "have to await a schooner called *The Active*. It's loaded down with South American turtles being transported in a terrible state, or so I'm led to believe." He patted Evans on the shoulder and added, "I'll need you because of your size, Alonzo. You know those shipboard men can be a tough crowd."

The burly young Evans smiled, his large, round face beaming. "I'll be glad to help, Mr. Bergh," he said. "My father always said I should use my size for good things, not bad." His blue eyes twinkled with excitement.

"That's fine, boy! And I think this is about as good as it gets!" Bergh pushed out the door and the others followed. Within an hour, Bergh, Evans, and six other agents waited patiently on the wharf as *The Active's* crew secured the dock lines. The skipper was the first man down the ramp. Bergh wasted no time in approaching him.

"I'm Henry Bergh with the American Society for the Prevention of Cruelty to Animals," he said. "Who's in charge of this ship?"

"I am," called a crusty looking, bearded man from atop the ramp.

"And what is your name, sir?"

"I'm the captain of *The Active*, that's who I be," he croaked. "Nehemiah Calhoun."

"I'd like permission to inspect your cargo."

"My crew's tired, Mister. They've been at sea for a long while," Calhoun said.

Bergh held up his society badge. "I'll ask you just once more, Captain Calhoun. Then you'll be off to the Tombs."

Calhoun stood silent, unsure. His men stopped and waited to see what

114

would transpire. "Go ahead, then!" he shouted. "But be quick about it. My men deserve every minute ashore they get."

"A wise decision, Captain Calhoun. Please, won't you assist me in my inspection?" Bergh led his agents up the ramp, while Calhoun stomped along behind them. Bergh was appalled at what he found.

Rows and rows of large turtles lay on their backs. Several of them were dead, many others near death. Hundreds of them stacked two and three high. The stench of rotting meat emanated from the carcasses. Bergh was angry and sickened, but remained calm. His eyes met the captain's. "Did these animals receive any nourishment on this voyage?"

The gruff old man with gray hair and bushy eyebrows answered, "We doused 'em with water a couple of times a day, just like we always do. Now, clear out and let us get 'em on the wagon to Fulton's Market. I'll get paid nothing for dead turtles."

Bergh ignored his command. "They've eaten nothing? Had nothing whatever to drink?" He stared in disbelief. "Sir, do you have an ounce of decency in your soul?"

"You've wasted enough of my time, man!" the skipper shouted, then barked orders to his men. "Untie these goddamned turtles and get them ashore!"

Two young deck hands set about untying the ropes that held the turtles in place. As they pulled the rope from the first animal, Bergh discovered yet another horror. Brutal holes had been bored through the turtles' flippers with some sort of jagged tool, and a single rope ran from animal to animal—right through the wounds—lashing them to the deck. All of the turtles were wounded like this, with blatant disregard for their suffering.

Bergh stood. "Calhoun, you and the rest of your heartless crew disgust me." He held up his society badge once more, this time so everyone could see. "I'm placing all of you under arrest, by authority of the American Society for the Prevention of Cruelty to Animals." And with that, Bergh rounded the men up and marched them all to the Tombs.

The days that followed were hard ones for Bergh. In court, the defense attorneys argued that the cold-blooded turtle wasn't an animal. "What then, is it?" Bergh asked, in court that day. "Since there are but three kingdoms in nature, is the turtle a vegetable or a mineral?"

The day after that, newspapers all over the city ridiculed Henry Bergh and his society. Cartoonists depicted Bergh as half donkey, the huge ears protruding from his characteristic top hat. The judge wasn't sympathetic to his plea, either. It was far more difficult to gain sympathy for a cold-blooded animal than a dog, cat, or horse, and Bergh quickly lost the case.

One city paper devoted six full columns to what they called Bergh's "turtle incident". Bergh paid it no attention. Any public awareness of the cruelties imposed upon animals was better than none. At least people knew an organization existed that cared about the rights of all animals.

A week after the trial ended, Bergh took his wife, Matilda, to dinner. Upon entering the dining room of the restaurant, he saw a live turtle resting on a silk-covered pillow, high above the door of the restaurant. A sign above it expressed:

> Having no desire to wound the feelings of the SPCA or of its president, Henry Bergh, we have done what we could for the comfort of this poor turtle during the last few remaining days of its life. He is appointed unto death, however, and will be served in soups and steaks on Thursday. Come dine and do justice to his memory.

Bergh and Matilda turned and walked out of the restaurant, the quiet laughter of the patrons echoing in their ears. That night, in the quiet of his home, Henry Bergh cried.

Matilda held him and tried to comfort him. "Now, Henry," she said softly. "You knew from the beginning what you would face. You must remember how many there are who believe in what you're doing. They're the ones who support you, not the others."

"I didn't expect to find such indifference, Matilda! Even when I expose abuse, it's laughed at! Where's their sense of decency, of right and wrong?"

Matilda nodded and hugged her husband. As a girl, she had married Henry because he was exciting, and though their lives had changed drastically, he still *was* exciting. From the moment he looked her in the eye on their wedding day—the crowd of guests in the other room—and suggested they elope then and there, she had known life as Mrs. Henry Bergh would be entertaining. And they *had* eloped, leaving the room full of guests dumbfounded.

Anything, any challenge he faced, he did with such zeal, Matilda some-times just liked to stand aside and watch what would happen next. No matter what the future held, she was already very proud of her husband. "You'll educate them, Henry. That's all. It will take time, so don't expect to win the world over in the first year." She hugged him again.

"I'm crying like a child," he said.

Matilda smiled. "Nonsense. Those tears are from your heart, and I want you to shed them whenever you feel the need." She hesitated for a moment, then added, "It may be a good idea to do your crying at home, though, dear. No sense in giving the cartoonists any more ammunition."

He looked at her for a long moment and his eyes lit up. "You're right!" he said. "I shall write Professor Louis Agassiz immediately, outlining the meth-ods of transport of these poor beasts. He, above all others, should have quite a say in the matter."

"The turtles again?" Matilda asked, rolling her eyes.

"What else?" Bergh grabbed some paper, dipped his pen in ink, and started scribbling out the letter.

He sent the letter off, and within a week, a reply from the great naturalist came. It read:

Mr. Bergh:

I need not tell you that men have always excuses enough to justify their wrongdoings. So it was with the slave trade, so it is today with the turtle market; and though black men are more likely to be protected hereafter, their former suf-ferings during long sea voyages are on record, and human-ity shudders at the tale. Whether men may ever be refined enough to feel their guilt when they torment animals re-mains to be seen; and your Society will no doubt do its share in educating them in that direction.

But to say that turtles do not suffer when dragged from their natural haunts, tied that they may not be able to move, turned upside down, etc., etc., is simply absurd. It is true that they can live for a long time without food or drink, but they do feel pain, and are indeed very sensitive to some injuries. That of turning them upside down among others is sufficient, for instance, to prevent their eggs from hatching. Their suffering may be inferred by the violent and convulsive movements to which the perforation of their fins gives rise; and yet to this proceeding dealers in turtles generally resort in order to tie them more closely and pack a large number in a smaller space.

Of course, when tied in this manner they may suffer less by being turned on their backs, because the fins are relieved from the pressure of their whole weight. But the best evidence I can afford that they suffer in that position is that they die if it is much prolonged; and yet turtles are among the animals which resist longest privations of all kinds. Is not the fact that they may die merely from the attitude in which they are forcibly kept the most complete evidence of their suffering?

Sincerely,
Professor Louis Agassiz

Bergh was astounded at the reply and forwarded the letter to *The New York Times*. Afterward, he checked the newspaper each day until he found the following editorial comment on October 2, 1866:

It was hardly creditable to this city that Mr. Bergh should have found it necessary to fortify the commonsense opinion that boring holes through live turtles' claws gave them pain, by an appeal to Professor Agassiz, but there was no alternative. The opponents of the SPCA assailed him with vituperation, and found coarse jokes and supercilious ridicule their most effective weapons. We hope that the general subject will receive more attention. The young men and children who are to be entrusted with so great an inheritance as our Republic should not be indifferent to the torturing of poor creatures, at the mercy of us who call themselves a superior order of beings.

Bergh was thunder struck. "Matilda! Come, read this article!"

She read the article slowly, put it down, and said, "You see, Henry? I was right. Never give up."

"Tildy, I always knew why I married you," Bergh said. "My dear, I'm so pleased with this *Times* article, I shall write to thank Mr. Raymond myself."

A few days later, Alonzo Evans came in carrying a copy of a small magazine called the *New York Day Book*. "I found this," he said, giving it to Bergh. "You might want to read it right away."

"So it continues," Bergh said, taking the paper. On the front page was an article entitled, "Cruelty to Turtles and Negroes". The article read:

> We desire to ask the Professor a question. If Negroes, thrown out of a certain position, die at the rate of ten percent per annum, while in another position they increase at more than the usual rate of the white population, which is the natural position? The position to which they increase and multiply, or that in which they perish from the face of the earth? If turtles die when on their backs, is not the Negro as emphatically on his back when he dies out as the turtle is? If the best evidence that a being suffers in a certain position is that it dies out, what more proof do we need of the inhumanity and cruelty of tearing a race from its natural protectors? We pause for a reply.

"Preposterous!" Bergh shouted. "This . . . this is typical of the newspapers . . . the silent enemy! They take a simple comparison of inhumane treatment and try to use it as a defense against freeing the Negro from slavery!"

"What'll you do about it?" asked Evans.

"This is directed to Professor Agassiz. All I can do is make sure he sees it and that he has the chance to respond. I'll mail him a copy of the article immediately. I only hope he isn't regretful he ever became involved."

Bergh sent off the article the next day. A short while later, he received a clipping from Professor Agassiz—a letter responding to the *Day Book* article that he had written for publication in the *Boston Transcript:*

> It is true that the Negroes have been dying at a fearful rate during the trial of their passage from bondage to freedom. But the comparison of the article in Day Book is not applicable in this case. Let the editor remember that Negroes were formerly brought from Africa to this country in slave ships pretty much in the way in which turtle dealers now forward their ware to New York. If the Day Book will directly affirm that the practice should be resumed, I will admit that the turtles may with propriety be treated henceforth as they are now.

"The professor is a quite a scholar," Bergh said. "Matilda, as long as I have philanthropists like this gentleman on my side, there is no reason to despair!"

Matilda came up behind him and rubbed his shoulders. "Professor Agassiz's response will help, darling. Just remember there will be many more triumphs, but there will also be frustrations to equal them."

11

November 1868
Two Years Later

Fanny sat alone in her apartment, shivering as she drank from a half empty bottle of rye. The lamp had burned out hours ago, but she didn't bother to relight it. The darkness had become a friend to her. It blocked out the dinginess of her apartment and let her imagine she was anywhere except this horrid place.

She wiped a dirty hand over her face and sighed at the pale, cheerless walls of her single room. Terry had closed the pub over a year earlier when he decided to return to Ireland in an attempt to rebuild his family home. He had received an appeal from his young brother who remained there, and the pull homeward was too strong for him to resist. When he told her about his decision, Fanny had almost asked him to let her go along.

Being Mrs. Joseph Gibbon was not what being Mrs. Thomas Wilson might have been. Fanny tried her best to hide it, but her misery was obvious to Joseph, and she could never hide how much she missed Mary Ellen and Thomas. It had been over four years since Thomas was killed—more than two

121

since Mary Ellen—and it still felt as though it all ended yesterday, so alive was the pain in her heart.

A year earlier, she and Joseph had both started working out of their room rolling cigars, and for a while, it supplied them with enough income to survive. New machines had been invented that allowed anyone to fill the leaves with tobacco and roll them evenly. The money wasn't much, but Joseph had never seemed interested in earning more than a meager living anyway, something Fanny had come to accept.

They would work side-by-side in complete silence for hours at a time. Often, Fanny would leave the room to take a quick drink from a stashed bottle of brandy or rye. Her absences became more and more frequent, and each time she returned, Joseph knew. He would look at her and shake his head, but after a while, Fanny ceased to care. The numbness was all she lived for. Joseph finally responded to her despair by enlisting in the Army. Stationed on Governors Island, he had only been home twice in the last six months.

So here she was, alone, just as she had been when she first came to this country from England. But how different things were now. She had made the worst decisions, never knowing then how they would shape her life in years to come. Now it had come to this darkness. Here, alone in this pitiful room, alcohol was her only light.

Fanny tipped and drained the last of the rye into the glass, then dropped the empty bottle on the table, where it rolled to the edge and fell to the floor with a crash. It didn't matter. Fanny couldn't see the glass, or feel anything except her pain.

Nothing really mattered anymore.

* * * * *

December 1869
Thirteen Months Later

Henry Bergh and several SPCA agents were spread out at the Spring Street intersection near Bowery, where six different car lines converged. The five o' clock rush hour traffic was heavy, and an ankle-deep slush covered the streets. The blustery weather showed no sign of letting up as the straining horses struggled to forge through the snow, pulling overloaded cars carrying heavy freight and passengers only interested in one thing: getting out of the weather. The SPCA movement had grown as quickly as the years had passed. By 1867, Buffalo had established a branch. Brooklyn had its own SPCA, Pennsylvania chartered another branch in 1868, and San Francisco and Boston were next. By 1869, New Jersey and Maine had opened offices and even Canada chartered its own SPCA. Each independently controlled, they had all been designed after the organization Henry Bergh had begun. From coast to coast, all across North America, Bergh's dream was being realized in leaps and bounds.

As Bergh eyed the scene, his heavy woven scarf wrapped tightly around his neck, the Third Avenue streetcar, overloaded with passengers, approached Spring Street with two sweat-covered, fatigued horses in the traces. The driver whipped the horses again and again, the car barely moving along the tracks. Bergh knew with certainty that the driver would not see him, but he *would* make sure his voice was heard.

"Stop! Unload!" he called, moving onto the tracks, his hands upraised.

The driver saw him at the last moment, tugged on the reigns, and cursed aloud as the horses slowed to a walk. Bergh could tell the man was in no mood to be confronted, but he hardly cared. "Unload this car!" he ordered again.

"Move off the tracks, Bergh!"

"When you unload this car, I shall move, sir!"

The horse car drew to a halt three feet in front of Bergh. He stepped forward to inspect the horses, and as he did so, the irate driver leaned forward and knocked Bergh's hat from his head, screaming profanities.

Bergh looked at his hat for a few moments, then met the driver's eyes. Without a word, he reached out and took the man's collar with one hand and the seat of his pants with the other. Still perfectly silent, he hauled the driver from the car and tossed him head first into a snowbank. Bergh then retrieved his hat from the snow and dusted it off.

Cheers arose from the passengers of the car, but their cheers soon turned to grumbles when Bergh removed the horses from the traces. He hitched them to a nearby post, leaving the crowd to stare at the horseless car in disbelief and growing anger.

The embarrassed driver of the overloaded car pulled himself from the snow and blended in with the other passengers as they abandoned the disabled transport and trudged their way down the street.

The cars stacked up behind the empty rail car and soon the blockade carried all the way to Chatham Street. Bergh, wearing his heavy winter boots, crunched a path of snow directly through the intersection, carefully inspecting the overburdened horses harnessed to public and private wagons. Other agents of the ASPCA fanned out through the tangle.

"There!" Bergh shouted. "Alonzo! Hold up the driver of that dray!"

"The yellow one with the single horse?" the agent asked.

"Yes. Don't let him away. Hurry," Bergh said.

Bergh approached another driver, his horse harnessed so tightly the leather had embedded itself into the animal's now bloody flesh. He held up his badge and said, "I'm Henry Bergh of the ASPCA. Please direct this vehicle to the side of road."

"Forget it, pal," the driver said. "I've heard about you. You won't impose your silly sentiments on my animals." The driver stepped from his dray, his fists balled as he approached Bergh. He faltered when he saw the muscular old gentleman towered over him—a good six inches.

"It's . . . too damned cold to lose my horse!" he said, his courage suddenly wilted.

"Not my concern," Bergh said. "Mine is the poor condition of this draft animal. Besides," he added. "I'll make a bargain with you. Remove the animal from the traces this instant and I won't file charges against you."

Soon, there were so many abandoned drays parked in the street that even those led by healthy animals couldn't pass through the intersection. Before long, hundreds of enraged, cold, tired New Yorkers made their way on foot through the icy slush.

Many of the ailing horses would have to be taken to shelters by SPCA agents. Because some of the horses were so grossly abused, misdemeanor charges would be filed against the owners, and they would not take the animals home tonight.

"Henry! Come look at this!"

Bergh made his way over to the cart. "What is it?"

"Take a look." Alonzo pointed to the cart.

Bergh leaned into the cart and found it to be filled with live geese. "What is it, Alonzo?"

"Their feet, sir," Evans said. "Look at the nails."

Bergh moved to the back of the wagon and opened it. He leaned down to get at better look. "What the—"

He stood and gawked at the butcher, then leaned down once more to make sure what he thought he saw was true. "My God," he whispered.

The butcher had nailed the geese's feet to the wooden floor of the cart to prevent them from flying out.

"Arrest this man and call someone over to remove these nails as gently as possible."

The night was long, but many injustices were put to a halt.

* * * * *

The following day, Bergh sat in his office on Fourth and Broadway, sorting through the many names and filling out the required forms to complete the previous night's work. Across from him sat Jack Smyth, another of his agents. He, too, had a stack of papers in front of him. It was tedious work, and the young agent was more in the mood to chat than do paperwork.

"So . . . Mr. Bergh," he said. "How did you come to love animals so much?"

Bergh smiled, then put the paper he was reading aside. "I can't really say it's a love of animals," Bergh said. "It's simply a matter of right and wrong, just as I've always said."

Smyth nodded. "I agree with that, but we do have a little dog in our home. My wife has always loved them."

"I've never really cared for pets," Bergh said. "Have you heard many— how should I say—*stories* about me?" he asked, toying with the corner of his mustache, his mouth turned up in a slight smile.

"No, sir. Only what I've read in the papers. Cartoons, mostly. Silly ones." Smyth looked embarrassed.

Bergh laughed. "Ah, the lifeless enemy. Ignore them, Jack. Do that and you're sure to find success."

"I'll remember that."

"Once, when I was still in my twenties," Bergh said, "and my wife and I were on an extended honeymoon, we visited Seville. While we were there, we decided to attend a bullfight, since it was one of the favorite local attractions in that country." Bergh leaned forward on the desk and remembered. "During that bullfight, we witnessed the brutal killing of eight bulls and over twenty horses, many of them with their entrails gored from their bodies. We left Spain with sickness in our hearts, needless to say. My wife, Matilda, was particularly horrified. I think that was when I realized something had to be done to protect animals, though I had no idea that I would be the one to begin the movement in America."

Smyth shook his head, smiling.

Bergh waved a hand in the air. "The bullfights still go on. Probably always will, as long as people frequent the tournaments."

"It's a pity," Smyth said. "Slaughtering animals for nothing more than sport."

"It is, but I had an interesting revelation while watching the spectacle," Bergh said, reflectively. "One of the young picadors—a horseman—was badly hurt by a bull, but my sympathy wasn't with him, for the men who do this have reason. At first I was surprised that I felt nothing at his injuries, but I cannot help reaching the conclusion that the picadors know their danger, are the inventors of the scene, and therefore richly merit death in any shape."

Smyth appeared to think about it for a moment. "I see the logic, Mr. Bergh. And allow me to add that it is a great honor working with you."

"It is an honor to have you beside me, young man. I hope to have many more like you join our forces."

"I'm sure many more will, Mr. Bergh."

Both men turned as a man walked through the door and caught his foot on a hole in the carpet. He stumbled into the nearest desk and looked at Bergh, his face red.

"I apologize for that," Bergh said. "Priorities, you know. I'm Henry Bergh, sir. How may I help you?"

The man recovered quickly and said, "Hello, Mr. Bergh, my name is Jason Shockley, and I've come to make a donation." He looked back at the hole in the carpet and added, "I see I've stumbled into a perfect way to be of service to you. Please, Mr. Bergh, buy a new carpet and send the bill to me."

Bergh shook his head. "No, thank you, Mr. Shockley," he replied. "But please leave the money and I'll put it to better use for my animals."

* * * * *

Mary Ellen stared down at the alley below and watched the many children playing tag together. She enjoyed hearing their laughter, but more than anything, she wondered what it would be like to play with them. That was something she wasn't allowed to do. She knew all their games, and over time, had learned all the rules, but she would never be able to join in.

Some of them used to see her in the window and call her to come down and play with them, but not any more. Now they made fun of her, calling her things like 'simpleminded' and 'feeble'. Mary Ellen didn't know what feeble meant, but the way they said it hurt her feelings and made her cry.

Mary Ellen slid down into the chair and rested her head against the window frame. She sat like this so she could hear them better. Her new papa, Mr. Connolly, had hammered nails into the window slider so she couldn't raise it more than an inch. Mama said it was for her own good, because she might fall out and hurt herself. Mary Ellen knew that was silly because she was a big girl now, and big girls didn't fall out of windows, at least she didn't think so.

One day she had been prying on it with a knife from the kitchen, trying to raise the window just a little more. Mama opened the door real quiet and sneaked up behind her, and it was a day Mary Ellen would never forget. She couldn't sit down for two days, and she had to sleep on her tummy for a week.

The six-year-old sat up again and rested her chin on the sill, dreaming of the feeling of the rough street touching the bottoms of her bare feet. As her mind drifted away, far outside the walls of her home, something caught her eye in the street. A feeling of panic overtook her as she ducked down and slid to the floor.

Mama was walking up the sidewalk! She might have seen her peeking through the window. How stupid of her! She'd sneaked out of the closet enough times to know better than to be careless.

Mary Ellen hurried to the closet and slipped inside. She looked at the room one last time, making sure there was nothing that would tell mama she'd been out in the room. Mary Ellen saw nothing that would tattle on her, closed the door behind her, and sat silent in the darkness.

Once she was comfortable, she felt on the floor for her tiny pieces of string. She had collected them over time, and each was special in its own way. Some were longer than others were, and she could wrap them around her finger many times. Others were softer, and she would dangle them against her face, letting the silky threads tickle her nose and cheeks. She loved the feeling of things touching her face like that. Mama never did that. She slapped her face when she was naughty. Sometimes even when she wasn't. Mama could get . . . upset, she said it was.

It wasn't good when Mama got upset.

Mary Ellen played with the string and waited to hear Mama open the door. Mama would remember she was in the closet right away today because there was some sewing that needed to be done and she usually let her help with it. Mary Ellen liked helping Mama. When she did things just like her mama said, she didn't act mean or hit her, but sometimes she didn't understand what her mama *wanted* her to do. She could tell when Mama was getting mad, but she didn't know what to do to fix it. It always ended up bad, with Mama slapping her in the face or whipping her bare legs with the horse rope .

Mary Ellen ran her hand over her legs as she thought of this. The whip hurt more than just about anything except the iron. The whip marks quit stinging by the next day, but the burns from the iron stung for a long time! She didn't have any burns that hurt now. Mary Ellen made herself real quiet when Mama was ironing. It was just a good thing to do that.

Mama did get mad when she went into the closet without being told. She said it was disrespectful for a little girl to ignore grown-ups unless she was told to, or if she saw they were having relations. Mary Ellen didn't like to be in the room when they were having relations anyway. Mama and Papa acted like they didn't even know she was there and they made scary noises. Plus they were naked, and that made her feel funny inside.

Mary Ellen knew when to be quiet, when to act like she was invisible. But there were times it didn't matter what she did, for Mama would turn angry and beat her no matter what. Mary Ellen could tell when she was in a mood like that. During those times she would rather stay in the closet and wait for Papa to get home. The beatings were never as bad when he was there. He took most of Mama's attention and she quit noticing her. That was okay.

She did like it when Mama would let her practice saying her letters, though. That was her favorite thing in the whole world. She almost knew what all the letters were now, and she could even read some little words in the two old books Papa had brought home for her one day. He said he found the books in a garbage bin, and though they were dirty, they were still full of pretty pictures of smiling girls and boys with their families. Maybe if she could read them she could tell Mama how things were supposed to be. Everyone should be happy, like in the picture book!

I would love that, thought Mary Ellen. She decided then and there that she would beg Mama to let her sound out some words after she was done helping her with the sewing—even if it meant a beating later.

Mary Ellen's heart leapt into her throat. The book! She'd been looking at the pictures and left the book on the windowsill! And Mama told her not to leave the closet.

Mary Ellen held her breath and listened. Mama's footsteps weren't in the hall yet, and that meant she had time. She pushed open the closet and looked at the front door. Still closed. No sounds but her own breathing and her heart pounding in her ears. Mary Ellen saw her book on the sill, and tiptoed toward it. How dumb for her to forget it!

She reached the window and peeked outside. Perhaps Mama had stopped to chat with one of the men who worked on the street. Mama did that sometimes, but she wasn't there, and Mary Ellen still didn't hear her coming up the hall. Perhaps she was in one of the shops. Mary Ellen turned and hurried toward the closet, the book in her hand.

The door flew open and Mama was there, staring at her. Her eyes were wide with disbelief, but the look turned quickly to anger.

Mary Ellen babbled, "Mama! I'm sorry Mama! I wanted to see if you were coming—"

"Shut up!" she shouted. "You know what to do, so do it!"

"No, Mama! I only needed light to see! To look at my book!"

"Don't you dare disobey me, you little devil. Give me that silly book!" She grabbed the book from Mary Ellen's hand and opened it. Mama ripped the pages from it one by one, wadding them up and throwing them at Mary Ellen.

Mary Ellen fell to her knees and cried as she watched her mama destroy her only love.

When she finished she said, "Against the wall, child, and I mean *now!*"

She felt herself being pulled up by her hair and a second later the wall came fast toward her face.. She slammed into it and slid to the floor.

"Stand up! Now!"

Mary Ellen stood slowly, her legs trembling. Her chest heaved as she sobbed in fear.

"Face the wall and stay there while I get my whip!"

Mary Ellen did as she was told, the fear in her heart increasing with each passing second. She was sure that Mama knew that. She heard the awful creaking of the kitchen cupboard as Mama opened it and removed the whip. As it squeaked closed, she glanced over her shoulder. The whip was in her hand, and the many leather strands at the end of it were stained just a little darker than the rest of it. Mary Ellen thought she knew why. It was her blood that had turned the stinging strands dark. Blood was so scary, and it hurt, too.

"Face the wall!" Mama said.

Mary Ellen obeyed. As the whip came slapping down upon her, her tear-filled eyes gazed toward the torn, wadded up pieces of her life strewn about the floor, never to be whole again. She did her best to drift far, far away, into the deepest places of her imagination.

A place her mama could never find.

* * * * *

"I want a latch on that door," Mary said. "She gets into things, Francis, and I won't have it!"

"You intend to lock her in the closet all day?"

"I said she gets into things, didn't I? I caught her with one of my dresses last week, I'll have you know. She was dragging it on the floor like an idiot."

"The child has no clothes of her own. She's probably envious," Francis said.

"And it shall remain so," Mary said. "She has what I happened upon, and nothing more. My time shall be spent making clothing for you, not that mis-begotten child. Now, about the latch?"

"Fine," Francis said. "I'll put a hook on the door tomorrow. I've just got one question. Why don't you get rid of the child if she bothers you so much?"

"Out of the question," Mary said, laughing. "If I did that, I'd have to clean the dishes, wash the floors and walls, and do all the other chores myself. All that besides making your clothes. The older she gets, the more use she'll be to me."

Francis looked at Mary Ellen, whose eyes remained fixed on the basin of dishes. "Maybe when she's older, she'll be of some use to me, too."

"I'd see her dead first," Mary said, rubbing Francis's shoulders. Francis smiled too, but as Mary massaged him, his eyes lingered on Mary Ellen.

12

January 1871
Two Years Later

"Thank you for seeing me Mr. Bergh," the young attorney said, squirming to sit comfortably in the wooden kitchen chair. "My name is Elbridge Gerry." The dark, mutton chop whiskers on his round face were well trimmed, and his eyes glimmered with intelligence. A man of considerable size and obvious confidence, and the suit he wore was of the highest quality.

Bergh smiled. "It's certainly my pleasure, Mr. Gerry, and I do apologize for the furnishings here. The money is primarily for the animals, so I don't have the creature comforts, as it were." He held out his hand. "I'm well aware of your family's work. What can I do for you?"

Gerry shook Bergh's hand. "I've heard your organization has become overly burdened with cases," Gerry said. "I'd like to offer my services if you feel you can use them."

Bergh raised his eyebrows in surprise. His cases had increased substantially of late, and it seemed the word was out around the city. "Mr. Gerry," Bergh said, "I'm afraid we're not equipped to pay an attorney just now. Especially one of your stature."

Gerry put up his hands and said, "I'm afraid you misunderstand, Mr. Bergh. I meant to offer my services to your organization free of charge."

Bergh sat up in his chair. "Are you sure you can spare the time? I assure you I'll gladly accept your offer, Mr. Gerry, and anything you can do will be appreciated."

Gerry smiled and said, "I've spoken to a friend of mine, Eddie Price, and he tells me you're quite a prosecutor yourself. I want to take some of that off your hands, and because I support your cause, I'd like to get involved."

Elbridge T. Gerry was a wealthy man with a love for yachting and a keen legal mind. As they spoke, Bergh further learned that the attorney had watched the progress of the society for years, and believed, as did Bergh, that all animals had a right to kind treatment. After talking for over an hour about the daily operations and case load of the society, Bergh stood.

"Mr. Gerry, this is an extraordinary offer, and one I would be a fool to decline, though for what reason I would do that, I can't imagine." He held out his hand. "Welcome aboard."

Gerry shook his hand again. "Thank you, and believe me, it's my pleasure, Mr. Bergh. I understand you have several animal protection bills you'd like the legislature to consider. If you don't mind, I'll review them and prepare for a trip to Albany."

"Mr. Gerry, you're a sight for sore eyes, I must say. Without dealing with those bureaucrats I can put my attention where it is required. Now, the first order of business is for you to call me Henry," Bergh looked around the crowded office and said, "I'll get the files straight away, but you might want to take them back to your building. We're a bit pressed for space."

Gerry nodded agreement. "Absolutely. You don't need another body in here, Henry. Let me review these in my office and if I need any further clarification on anything, I'll put together a packet of requirements and send it by messenger."

"Good luck, sir," Bergh said. "I'm truly grateful."

"It's my pleasure, Henry," Gerry said. "And you may call me Elbridge."

* * * * *

133

Bergh sat at a desk in his office wondering how he would ever balance the ledger book open in front of him. The hands of his pocket watch told him it was nearly ten in the evening, and he knew Matilda would be waiting for him, as usual. He ran down the columns of figures once more, knowing he would never make the numbers balance any differently. He slammed the ledger book closed, the gaslight flickering wildly as he stared out the window, wondering if everything he had accomplished would be snuffed out for lack of financial support.

So many reports of animal abuse came in daily that the ever-growing staff of agents could hardly investigate them all. Still they worked diligently, with dozens of agents fanning out over Manhattan and fifty more carrying the load in New York State. Asking his friends for donations was no longer an option. Bergh had extended his palm so many times it was becoming an embarrassment. So many had given generously, as had he, but it was not enough. He needed a miracle, and though Bergh had seen his share of them, he knew they were still quite rare in New York City. It seemed he would have to eliminate some agents immediately or risk insolvency, whereupon he would risk losing the society entirely.

He turned out the lamp and tucked the ledger back into the file drawer. The uneven figures would still be there tomorrow. He put his hat atop his head and slipped into his coat as he opened the door. To his surprise, a messenger stood outside his office, his hand poised to knock.

The young man was startled at Bergh's appearance in the doorway and stuttered, "He-hello, sir. I've got a message for Henry Bergh."

"You have found him, young man," Bergh said.

He gave Bergh the letter and said, "I'm supposed to wait while you read it, sir. If you cannot meet the request, I'm instructed to return with a written response from you."

Bergh took the letter, wondering from whom the appeal for help came this time; what poor creature was in need of the society's intervention. So many came in each day, he was elated and afraid at the same time. Would he be able to help them all? He knew it was impossible, but each appeal received his full attention, and was dealt with according to severity and need. He unfolded the paper, and read it. The handwriting was scrawled and frail, the message quite simple:

Mr. Bergh:

I respectfully request that you come to St. Vincent's
hospital as soon as possible to see me. I have some news
that should come as quite a pleasant surprise.

Monsieur Louis Bonard

Bergh read the letter twice, then looked at the messenger, a frown on his
face. He couldn't place the name. "I'll call on Monsieur Bonard tonight,
young man. I guess that means your work is done."

"Thank you, sir. Have a pleasant evening."

Bergh flipped the boy a bit and locked the door behind him as he stepped
onto the sidewalk of Broadway. So it was to be good news Monsieur Bonard
had for him. That would be a welcome change from the distressing condition
of his ledgers. It would be nice to have something to feel encouraged about.

Bergh breathed in the warm evening air, glad to be out of the stuffy attic
rooms. The walls inside seemed to be closing in as the facility grew and more
agents completed paperwork inside, but with money so scarce, it would be
impossible to consider expanding. Bergh found himself thinking about it at
every spare moment, always considering going back to past supporters for
donations, but hesitant to be more of a pest than he'd already been.

The waiting coachman opened the door for Bergh. "Home, Mr. Bergh?"

"No," he replied, stepping into the carriage. "Take me by St. Vincent's
hospital, Roger. I've received quite an intriguing message. It won't take long,
I'm sure. You'll probably want to be getting home soon."

"If I've got plans other than sleep tonight, it's news to me," Roger said.
"I'm in no hurry to do that."

"Oh, you need a woman, Roger. One like my Matilda."

"Someday," chuckled the driver, closing the door and hopping into the
driver's seat. He guided the coach up Broadway, turned left on 12th Street,
and within ten minutes they had arrived at St. Vincent's Hospital. It was now
nearly ten-thirty, and the hospital was quiet. Only one nurse sat at the counter
inside when Bergh walked in.

After showing her the message, Nurse Hetrick led him to Bonard's room.

The man in the bed looked older than his years. As Hetrick had said, he was awake, reading *The New York Times* with an unlit pipe clenched in his teeth. He looked up as Bergh entered.

"Henry Bergh!" he said, a thick, French accent affecting his words. He removed the pipe from his mouth. "It is you! I would know that face anywhere!" He held out a thin, shaking hand.

Bergh stepped forward and shook it gently, feeling the feebleness in Bonard's grip. A distant agony was evident on his face, even though the broad smile he wore did its best to deny it.

"How do you do, Monsieur Bonard. I came as soon as I received your message."

"Ah, the messengers, the boys work hard, no? I thought I gave him more money than it was worth, but now that you are here, I wonder! To speak with you is an honor beyond price!"

"I'm not sure why you feel so strongly, sir, but I am grateful. Since the hospital is only a short distance from my office, I came without delay. I hope it's not an inconvenience."

"Not at all, Mr. Bergh. Let me tell you who I am, before you take me for an extravagant European! I'm a trader . . . or rather, I *was* a trader before my illness caused me to retire."

Bergh sat in the chair beside the bed. "Surely there's a good chance for your recovery, Monsieur. You're under constant care, and you're still quite a young man."

"Not so young, and not such a good chance to overcome whatever it is that kills me. The doctors don't know how to stop it, and each day I grow weaker. A man knows, Mr. Bergh. He knows when he is going to die, and I can tell you with certainty, I may not see next Sunday, much less Easter Sunday."

"I'm very sorry, Monsieur."

The Frenchman shook his head, and his bald scalp reflected the lamp light. "I've had a good life, Mr. Bergh. And though I will not see Easter, *you* will, which is one reason I called you. Now, back to my story. I traded with the Indians for many years. Liquor, oil, tools, blankets, whatever they needed. Guns, too. Why should they not be able to protect what is theirs? It is the right of every creature not to be driven from his home, no? Is that not what

136

you preach, Mr. Bergh?"

"You will receive no argument from me, Monsieur," Bergh said. "What we've done to the Indians is an injustice, and convincing ourselves they're savages doesn't change that."

"*Mon ami*, this dedication, this . . . this *conviction* is exactly why I contacted you. I shall help you! I have not chased the dollar all these years without catching him now and then. What is mine is mine alone, to do with as I please," Bonard said. "I will give you all that I have, and ask only one thing."

Bergh smiled at the good-hearted man. However small his gift, it would be appreciated, if only for the sincere intentions behind it. "What is that, Monsieur Bonard?"

"That if you ever have the power to reach so far, you will extend your protection to the tormented wild things of the forest and the plain."

"I will tell you sir," Bergh said, "our society has already spread westward. Even as this conversation takes place, we're working to protect the hunted animals of which you speak."

Bonard squeezed Bergh's hand and tears came to his eyes. "I cannot tell you how much it means to have met you. Perhaps I will see you again, later, in some other place."

Bergh nodded. "Perhaps, Monsieur Bonard. Perhaps you'll join my wife and me for Christmas dinner."

Bergh spent a few more moments with Bonard, giving him information on how to make the donation. He then bade the Frenchman good-bye, his mind occupied with so many things. The sick man had made an impact on him. On his deathbed, his only concern seemed to be his bequest to the society! An unselfish man; a rarity in the world today.

As he returned to his carriage, Bergh's mind drifted back to his most pressing problem; how he would see his organization through another month. It occupied his thoughts until the coach pulled into his drive, then it kept him awake most of the night.

He lay there in bed tossing the society's troubles over in his mind until the sun broke through the window, reminding him he was not out of time. As long as there was another day, there was hope.

Always hope.

* * * * *

Louis Bonard passed away less than two weeks following his hospital room visit. Bergh's mouth hung open as he stared at the paper in front of him. The digits were too many! It couldn't be!

"It's correct, Mr. Bergh," said Bonard's attorney. Monsieur Bonard has bequeathed to your society a sum of money somewhere in the neighborhood of $150,000."

Bergh read the words again. It was a miracle! That sickly man in the hospital who knew so well he would never see Christmas had not only been wise, he had been wealthy! And leaving it all to the SPCA! He gaped at the attorney representing Bonard's estate. "I don't know what to say. It's come at such a perfect time! I've got to tell Matilda immediately!"

"There are a few things that must be taken care of beforehand, Mr. Bergh. We are still in the process of trying to locate his closest relatives. So far, there are none to be found."

"How long before the money can be put to use?" Bergh asked. It would, after all, save the society from financial ruin, and was needed without delay.

"Keep in mind, what you've seen is the value of the entire estate. Approximately $40,000 is in currency, the rest is in real estate. Still, if no relatives contest Mr. Bonard's will, I don't see any reason why you can't have it."

"Contest his will? Why, surely his signature can be verified somehow."

Louis Bonard's attorney nodded. "Of course, but that means little if he has family who oppose the bequest. Our wonderful laws supply that opportunity, you know."

Bergh shook his head. "When a man's deathbed wish can be overturned, nothing else in this world should surprise me."

"Give me thirty days, Mr. Bergh. We'll have to correspond with the French government to get the necessary information. Hopefully, there won't be any delays."

* * * * *

August 1871
Seven Months Later

Etta Wheeler walked along the sidewalk of 41st Street, saddened by the advanced deterioration of the neighborhood since she'd left it. Not only had the general condition of the area taken a nasty turn, there was such awful overpopulation that she could barely walk forty yards without tumbling over another group of children. Some of them were of toddler age, others old enough to go to school, but all of them were filthy and near starving.

Etta cringed as she looked the neighborhood over, the dilapidation more apparent as she made her way south on Ninth Avenue. Unfortunately, Margaret Bingham's building—which was still upscale for the area in which it was located—was smack in the middle of a part of New York City that had recently become known as *Hell's Kitchen.*

On a hot day like today, Etta couldn't argue the name, though it seemed to give the area little hope. The August sun beat down and turned the streets into griddles, wilting the spirits of the children who crawled under whatever they could find that would provide them shade. Certainly the interiors of the buildings sweltered—no place for so many little ones.

On her way to Mrs. Bingham's building, Etta wondered if the barrenness around her had grown to a point beyond the coffers of St. Luke's Mission. The funds available to Pastor Jameson's charities had not increased over the years; in fact they had diminished considerably. Still, the pastor refused to quit offering services to the poor. Just when Etta became depressed enough to believe that her efforts made no real difference, there would be that one child, that one mother who would gaze at her with such gratitude, it was all worthwhile.

The building just down from Mrs. Bingham's had only fifteen rooms, yet it accommodated thirty-six families with fifty-eight children all told. The only breathing space for them was a filthy yard just twelve feet square, surrounded by walls, six stories high. Again, it was the children who suffered, for they had no means to help themselves.

Etta's husband, Charles, worked as a reporter for a small newspaper, and though his income was meager, his father had left them a lovely home away from the slums in which to live, so there was no rent. Still, Etta walked out the front door of their comfortable home each day to come here, to the tenements. She was fond of the people she had come to know, and loved seeing to them. It gave her peace, and a feeling of well being. When she and Charles decided to marry, they had agreed not to have children. There were too many unloved children in the world already, and Etta had devoted her life to the church and the needy. It wouldn't be right to bring children into a world such as this one, and her work for the mission didn't allow her the time anyway.

She arrived at Margaret's building and knocked on Mary Litzbeney's door.

"Etta!" Mary opened her arms and scooped Etta into them. They embraced for a moment, then Mary said, "Is this just a visit, or are you back to our buildings again?"

Etta shook her head. "Just a visit, I'm afraid, Mary. I just feel better when I come by and see you now and then."

The building was noisy, with voices echoing through the halls and making it almost impossible to hear. "Let's go inside and spend some time together, Etta. I've got a glass of water to cool you."

Etta stepped inside Mary's apartment. It was neatly furnished, in sharp contrast to the outer halls and the rooms Etta had passed on her way in. Etta relaxed on the sofa and the weight off her feet was glorious. "Mary, you keep your place so nice . . . surely you've noticed how crowded this building has become lately."

"It's the way these days," Mary said. "Too many people."

"Have you spoken to Mrs. Bingham?" Etta asked. "To find out why she allows the tenants to fill their rooms as they do? There must be a limit on the number of occupants per room."

Mary sighed and nodded. "Yes, Etta, and I do know why she allows it. You're correct. She does have the rules, she just doesn't enforce them." She gave a glass of water to Etta.

Etta drank half of it, surprising herself. "Why not? Isn't it a matter of health to keep the limit?"

"Their lives are difficult enough as it is," Mary said. "Margaret says she hates to make it harder for them."

Etta nodded, listening to the cacophony of voices, adults and children alike, around her. "I hate to think what they would do without her charity," she said.

"Speaking of charity, look outside my window," Mary said. "So many poor souls there, on the street. People like you make all the difference for many of them, Etta. Don't forget that for one second."

"I've always said, Mary. If I can save the life of just one child, I've given meaning to my life."

Mary laughed. "Etta, you've done that a hundred times over. You should be made a saint!"

* * * * *

"They *what*? We've been waiting for months already!" Bergh said, his face suddenly drawn and pale.

Gerry put a hand on Bergh's shoulder. "Come now, friend. It's politics as we've always known it. The French consul says they have rights to their countryman's money."

"Just because he's French?"

"Apparently. It's a lot of money, Henry. What do they have to lose by trying?"

"They *will* lose, Elbridge. You'll see to that, won't you?"

"It may take some time. You know what they're saying, don't you?"

"I hate to ask."

"Some of the Frenchmen with whom he dealt are claiming he was a miser; he kept his gold in barrels and boxes inside his room, protected by no fewer than eight separate locks."

"And what difference does that make?"

"They're trying to convince our government he was insane, their obvious intention to declare his will meaningless. They even say he believed in the transmigration of souls when one dies, presumably from man to animals. That is the reason, they say, the chap wanted the animals protected."

Henry paced back and forth. "And do they have evidence contrary to this belief?"

"Henry . . ."

"All right, all right. The important question is, are you prepared to go to Albany and fight for us?"

Gerry smiled broadly and his thick sideburns parted even further down the sides of his round face. "Of course, Henry! These confrontations are what I live for! There is one thing that might hold up our progress some, though."

"I hesitate to ask just what that might be."

"It's the land, Henry. We'll need to appeal to the legislature to approve an amendment to our charter empowering the society to hold real estate."

"God, I never thought of that."

"That's why you have me, friend. I don't see that it will be a problem, but as you know, it takes time and money to do these things."

Bergh shrugged. "Meanwhile, I'll try to use this endowment to gain the trust of some choice financial institutions. What do you think our chances are of everything turning out?"

Gerry put a hand on Bergh's shoulder and said, "Excellent. These disputes are expected, and all things considered, these are relatively inadequate claims. In this country, a man's will still holds exceptional weight. The bequest to the society is certainly stated clearly enough."

Bergh sighed, trying to force a smile. "So you're confident, then."

"Having to litigate to obtain it will likely reduce the net amount, but there is room for reduction considering the initial sum."

Bergh threw his arms around Gerry and hugged him, patting him on the back.

Gerry laughed heartily. "Henry! What on earth was that for?"

Bergh smiled. "Everything, Elbridge. It was for absolutely everything."

13

Late that afternoon, Henry and Matilda Bergh strolled down 6th Avenue, enjoying the light cloud cover that made the sunny day tolerable, even pleasant. Bergh breathed the warm air of the New York summer into his lungs. He left his overcoat home today, but the top hat came in handy as a shield from the sun, so it sat atop his head. Matilda on his arm, he looked around him, rejoicing in the observation that all the draft horses within his view appeared well watered and free from abuse.

He and Matilda visited Central Park, enjoying the beautiful scenery, the gracefulness of the water birds soaring over Manhattan Lake, and the children celebrating the wonder of youth in the playgrounds. Many people recognized him, most of them simply tipping their hats, some of them thanking him for his efforts in the interest of animals.

To Bergh, this made it all worthwhile; knowing somebody *did* care.

They approached 47th Street where a building was under construction. Bergh tilted his head back and shaded his eyes as he stared up at the tall framework. "It's going to be a big one, Tildy. Before long they'll block out the entire skyline."

Matilda nodded. "They practically do that already," she said. "Thank goodness for Central Park. A place to retreat from the congestion."

As they passed by the marble front of what would surely be a grand new store, he heard the smallest of sounds, but one that caught his ear as if it were a tuba. "Stop a minute," he said, putting up a hand. "Listen, Tildy. Do you hear that?"

Matilda stood close to him and listened. "No," she said, shaking her head.

"Come closer." He stood right up next to the building and stopped to listen. "See? There it is again! By the way, I like your perfume."

"Why thank you, dear. Is it a cat?" Matilda asked. "Or a kitten?"

Bergh leaned inside the building and saw a new wall, obviously just con-structed. He heard the mewing again. It sounded as though it came from inside the wall.

"Hey, Mister! Get away from there! This area is off limits to the public!" A sweat-drenched construction worker stood directly behind Bergh.

Bergh turned to look at the gruff old man. "I'm on official business, sir," he said with authority. "Henry Bergh, ASPCA." He glanced at Matilda, who shrugged and smiled.

"A-S-P what?"

"The American Society for the Prevention of Cruelty to Animals, my good man. I believe there is an animal of the feline variety trapped within this marble column." He glared at the workman and added, "I was under the im-pression that the practice of installing cats into the walls of buildings for good luck was abandoned some years ago."

"What?" asked the worker, perplexed.

"Listen to that," Bergh said, leaning toward the wall. The faint mewing sounded again through the thick marble. "I told you there's a cat trapped inside this marble facing. This wall must be taken down and the cat freed."

"Sure, Mister! First the niggers, now the cats! I'm sure the foreman's gonna give us the go ahead right away for a damned cat!"

"You disgust me, sir. Get the foreman, and I'll be sure he does what I say," Bergh said.

"Yeah, sure," the worker said. He went inside, and a few moments later, returned with the job foreman.

"Yeah, what's the problem?" asked the man, his eyes squinting against the brightness of the day.

"A cat," Bergh said, "is built into the wall here." Bergh patted the smooth, relatively cool surface. "You must take whatever measures are necessary to free it—immediately."

Bergh glanced at his wife again and saw that Matilda was enjoying herself immensely.

"Get the hell out of here, mister," the foreman said. "I ain't got time for your games."

"I assure you it is no game, Mr.—"

"Don't you worry what my name is. I got a building to put up. Piss off!"

Bergh spotted a policeman standing on the opposite corner of the intersection. "You wait right here, sir," he said. "And I advise you to do what I say." Bergh made a beeline toward the officer and spoke to him for five minutes, his hands gesturing excitedly toward the building. A moment later, the officer accompanied him to where the foreman waited, his hands balled into fists of rage.

Bergh removed his badge from his pocket and showed it to the construction foreman. "I'm Henry Bergh of the ASPCA, and I'm ordering you to remove the animal trapped within this wall immediately. This officer will stand by to arrest you if you disobey the command." Bergh raised one eyebrow and stared at the construction worker. A crowd had gathered, waiting with anticipation to see what would happen next. It was what Bergh lived for.

"Damn it all to hell! What the devil's happening to this city!" He stormed inside the building and screamed, "McKinley! Get out here and figure out where this damned cat is!"

Soon, several construction workers dismantled the block wall. Bergh smiled and put his arm around Matilda's shoulder as he watched with a slight smile on his face. A crowd of nearly fifty people had gathered and now stood around Bergh, watching and discussing the latest escapades of the Society for the Prevention of Cruelty to Animals.

"It's a yellow cat," some said. "Black, I'll wager," said others. And wager they did. Bergh later laughed at what might have been the first time money was gambled on the life of an animal being spared rather than being ended.

After an hour's work, the last big block was removed, and an emaciated cat jumped out from the darkness beyond, its fur matted, ribs clearly visible.

145

The feline had probably been in there for two or three days, using its last bit of strength to lament its misery.

At its appearance, much of the crowd cheered, except for those who had lost their bets. The cat was black with white paws, with a blob of dried mortar on top of its head.

Bergh bent down, and as if he knew who his savior was, the cat went to him, rubbing against his legs. "There, there, little fellow," he said, lifting it up. "You'll accompany my wife and me back to the shelter."

He stood, and the cat seemed content in his arms. "And you, sir," he said to the foreman, "could have saved your men a lot of work by paying a bit more attention to the more humane aspects of this building's construction."

* * * * *

September 1871

"Here now, hold it right!" Mama shouted, as Mary Ellen tried to lift the hot iron.

"It's too heavy, Mama! I can't pick it up with one hand."

"It's like this, child!" Mary took the iron from her and ran it over the skirt twice, then put it back on the table. "Now hurry before it cools!"

Mary Ellen reached for the iron and wrapped her hand around the thick handle. She looked up at Mary, then strained to lift it again. Before she even lifted it entirely, it fell onto the ironing board, face down.

"Stupid child! I try to teach you cleaning and taking care of the home and you don't try!" She seized Mary Ellen's wrist. "This iron is hot. It must be so to smooth out the wrinkles in our garments!"

"I know, Mama—"

Mary touched the flat of the iron to the child's arm, and Mary Ellen screamed, jerking her wrist from Mary's grasp.

"That's what happens if you mishandle an iron, young lady! You'll not forget that by the next time we do laundry!"

Mary Ellen fell to the floor and scooted into the corner by the window, clutching her wrist and sobbing. The large, enraged burn was already bubbling up.

"That will be a lesson to you! Now get into the closet if you intend to carry on like that! I don't want to listen to it."

Mary finished the ironing by herself. There was only the skirt and one blouse left anyway. Francis Connolly walked into the apartment and Mary knew something was going on. He wore a bigger smile than any she'd seen since before they were married. "What are *you* wearing under your clothes today?" she asked.

"I have good news, woman. A man has a right to wear a smile when he's got good news, doesn't he?"

"Well, out with it then, husband!" she pleaded.

"I found full time masonry work just off 6th Street, by 47th," Francis said, obviously pleased. "A new store going up over there."

"Does it pay enough?" asked Mary.

"Plenty. I wanted the chance to show him how good I was so I worked today for no fee. He was so happy with my work he hired me right after quitting time."

"How do you plan on getting over there, with no horse to speak of?"

"That's what I haven't told you yet. He said he'd forward my first week's pay to put down on an apartment. Said we ought to look over on 41st Street. According to him, there's plenty of rooms over there."

"I'd better do that," Mary said. "You'll have us in some rat ridden shack if I leave it to you."

Francis waved her off. "Please yourself, woman—just get it done tomorrow. I don't want to have to beg rides all week!"

* * * * *

Mary opened the door to the apartment, her purse in her hand. "I'm going out for a time," she said. "In the closet with you."

"I'll be quiet, Mama! I won't touch anything that isn't mine and I'll be very quiet!"

Mary let go of the doorknob, dropped her bag on the table, and walked directly to the kitchen cupboard. Mary Ellen ran to the closet and opened the door.

"It's too late, idiot. You must learn to do what I say the first time!" She took the rawhide whip from the cupboard and slipped her hand through the leather loop attached to the handle. Mary Ellen had scrambled into the closet and now cowered inside, trembling with fear, her hands over her head.

Mary lashed her with the whip.

"Don't . . . ever . . . disobey me . . . again!" she screamed, as she brought the whip down on the head and upraised hands of the seven-year-old.

"Mama, I'm sorry! Please!" cried Mary Ellen, her voice quivering.

Mary gave the wailing child one more lash on the head, then slammed the door and threw the hook in place. She listened at the closet door for a moment, then stepped into the hall, where her neighbor, a woman who had earlier introduced herself as Theresa Salton, gaped at her in horror.

"Were those . . . those *horrible* sounds I heard—Madam, were you beating your child?" she asked.

"You'll do well to mind your own business. Nosy people like you are the reason we're leaving this building!"

* * * * *

Inside the closet, Mary Ellen gently touched her arm where the blister from the iron had ruptured when the rawhide struck her tender skin. The oozing sore stung more than all the places the whip had ripped at her hands and ears, and in the darkness of her prison, Mary Ellen allowed the tears to fall, without fear she would be punished for crying.

She rolled onto her back and rested her head in the corner of the cramped, dark room, relieved her mama had finally gone away. She stared into a darkness that revealed nothing even long after her eyes had adjusted to it, and involuntarily, her hand searched for her precious pieces of string. Her fingers eventually brushed over one, she picked it up, and immediately felt more at ease.

After a while, Mary Ellen imagined she could hear the laughter of the children in the street. Were they really out there, playing with their stones and sticks? Oh, how she longed to at least watch them from the window, for she knew their names, and knew which ones she liked and which ones she didn't. It was so nice to pretend they were her friends. It was only the last time she

148

watched them that she realized she had never had a friend before. Not one. She had never so much as spoken to another little girl or boy as far as she remembered.

She twirled the many pieces of string around her fingers, lost in thought. She put one piece in her mouth and pulled it out slowly, the tickle on her lips making her face tingle. She knew many of the strings were every color of the rainbow, but since she couldn't see them, she simply remembered how brightly they were colored.

I must remember to hide them good, she thought. Otherwise, Mama will take them away. They were almost the only toys she had, now that her favorite story book was all torn up and gone.

Mary Ellen hummed the little pieces of a song, one that seemed to have always been with her. She never thought to wonder how she knew the tune, nor did she have any way of realizing it was one of the last remaining fragments of an ever-dimming memory of her natural mother, Fanny Wilson.

* * * * *

Margaret Bingham swept the dust from the front stoop of her building, her feet swollen and painful. She should be sitting inside out of the baking sun, but the porch was a filthy mess with all the neighborhood kids sitting in the shade there, leaving their refuse behind. Margaret never shooed them away, though. They had to have somewhere to go, as they had no homes, and no one who cared for them. As she finished up, she saw a woman walking up the street.

The lady wore a simple dress and flat shoes, her hat a plain black, having seen many a day before this one. She was of generous build, her short, dark hair framing a rigid face that seemed incapable of any expression but a frown.

"Good day, madam," the woman said, when she arrived at the foot of the stoop.

Still no smile. "Hello," Margaret said, forcing one herself.

"My name is Mary Connolly, and my husband and I are looking for some rooms to let. Would you know where I could locate the landlord of this building?"

"You seem to have stumbled into a bit of good fortune, Mrs. Connolly.

I'm Margaret Bingham, and I own this building. A family just moved out yesterday, so I do have a vacancy."

"I prefer the rear house. They tend to be more affordable and a bit more private."

"Once more, good fortune is on your side. The rooms are on the first floor, in the rear house."

"May I see them?" Mrs. Connolly asked.

"Yes, of course. Follow me." Margaret climbed the steps, her legs and hips aching from the rheumatism her doctor told her would simply have its way with her. After all, she was sixty-six years old, and these were the pains of age. Margaret dealt with it, thankful she could choose her own rooms on the first floor of the front house.

"Jenny!" she shouted, then looked at the Connolly woman. "She's my daughter. Jane's her name, but I call her Jenny. She and my son-in-law live across from me."

"That's nice," Mrs. Connolly said. Margaret noted the woman still had not smiled once.

Jenny came down the steps. "Yes, Mother?" She wore a light summer dress, and had her blonde hair tied up off her shoulders. She smiled at Mrs. Connolly.

"Jenny, this is Mary Connolly, and she'd like to see the vacant rooms in the rear house. Could you show them to her, please?"

"Pleased to meet you, Mrs. Connolly. I'm Jane Slater," Jenny said, holding out her hand. "You can call me Jenny if you like."

Mrs. Connolly shook it quickly. "Pleased, I'm sure . . . Jenny."

"I already have the key," Jenny said. "Follow me."

"I'll wait here, if you don't mind," Margaret said. "My legs pain me these days."

"I understand," Mrs. Connolly said. "Don't trouble yourself."

A few moments later she came back, Jenny behind her making silly faces. Margaret suppressed a smile, and gave her a sharp look meant to say, 'Stop that!'

"I like the rooms well enough," Mrs. Connolly said. "May I bring my husband around this evening to see them as well?"

"Well, you can't very well pick the rooms without your husband. I'd like to meet him, but I'm an early sleeper," Margaret said. "I'll ask that you come before eight o' clock."

"We'll be here no later than seven. Does that suit you?"

"Yes, thank you. I'll see you then."

When Mrs. Connolly walked away, Jenny said, "I don't like her, Mother. I'm not sure why."

"I don't either," Margaret said. "I only wish the money weren't so important. I've had no one else asking that can afford to pay for the rooms."

"Yes, I suppose so," Jenny said. "And vacant rooms aren't profitable."

"I'll tell you what," Margaret said. "If her husband's drunk on liquor when they come this evening, I'll make up an excuse why they can't have the rooms."

Jenny laughed. "Good. We have to have some standards, don't we?"

"Of course we do my dear."

* * * * *

It was ten minutes of eight when the knock came upon the door. By seven-thirty, Margaret had decided the Connollys would not be coming, and almost hoped they didn't. Still, to have the rooms occupied would be far better than having them empty, and inconvenience was part of being a landlord.

She opened the door, and Mary Connolly stood outside her door with a decent-looking, though unshaven man of medium height and slim build. His salt-and-pepper hair was thinning, but his eyes and the smoothness of his skin indicated he was in his middle years.

"Mrs. Bingham? We're here to see the rooms."

"I'd hoped you would come earlier," Margaret said, wanting them to know she was inconvenienced, but not enough to send them away.

Mary Connolly didn't appear perturbed. "You said before eight," she reminded Margaret.

"Yes, yes, I know. Just give me a moment while I fetch Jenny."

"I'm Francis Connolly," the man said, holding out his hand.

Margaret took it. "Pleased to meet you Mr. Connolly."

"If you have the key we can have a look ourselves," he added. "I suppose

Mary here already knows which rooms they are."

It was a good idea, and Margaret could see no reason to decline his offer. "Yes. That would be much better. Please look quickly, though. I'll be retiring for the evening very shortly."

Margaret gave the key to Mr. Connolly. He didn't appear to be drunk or anything else that might give her reason to turn them down. Ten minutes later, another knock came upon her door. Margaret opened it.

"The rooms will do fine," Mrs. Connolly said, "and Francis wants us to take them."

"Wonderful," Margaret said. "Have you any children? Or any other family that will be living here?"

Mrs. Connolly's face became stern once more. "Well, I haven't any family. Yes, we have one child, but she won't give you or anybody else any trouble."

"Oh, please don't misunderstand me, Mrs. Connolly. It's not for worry of trouble that I asked you. Where the parents live, so must their children. Your little girl is welcomed here."

"She is near seven years," Mrs. Connolly said. "A very quiet child."

Margaret smiled. "Half-grown boys can sometimes be very troublesome, but I don't mind the little ones at all. Jenny has some of her own."

"How much are the rooms?" asked the husband, apparently tired of the chitchat.

"For third floor, rear house rooms I charge eight dollars per month."

Mary Connolly looked at her husband.

"Sounds reasonable to me," he said. "When can we occupy them?"

"As soon as you pay your first month's board."

"Tomorrow, then. Thank you, Mrs. Bingham."

"You're welcome, Mr. and Mrs. Connolly. I look forward to seeing you both then. *And* meeting your daughter. Perhaps she'll have fun playing with my grandchildren."

Mary Connolly's face seemed to change. She said nothing, but turned and walked toward the front door, her husband in tow.

"Odd woman," Margaret said, closing the door. "Very odd, indeed."

14

January 1872
Four Months Later

Etta Wheeler knew that the freezing temperatures had everything to do with the fire. As the cold set in, efforts were made to stay warm, many of them hazardous.

Forsaking her own safety, Etta rushed inside the building. She threw her cloak over her head, and crouched low as she ran through the smoky hallways screaming for anyone who might be trapped or lost in the dark, hot fog. She could feel the flames closing in on her from what felt like all directions, and she did her best to concentrate on one area at a time.

"Hello! Is anyone in here!" she called, but through the thunderous crackle and roar, she only heard a faint cry. She saw a basin of water in the hall and knelt next to it. Removing her cloak, she pushed it into the basin, soaking it, then wrapped it over her head and face, leaving only her eyes exposed. Prepared now, she rushed inside the smoky apartments from which she heard the cry.

There was a crib by the window. Etta rushed over to it and saw a baby inside. As she reached for it, the wall to her left exploded and embers flew toward her, tiny sparks stinging her exposed face and hands. Etta dropped to her knees and saw the mother of the child lying on the floor, unconscious.

She had to save them both quickly or risk perishing herself. The fire now crept across the dry floor and along the wall behind the crib as Etta got to her feet and reached inside for the child, then tucked it into her wet cloak and bent down to seize the arm of the unconscious woman.

Keeping her eyes on a door, hardly visible through the thick, pungent smoke, Etta prayed to God to give her the strength as she dragged the woman slowly along the floor. She was not a large woman, and that was fortunate, for neither was Etta. It hurt to breathe. Etta pulled with all her might.

"Just . . . a few . . . feet to . . . go!" As the last word exited her lips, she was through the door and only ten more feet from the front entrance to the building. "Help me!" she shouted, but there was no force behind the words. Her lungs burned, and only a dry croak came out.

With no one to come to her aid, Etta dragged with all her might, but the woman's arm slipped from her perspiration-slickened grasp. Etta fell to the floor, shielding the child from harm. She stood and lifted the woman's arm again, then stopped.

There had been no movement, no sound from the blanket in her arms at all. The baby should be crying, wailing, by now. A sudden panic overtook Etta, and she reached down to pull the blanket from over the baby's head.

The child lay motionless in the blanket, its face bluish-purple. It wasn't breathing. Etta said a prayer as the licking flames devastated the hallway just fifteen feet from where she and the unconscious woman lay. Etta left the woman for the moment, bolting through the front door and down the front steps of the building, the baby clutched in her arms.

As she passed a fireman just outside the door she shouted, "A woman! Just . . . inside the entry! Hurry, the fire . . . it's coming . . . down the hall!" The fireman ran past Etta and into the building. Etta dropped to the ground when she got far enough from the flames and put the blanket down, resting the baby on its back.

She puffed air into the baby's mouth. One breath . . . two breaths . . . another breath . . . nothing. "Help me!" Etta called, but nobody heard. Too much commotion. Her voice too weak. She would have to do it herself.

She picked the baby up and pressed it against her chest, rocking back and forth. She patted its back hard. Harder. She prayed. And rocked. She heard a cough from its tiny mouth, then a sudden breath. "My God!" Etta shouted. "Oh, thank you, Lord!" The baby started to cry, and to Etta it was the sound of life itself. For a long moment she stared at the infant in wonder, then wiped its tiny mouth. The color slowly returned to its face and Etta rested the baby across her shoulder again, patting its back.

As she held the child and rejoiced in her heart, tears ran down her smoke-blackened cheeks. A miracle had just taken place and she had seen it; she had even helped to make it happen. She watched the building for the child's mother. They had not yet emerged, and it seemed to be taking too long.

As the thought crossed her mind, the fireman she had called to when she left the building struggled down the steps one at a time, the woman over his shoulders. His face was contorted from effort and exhaustion as he erupted into a coughing fit. He labored to take ragged, painful breaths as he rested the woman in the grass. She moved her head, convulsed, and began coughing herself.

Etta was several yards away from them. She wrung the remaining water from the blanket, shook it out, and covered the child with it again.

As she drew close to the woman, who now sat up with the fireman's help, she heard her say, "My . . . baby's in there. My poor little Rebecca."

Etta knelt beside the woman and folded back the blanket. "She's here. Rebecca's safe."

Life flooded back into the woman's eyes. "Oh, Rebecca!" She reached for the child and Etta gave her over willingly. The woman touched the child's face and mouth with her trembling fingers. "How can I thank you!"

"Hold her close to you, Ma'am. She's wet from the blanket I wrapped around her. I wouldn't want her to catch cold."

The woman looked at Etta, then placed a hand on the side of her face. She stroked her cheek and said, "Thank you. I just know I couldn't have gone on without my little girl."

"You needn't think of things that don't come to pass," Etta said. She wanted to stay with the woman, but she was all right and there were others who might need her. She spotted a commotion just below the base of the building.

There was a boy, perhaps thirteen years old, standing in a third floor window, the useless fire escape just a few feet away. The stairs hadn't been lowered in so long they had rusted in position, useless to anyone. Looking at the crowd below, the young man climbed tentatively out onto it, and stood gripping the rusted metal.

"Jump up and down!" shouted a young fireman, a cone-shaped megaphone pressed against his lips. "Try to break the stairs free!"

The boy was frightened, but followed the command. He held tight to the rails and jumped twice without any visible effect on the corroded pivots.

"It'd take an act of God to move those escapes," the firefighter muttered. "Get that oversized blanket from the wagon! You men, get beneath him and make a net!"

Moments later, six volunteers gripped a heavy blanket, stretching it tight with all their strength. Yellow-orange flashes could be seen licking out from the window behind the young man, and he kept glancing back as if he feared the flames themselves would reach out and pull him back inside the building.

"Jump, boy! Jump now!" the man with the megaphone shouted.

The boy didn't jump. His fear was too great.

An elderly man dressed in his nightshirt—probably a neighbor of the young man—snatched the megaphone and yelled, "You gotta jump, David! You got Hell's fire burning right behind you!"

The firefighter looked at him, aghast. "He obviously ain't scared enough, captain!"

The boy suddenly dropped to a sitting position, then grabbed the edge of the fire escape with this hands. Seconds later he dangled from his straining fingers as the rescuers scrambled to get directly beneath him with the blanket.

"Okay, we're here, son! Let go, now!"

The boy's fingers slipped from the rail, and he plummeted the three stories toward the men. Etta watched him fall, the surreal scene appearing to happen in slow motion, as though he were floating instead of falling.

Before she knew what happened, the boy lay flat on his back in the dead center of the stretched blanket. As he lay there stunned, he stared up at the ring of frantic faces over him and said nothing. In his wide eyes was a reflection of the fire exploding from the window three stories above him; the window of the room he had, only moments before, occupied. Etta rushed to his side and helped him away from the building while the tired men hurried to take care of others desperately in need of rescue.

It was a long night, but Etta remained until she could stand on her feet no more. When she finally left, the building was too far gone to expect that any more survivors would be found. Etta didn't sleep that night. Instead, she prayed for the souls of the dead and thanked God for the strength He had given her.

* * * * *

March 1872
Two Months Later

Jenny sat in her chair, rocking as she mended a torn pocket on her husband's favorite pair of striped pants. Stuart, on the other side of the room, was busy fixing the broken leg of a chair. As he finished the repair and flipped it over, Jenny heard Margaret's door close across the hall.

"Stuart, could you open the door and call Mother, please?" Jenny asked.

Stuart reached over and flipped the door open. Margaret smiled when she saw him. "Hello, Stuart. I see you've gotten tired of teetering in your chair."

"Yes, Ma'am. Just been trying to find time to get this done," he said. "Oh, by the way, I found out last night that I'm finally getting my transfer to the day shift."

"Oh, Stuart, that's wonderful. I know you've been worried about leaving Jenny home alone all night."

"I've been fine, Mother," Jenny said. "Besides, you're the one worrying. I'll be glad just to know you'll feel better."

"I've got to walk to the dry goods store," Margaret said. "Do you need anything while I'm out?"

Jenny crinkled her forehead. "Mother, you shouldn't be walking any-where with—"

"Now, now Jenny, the store's just down the street. Don't you fuss over me."

Jenny shrugged. "It's pointless to argue with you mother," she said. "But

157

before you go, I did want to ask you about those people in the rear house, the Connollys."

"What about them?"

"Where *is* their child? I've never seen it."

"Yes," Margaret said, "I've wondered, too. I only laid eyes on her once, and that was the evening they moved in."

"Mother, they can't have a child there. I've watched both the husband and wife come and go several times, and I've never seen a little girl."

"Mrs. Connolly told me she's just the age of your Melissa." She looked into the other room. "Where are those children anyway?"

"Outside, where else? Their friends call them and they go running."

"Why do you ask about the Connollys' little one?"

Jenny shook her head. "How can they keep her in there? The windows are always closed and the blinds down. The poor child must feel like a prisoner."

Margaret nodded. "I suppose she's a well-disciplined child. She must take care of herself quite often."

"Well," Jenny said. "I'm going to watch for her. If I see her out I'm going to ask her how she's treated."

"You both know it's best not to interfere with a man's family," Stuart said. "I'm a policeman, remember? I should know."

"All the same," Jenny said. "I'll keep my eye out anyway. I'd like to know if she's mistreated, at least."

"And keeping her a prisoner is mistreatment," Margaret said. "I do have an idea, though. Stu, how about if you find an excuse to go inside to make a repair of some sort. You *are* the custodian here and that would give you the perfect opportunity to see the child."

"C'mon, now ladies. I told you it's best not—"

"Now Stuart," interrupted Jenny. "You'll do this one little thing to make us feel better, won't you? In the interest of a poor little girl, no older than our own?"

Stuart's face told Jenny she had won her appeal. He would do anything for her. "Thank you, dear," she said, putting an arm around him and planting a kiss on his cheek. "I knew you'd do it."

"Just once," Stuart said. "I'll check on her once, and I never want to hear about it again, unless she's hanging from the ceiling by her feet."

* * * * *

Stuart Slater's opportunity came a week later. Jenny happened to see Mrs. Connolly go out without the child, and less than an hour later, Mr. Connolly left the building, too.

That Stuart was a policeman would help him if he were caught, but he planned to say he smelled smoke and was investigating all the rooms to make sure no fire was burning inside. Stuart was, after all, responsible for taking care of the building.

He climbed the steps on tiptoe, then laughed aloud. Why was he sneaking? He had a perfect right to be anywhere in the building! He tromped up the last few steps noisily, a smile on his face.

Stuart hesitated at the top of the stairs, realizing he should check some of the rooms around the Connollys' just to make sure his excuse held up under scrutiny. He turned right at the top and knocked on Mary Litzbeney's door. She lived at the opposite end of the hall from the Connollys. He would have asked Mr. and Mrs. Kemp, but he knew they weren't at home through the day. Mr. Kemp owned a hat shop on Mulberry Street, and his wife helped him in the store.

"Who's there?" she called.

"It's Stuart Slater, Mrs. Litzbeney. I smelled smoke and wanted to check the rooms for anything burning."

"Hold on, please." He heard the lock turning, and a moment later Mary stood at the door. "You say you think there's a fire?"

"I don't really smell it anymore," Stuart said. "but I thought it better to investigate anyway."

"Good idea, young man," Mary said. "But there's nothing burning in my rooms."

"Thanks, Mrs. Litzbeney."

"You're welcome, Stuart," she said. "You will let me know if I need to leave the building?"

Stuart waved as she closed the door. He walked down the hall to the Connollys' rooms.

The hall was quiet again, and Stuart waited for a few moments before sliding the key into the door of the Connollys' apartment. As he turned it, he heard a scuffle inside. He jumped back and let go of the doorknob for a moment, his heart pounding as he listened.

It's probably just the child, he thought. She was probably in there, left alone for the day, and would no doubt be frightened at the sight of a stranger. He pushed the door open and peeped his head inside. The furniture was simple, only a few wooden chairs and a table, and a little tattered rug lay beneath the only window.

"Hello!" Stuart called.

He waited for a moment but no answer came. He stepped further inside and looked toward the bedroom. The main living room was typically small, not quite ten by twelve feet. As in many of the other units, the bedroom was really just a large closet, only four feet wide and six long, but the door was almost closed, preventing Stuart from seeing inside.

As he reached out to take the bedroom knob, the door swung away from him, slamming closed. Stuart turned and ran for the front door, stopping in the hall, his heart pounding. Why was he running from a poor, frightened little girl?

The hall was still empty, but Stuart looked once more to be sure the Connollys weren't coming. This time he walked inside the room, went directly to the closet, and tried the knob. It wouldn't turn. He twisted harder, and it started to give. Suddenly it spun freely and the door flew open, causing Stuart to stumble backward before catching himself.

Inside, a little dark-haired girl pressed herself into the corner, her body quaking with fright as she pushed and pushed with her feet to become part of the wall behind her. She squeezed her eyes closed and it was clear that she wanted, more than anything else, to disappear.

"Little girl," Stuart said, kneeling in the doorway, "there's no reason to be afraid. I promise." It was probably wise not to approach or touch her. "I'm Stuart. I live here, in the front house. My wife's mother owns this building."

The child peeked out from behind her folded arms. What he could see of her face was bruised, her dress worn and tattered. The petticoat, which could be seen through the holes in the dress, was filthy, nearly worn through.

"We were just wondering if you were all right," Stuart added, smiling.

She said nothing, but her eyes sparkled with fear, as though she believed he might strike her.

"What's your name, little one? I have a little girl about your age named Melissa."

The little girl lowered her arms. "My name's Mary Ellen. Is your little girl . . . is she pretty?"

"Yes, Mary Ellen, she is. Almost as pretty as you. How old are you honey?"

"How old?" She looked confused, then shrugged. "I don't know."

"Don't you ever celebrate your birthday?"

"I don't know what that is," Mary Ellen answered.

A powerful feeling of affection for the neglected little girl came over Stuart. He smiled and said, "It's the day you were born, sweetheart. Most people have a little get-together and celebrate it."

Mary Ellen appeared to consider the idea as she chewed on her bottom lip.

"Where are your mommy and daddy, Mary Ellen?"

She looked at him for a long time, her big brown eyes searching his face for something Stuart couldn't quite put his finger on. Her eyes darted back and forth from the open door to where he knelt, and each time he moved his hands, she responded with a flinch.

"Relax, honey. I promise I didn't come to harm you."

After another long moment of uncertainty, she finally released her breath as in acceptance, then stretched her legs out in front of her.

Stuart cringed. They were covered with vicious welts. Some were scars of days past, others still bore the crusted blood of recent wounds.

"You really think I'm pretty?" asked Mary Ellen, a shy smile on her face. The poor child didn't even realize her own pitiable condition, much less her plight.

"You're a beautiful young lady, Mary Ellen. My Melissa would love to play games with you sometime, I'm sure."

"Oh, no," Mary Ellen said. "I'm not allowed to play with other children. Mama says they're diseased."

Stuart laughed aloud. "Why, Mary Ellen! My children are quite healthy, I assure you, and wouldn't pass any diseases to you or anyone else!"

"Really?"

"Absolutely true."

She smiled, and Stuart's heart nearly broke in two. The poor thing was so pitiful. "Do you know where your mommy and daddy are?" he asked.

She shook her head. "The door's not hooked 'cause Papa was the last to go," she said. "Mama always puts the hook on."

Stuart frowned, then looked at the door. The front door opened into the living area, and a tiny bedroom no larger than a closet divided it from the kitchen. Mary Ellen now sat in this windowless room, the door behind her leading into the kitchen closed. Sure enough, a swing hook and ring had been attached to the outer door. They apparently locked her in this dark room when they went out.

"Are you hungry?" he asked.

She nodded. "Yes, sir. Mama left early and Papa doesn't do that."

"Do what? Feed you?"

She nodded.

Stuart looked around the small apartment, then reached over her and opened the door to the kitchen. He was baffled. "Where do you sleep? With your parents?"

"Oh, no! I sleep there." She pointed to the window.

Stuart followed her finger and saw only a tiny rug beneath the window.

"There? On that rug?"

Another nod.

"Do you have a blanket?"

"No," she said. "But I'm not cold."

Stuart was in shock. He stood and walked to the kitchen, which contained only some low cupboards and a small stove and wash basin. As he opened the cupboard, he heard the child scream.

He ran to her. "What's wrong, sweetheart? Are you all right?"

Mary Ellen trembled, pressing herself into the corner again as she'd done when he first arrived. "I was only going to see if you had any food in the cupboard," he said. "Really, darling. You said you were hungry."

Slowly, she showed her face again, and her fear was evident. "You . . . weren't going to beat me like Mama does?"

"God, no. I would never hurt a child, Mary Ellen. I told you that." He slid down to the floor next to her. "You do believe me, don't you?"

She nodded. "Yes, sir."

"Okay, that's good, but you call me Stu. Can you do that for me?"

"Yes, Stu."

"Good. There's nothing in there for me to give you, but I'm going to close the cupboard and go now. I don't want you to tell your mommy and daddy I was here, okay?"

Mary Ellen nodded, watching him carefully.

"I only came to see if you were well, Mary Ellen. I'll try to bring you back something to eat and maybe some candy later this week. How would you like that?"

"What is . . . candy?"

Stuart stared at her. "Candy? Why it's . . . um . . . sweet . . ." He laughed. "I'll just have to bring you some and you can find out for yourself. Don't worry, you'll love it. Now remember what I said about not telling your mommy I was here, okay?"

"Okay."

As he reached in to close the cupboard, Stuart's eyes fixed on a three foot long horsewhip lodged inside the cabinet. It was made of braided leather, at the end of which were strips of frayed rawhide. He knew then why the child had reacted so strangely. This was the instrument that had caused the welts on her legs. Stuart closed the cupboard, waved a silent good-bye to her, and walked toward the front door. Before he got there, he heard footsteps in the hallway.

He froze where he stood, then whirled around when the door behind him slammed closed. Mary Ellen had again shut herself in the small room. Turning back toward the door, Stuart didn't know whether to keep walking toward it, or turn away and act as though he were inspecting. A second later, it didn't matter. The door flew open and Stuart stood face to face with Francis Connolly.

"Who the hell are you?" Connolly demanded, his eyes flashing anger.

Stuart looked directly at Connolly. "I'm in charge of repairs here, Mr. Connolly. I smelled smoke in the building and I'm checking every room."

"I don't smell anything," Connolly said. "You're lying."

Connolly's blatant accusation took Stuart by surprise, but he refused to be intimidated. He was a large man himself, and could be imposing if need be. His police work had also taught him how to defend himself if necessary. "I don't care whether you believe me or not," he said. "I'm authorized to enter every room in this building if I suspect the need for repairs or for reasons of safety. If you want to confirm what I'm saying, ask the woman next door. I've been in her room as well."

"Did you find a problem here?"

Stuart shook his head. "I was just leaving. Whatever the source of the odor, it's not coming from here."

"Like I said before, I don't smell anything."

"Good. Then you have nothing to be concerned about." Stuart squeezed past the stern-faced man as he left the room, his heart racing. Despite Connolly's anger, Stuart would return to see the child again, if only to make sure she was all right week by week. Besides, he had to bring Mary Ellen the candy he promised her.

15

September 1872
Six Months Later

"My god, Thelma, get away from her! You can't possibly know what she's got!" Cedric Marks pulled his wife from the room and moved into the doorway to block his son's view of the scene.

Inside the room, Frances Gibbon lay face down on the glass- littered floor, her breathing ragged and hoarse. Her body was emaciated, and a drool of bloody phlegm ran from her mouth onto the floor.

"Billy!" Cedric called out the door to his son. "Run and fetch Dr. Moore. Hurry!"

The boy ran off, and Thelma turned to her husband. "It may just be the liquor, Cedric. My God, there must be eight bottles broken on that floor!"

"Leave the diagnosis to Dr. Moore, Thelma. Whatever's the trouble, she needs a doctor's attention, not yours."

Twenty minutes later the doctor arrived. A mere five minutes was spent inside with the woman before offering a diagnosis. His face was grim as he stepped out of the room. "It's consumption."

Both Thelma and Cedric took an involuntary step away from him. "Don't worry. I've got a pretty good stake in knowing how to protect myself from germs. Did either of you come in direct contact with her?"

Cedric looked at Thelma, dread in his eyes. "Did you, Thelma?"

She shook her head. "No, I had Billy call you as soon as I found her. I was about to move her when you pulled me from the room."

"Did your son touch her?"

"No. He never came in."

Dr. Moore looked squarely at Thelma. "Mrs. Marks, will you excuse us, please?"

Thelma glanced at her husband, then left the room wringing her hands.

Moore put a hand on Cedric's shoulder. "If I tell you what to do, will you help me move her to my carriage? I'll need to transport her to an asylum immediately."

"Is it . . . are you sure it's safe?"

"It is if you listen very carefully and do exactly as I tell you."

"Very well, then."

Moore pulled out a notepad and a quill pen. He placed a bottle on the desk and dipped the pen into the black liquid. "May I have her name, please?"

"Yeah, sure. Her name's Frances Gibbon. Thelma says her husband's in the army, stationed on Governors Island."

* * * * *

Fanny lay in the stark room lined with beds, knowing in her heart and soul she would never leave this foul place. The sheet below her chin was stained with blood, and though she tried her best not to, as soon as the bedding was changed, she would cough up more. Her lungs felt destroyed, so intense was the pain. The morphine they supplied was good; she only wished they would give her enough to kill her once and for all.

Her mind wandered, her thoughts alternately clear and foggy, her dreams sweet, then terrifying. One moment she would be cradling an infant Mary Ellen in her arms, the next she would be running from unseen demons through dark, frightening alleys, with no hope of escaping them.

Fanny felt the sweat on her face; felt it sliding down her cheeks and off

166

her neck where it rolled onto the sheets and mingled with the blood that had soaked them. Fanny hoped to die very soon, for no human being was meant to suffer so long. As she pulled in each breath, her lungs screeched and ached with excruciating pain. Fanny had no desire to draw another breath.

While she prayed for a gift of death, she also asked for forgiveness from God. The harm she had brought to her daughter was unintentional, and Fanny prayed she would be able to join her little daughter in Heaven.

Fanny opened her eyes, squinting against the brightness of the room.

Were her eyes really open? An image of her parents drifted before her and Fanny smiled. Yes, she was telling them good-bye before she left for America, so long ago. Next, Thomas's face appeared before her, so handsome and serious. He was telling her about the war, and how he must go fight for his new country to prove the integrity of the Irish American. And finally, she saw an image of herself, belly swollen with child, as she awaited her husband's return from the war.

After all of these images passed before her eyes, bringing smiles and tears to her subconscious existence, Fanny closed her eyes and passed away.

* * * * *

December 1872
Three Months Later

Mary Ellen stood in the hallway by the open door, hoping someone would come along. She didn't mind so much being home alone with Papa, because he usually left the door open and she could watch for people walking by. Mary Ellen knew everyone who lived in the same hall she did; there was Mrs. Litzbeney, Miss Kemp, and a man, Mr. Gregson, who didn't seem very friendly. She ran back inside every time she saw him coming, for his mean face told her it might be smart to do that.

As her papa read what he called the "work pages," Mary Ellen walked quietly to the midpoint in the hall where the stairs began and peered upward through the rails. It was a game she liked to sometimes play when she was allowed a few steps into the hall. She would wait until she saw someone coming down, then at the last minute she would run inside and close the door.

Sometimes she was slow, and she got a funny feeling when they looked at her. They all seemed so sad when they looked at her, even when they looked happy right before.

There was no one there now. She waited a little bit before going back inside. Maybe she would watch out the window and see who was in the yard. She would have to convince Papa to open the shutters though.

"Papa? Where's Mama?"

Papa looked up from his paper. "At her sister's house. She'll be back tomorrow afternoon."

"I . . . I found something under your bed, Papa. I think it's money."

Francis's eyes widened. "Well, bring it here now, girl!"

Mary Ellen ran into the back room and lifted the corner of the mattress. Beneath it she found some paper money and some coins. The amount always changed; sometimes there were only a few coins there, but now there was a lot of paper, too.

She gave it to her papa and he thumbed through the bills and dropped the coins from one hand to the other.

"How long has this been there?" he asked.

"I see Mama put it there sometimes," she said. She moved closer to him and whispered in his ear, "I'm not supposed to tell you about it."

"If you didn't you'd be in trouble. Never lie to me and never keep secrets from me, do you understand?"

Mary Ellen nodded.

Francis put the newspaper aside and tucked the money inside his pocket. "Come here and sit on my lap, Ellie."

He called her Ellie only when he was happy, so Mary Ellen knew it would be okay. He had once told her that there were too many girls named Mary in the world, and she should be called after her second name. It was a very cold day, and her clothes were thin, so sitting on his lap would be warm.

She crawled up and tried to snuggle against him, but Papa turned her over and made her lay on her tummy in his lap. While holding her with one hand, Papa slid his other hand underneath her petticoat, and she cried out with fear.

"Papa I don't—"

"Relax, now," he said, using a deep voice she had only heard when he and Mama were having relations. She kicked her legs; sure something was terribly wrong with what Papa was doing. Mama had told her never to touch herself there, or in front, and now Papa was doing it!

"Be still, Ellie!"

"No, Papa! I'll go to the bad place! I'll go to the bad place!" Mama had told her about the bad place. It was a horrible dungeon where fire burned you all the time and devils poked at you with pitchforks. Mama said it never ended, and that little girls who did bad things went there forever.

Suddenly, Papa stopped. He removed her quickly from his lap and stood up without saying a word.

Mary Ellen sat on the floor, relieved. She watched him cross the room to the door and close it. He turned the lock and looked at her again.

Mary Ellen was scared. More scared than she had ever been with Mama.

"Come here," he said, standing by the bedroom door.

Mary Ellen couldn't stop the tears that ran down her cheeks. "Papa—"

"Now!"

She walked toward him, and he pulled her down onto the mattress. "You stay still now," Papa said. "This will only hurt if you're bad."

Mary Ellen knew it was wrong. Whatever was happening, it was a bad thing she was doing. She went to Papa and lay there with her eyes closed, the tears already stopping, for she was drifting into her special place, her safe place.

In her mind, Mary Ellen was safe in the darkness of the closet, playing with her nice pieces of colorful string. She was alone, dreaming of the happy children and nice mommies and daddies in her favorite picture book. That was how it was supposed to be.

* * * * *

"Where is it!" Mary shouted, her hands clenched into fists of rage.

"Gone," Francis said, calmly. "Thanks to Ellie, there. You wanted to keep her here so much, now see what it gets you? She tells me everything!"

"I'll deal with her later!" she shouted, glaring at Mary Ellen. "But you have no right, you bastard! That was my money!"

"Where did you get it, woman? Did you steal it from me, little by little? Is that how?"

"You have nothing to steal, Francis! If I took your money in such a manner I would need to take it all, for a little is all you ever have! Surely then you'd notice it!"

"To hell with you, woman. I've got it, and that's all that matters."

"Give the money to me now, Francis!" Mary said, slapping her husband hard across the face.

Francis looked stunned for a moment, then seized his wife's collar in his hand. He pulled her face to within inches of his. "Never! Never do that again!" He pulled his arm back and landed a fist squarely against Mary's face. Her body went limp and as Francis let go of her she fell to the floor in a heap.

Francis stared at his wife for a long moment, but she didn't move. Blood ran from her nose and mouth into the cracks in the faded wood floor. Mary Ellen stood at her feet and screamed at the top of her lungs, the wail penetrating Francis's eardrums.

It went on and on, until Francis could take it no more. "Shut up!" he shouted. "Now!"

Mary Ellen kept screaming.

"Goddammit! Shut your mouth, Ellie!"

The little girl ran to the front of the room and buried her face in the tattered rug beneath the window, the one that served as her bed each night.

Francis walked out of the room, leaving the child's muffled cries behind.

* * * * *

Down the hall, Catherine Kemp paced back and forth in her apartment, angry at the lengthy disturbance which, to her relief, appeared to be over.

It wasn't the first time Catherine and her husband had tolerated such scenes. When the Connollys fought, they seemed to rattle the entire floor, and Catherine cringed at the thought of a little child—the little trembling thing she'd seen in the hallway on rare occasions—witnessing such a scene.

This time it appeared Mrs. Connolly had gotten the worst of the argument, for when Catherine poked her head out the door, she saw Mr. Connolly charging down the steps, cursing under his breath. No sound came from the rooms. She was tempted to go and knock, but Mary Connolly had been nothing but rude to her in the past, and it wasn't her place to confront the neighbors anyway. It was the landlord's job to do such things.

Her husband had gone to bed early, exhausted from a day at the docks, and had slept through the entire commotion. Catherine couldn't imagine him being able to, but was glad he slept so well. His twelve-hour workdays could be dangerous if he didn't get enough sleep.

Catherine hurried downstairs to Margaret's apartment. There was no time like the present to report a disturbance, and if too much time passed, Margaret may not feel right about confronting them.

Margaret answered the door just after she knocked. "Yes, Catherine? May I help you with something?"

"I'm afraid so, Margaret. It's the Connollys. They're at it again."

"The child?"

"Oh, I don't know if she's involved in this one. All I could hear were the Connollys, the husband and wife. It's absolutely frightful, Margaret. Something must be done about their quarreling. My husband and I work so very hard, and to have peace of mind at home is important. Besides, the poor child! She's never allowed out, so she must be horrified as these . . . these *battles* take place! Can you imagine!"

Margaret shook her head. "Ah, the child. She's pitiful, that one. I've had Stuart checking on her a bit. He brings her treats now and then." Margaret sighed. "I'll talk to them myself, Catherine. You're perfectly right. I mustn't have them disturbing good tenants like you and Stephen."

"I'm sorry to bother you with it, Margaret. I know you do the best you can here."

"Since Daniel died, this building has been quite a task, though the income is a blessing. I really don't know what I'd do without Stuart and Jenny to help me manage. Catherine, will you please sit for a moment? I want to ask you what else you know about the Connolly girl. Mary Ellen is her name, did you know that?"

Catherine followed Margaret inside and sat down at the table. "No, I've asked her name before and she just runs back inside the room."

Margaret sat across from her. "You've seen her out?"

"Yes. She's in the hall sometimes, when the door's open. I think it's when the woman is away."

Margaret nodded in agreement. She would go to the rear house more often to try to catch a glimpse of the child. "I think you're right. Mr. Connolly doesn't appear to be as curt as his wife is. I haven't seen that woman with a pleasant face in all the time she's lived here."

"I think I'd turn and run if I did, for it could only mean she's invited the devil himself to dinner!" Catherine said, laughing.

Margaret laughed despite her concerns over the problem. "Have you ever spoken to her?"

"I've never had the nerve," Catherine said. "The woman practically glares at me! I just turn away and go about my business."

"Catherine, with your blond hair, blue eyes and figure, I imagine she despises you unconditionally to begin with!"

Now it was Catherine's turn to laugh. "Don't get carried away. I'm no goddess, Margaret."

"Compared to Mary Connolly, *I'm* a goddess!" Margaret laughed so hard tears came to her eyes. She dabbed at them with a handkerchief and asked, "When did Mr. Connolly leave?"

"It must be near twenty minutes ago now," Catherine said.

"I'll go up tonight. Why don't you go back to your apartment so she doesn't suspect you told me, and I'll wait a bit more."

Catherine shook her head. "She usually takes the child down to the water closet early in the mornings, Margaret. Why not do it then? It won't allow her the opportunity to slam the door in your face. You'll be right out in the open, and perhaps you can see the little one."

* * * * *

The next morning, as expected, Margaret's chance came. Mary Connolly had come down to visit the privy in the courtyard. The child did not accompany her, but it was as good a time as any. She mustn't let too much time pass between the disturbance and her confrontation.

As Margaret walked into the yard, the incredible feeling she was being watched overcame her. She glanced up at the building, and there, in the window, was the little girl's face. Three stories up, but even from such a distance, Margaret could see the hopelessness in her features, the numbness of her expression. She raised one hand in a subtle wave, and the girl vanished.

172

Had there been bruises on her face? Was her eye blackened? Or was it merely a trick of the morning light, or a distortion cast by the reflection of the glass that imprisoned her? Margaret wasn't sure. Perhaps her eyesight wasn't so good anymore. She was nearing seventy, after all.

She turned to find herself face to face with Mary Connolly. The woman's nose was swollen and a dark purple bruise ringed her eye. Connolly moved to step around her, but Margaret spoke quickly. "Please, Mrs. Connolly," she said. "I'm sorry to bother you, but I must discuss the disturbance in your rooms last evening."

Mary Connolly's mouth became a hard, thin line. Her dark brown eyes glared at Margaret. "What disturbance is that, Mrs. Bingham?"

"The argument between you and Mr. Connolly. I had complaints from some of my tenants."

"It was a private matter, Mrs. Bingham," she said, curtly. "None of your concern, and certainly none of your tenants', either."

"I'm afraid when it disturbs the others in the building, it *is* my concern, Mrs. Connolly. It makes it very unpleasant and annoys everyone."

Mary bristled. "It is not mine, but my husband's fault. He's always fighting me to put Mary Ellen in an asylum or poor house. When I got the child I got a good fortune to take care of it, and I intend to do exactly that!"

"Mrs. Connolly, it seems very cruel to keep that little child locked up in the house all the time."

"I'll not let her out to learn foul language among the other children."

"We have four little ones, my daughter and her husband do," Margaret said. "We try to keep them as nice as we can, and we don't allow them to use bad language."

"Yours are not the only children out there, are they? Mary Ellen could be contaminated by the other filthy children I see playing here."

"Won't you send her to school?"

"The child knows enough," Connolly said. "I teach her myself, from reading books. Now, if you'll excuse me, I have things to attend to."

The conversation was over. Mary Connolly brushed past Margaret and stormed inside the building. Margaret watched her walk away, unsure whether her talk was anything more than wasted time.

Mary Ellen Wilson just after her rescue in 1874. (The front cover is a artist's drawing of this photograph.)

Mary Ellen's guardian angel, Etta Angell Wheeler.

Photo courtesy of the NYSPCC's George Sim Johnston archives

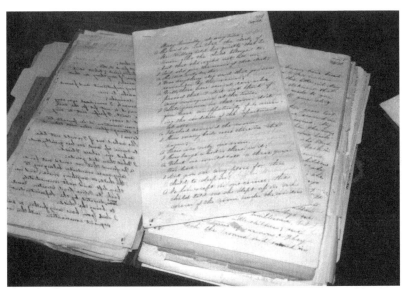

The original, hand-written court transcripts from the 1874 child abuse trial remain in the George S. Johnston archives at the NYSPCC

Original sheet music for songs written about Mary Ellen remains in the George S. Johnston archives at the NYSPCC

THE ONLY MOURNER.

Cartoonist Puck pokes fun at Bergh's cause . . . again.

Henry Bergh
Founder of the ASPCA
and Mary Ellen's rescuer.

Elbridge Gerry
ASPCA attorney and
child welfare proponent.

Artist's depiction of Officer Christian McDougal carrying Mary Ellen into the courthouse.

Mary Ellen Wilson, one year after her rescue.

Photo courtesy of the New York Society for the Prevention of
Cruelty to Children's George Sim Johnson archives

The tattered dress Mary Ellen wore into the courtroom and her other meager belongings can still be found in the George Sim Johnston Archives of the New York Society for the Prevention of Cruelty to Children (NYSPCC).

Eric A. Shelman & Stephen Lazoritz, M.D.

Rare photo of Mary Ellen taken circa 1880. That would make her around sixteen years old.

Photo courtesy of the NYSPCC's George Sim Johnston archives

Lewis Schutt, Mary Ellen's husband. He died in 1925 at age 72.

Mary Ellen with daughters Etta (standing) and Florence.

Mary Ellen attends a meeting of the American Humane Association (AHA) in 1913.

Mary Ellen lived a long life, surviving her husband, Lewis Schutt, by thirty-one years. She passed away in 1956 at the age of ninety-two.

* * * * *

Mary Ellen had only one tiny piece left of the lollipop Mr. Slater had given her. She wanted to eat it earlier, when Mama and Papa weren't home, but couldn't bear to think it would be all gone! It was so wonderful! Her heart sang when the sweetness touched her tongue, and it made her want to smile just thinking about it!

She decided then to save it for that night, but now Mama and Papa were staying up very late. She looked over at them and saw Papa was already asleep, and Mama was trying to keep her eyes open while she sewed. Soon they would turn down the lamp and go lay down in their bed.

Earlier that cold December evening, while Mama sewed Papa's pants and Mary Ellen washed dishes, Papa walked over and stood on the rug where she slept, beneath the window. How long had she held her breath? How long did he stand there, his foot just inches from where she had hidden her lollipop beneath the corner of her carpet? Forever, that's how long! What he could have been staring at out that window was a mystery to her, but when he finally did move, she swore they both heard her let out her breath. She just smiled and lifted another pot.

That night, she couldn't help herself. She ate the rest of it, letting the sweet flavor run down her throat as she lay on her carpet thinking of a room filled with the delicious lollipops. Sometimes she would lie awake at night, dreaming with her eyes open. She would imagine she was outside in the street with the other children, throwing balls of snow at them as she tried to dodge the ones thrown at her. She longed to touch the pretty white snow, so clean and cold, but Mama wouldn't allow her to go outside, except when the chamber pot was too full to use, and then it was only before she and Papa went to bed or very early in the morning, when nobody else was about. Otherwise, she just had to hold it in, the hours passing so slowly while she waited for Mama or Papa to awaken and give her permission to go out.

Once, early in the morning after Mama and Papa had been out very late, Mary Ellen had not been able to wait. She thought she might burst if she had to hold it another minute! Used to watching them, she could tell when they were near awakening, for Papa would start to toss and turn, and Mama would make noises and flutter her eyelids. On that morning, neither had shown any signs of waking up.

Mary Ellen stood over them for a long time, her pain so bad from having to go pee that she could think of nothing else. She had to do it. She moved as quiet as a mouse for the door, put her hand on the knob, and turned the lock. As she carefully pulled the door open, her eyes locked on the sleeping couple, she made sure neither stirred. Then she slipped outside into the hall leaving the door open just a little, and tiptoed toward the back door making no sound at all.

Once in the yard, she headed directly for the water closet. She pushed it out as fast as she could so she could make it back inside before either of her parents awoke. When she finished, she ran back toward the building, and smack into a woman coming out.

"My little child!" the lady said, "Why don't you put shoes and stockings on?"

"I dare not, Ma'am," Mary Ellen said.

"In Heaven's name, why not?"

"Mama won't let me."

The woman's eyes fell to her legs and she gasped. "What happened to your legs, child? Are those bruises . . . and cuts?"

She turned the child's arms over. "Where in Heaven's name did you get all these bruises, child?"

"I have to . . . please, Ma'am, I have to get back inside."

"You poor child! You must come to my apartment and let me give you a wrap."

"No! They might wake up! I have to go *now!*" Mary Ellen broke free from her grasp and bolted into the building and down the hall. She turned and saw the woman's sad face behind her, but kept running toward the door. As she approached the rooms she slowed to a walk and tried to catch her breath. The door was still open.

They hadn't found out. She breathed a sigh of relief and eased the door open.

The whip struck her across the face and she crumpled to the floor.

"Why did you go out!" shouted Mama.

"Please don't beat me, Mama!" Mary Ellen cried. "I had to go pee!"

She brought the leather crop down on the child's back. "You are never to

187

go out! Do you understand me!"

Mary Ellen scrambled to her feet and the whip slashed at her legs. She ran away from the pain, screaming, "Mama, Mama! Please, Mama, don't!"

Mary chased after her, whipping her back and neck. "Stop running from me, you demon! What were you really doing out there?"

"Please, mama! I had to go pee!"

Again, Mary Ellen lay down and drifted to her special place, deep within her imagination, until it was all over. She would be safe there.

The pain wouldn't come until later.

* * * * *

Outside in the yard, the woman cringed at the sound of the child's beating. She had heard it before, but had never laid eyes the child. The little girl was no more than five or six if she was a day, judging by her size, and her poor legs were striped with the welts of a whip, her body bruised from blows. Her hair was matted and infested with vermin, no doubt, and she did not appear to have had a bath of any kind for many days, if not weeks.

Suddenly, the child's wails ceased, and an eerie feeling swept over her. The sounds of the beating still met her ears, but the only response was silence. Dead silence.

Charlotte Fiehling did not hold back her tears as she walked back to her rooms. She would pray for the little girl—that she would find the solace and comfort of the Lord sometime in her miserable life.

16

Mary Ellen didn't go outside from that day on. The pretty snow, the sweetness of the cold air, those things were only for her imagination; it was safer that way. She could dream about what those things were like, and nothing could spoil the perfect pictures in her mind.

No matter how much she wanted to do the things other children did, she would satisfy herself by pretending she was hiding so well they couldn't find her. She could see where they hid and make believe she was seeking them out, always surprising them with a loud "boo!" She would tell Richie and Martha—her two favorites among the neighborhood children—to be sure to count all the way to twenty, which was as far as she learned to count by listening to them each time they played the hide-and-seek game she longed to join.

But she would never be allowed to join them. Mama said she could get a disease from those children, and if she did that, she would die. Mary Ellen wondered if dying would be so bad—at least she would be able to play with Richard and Martha once.

Just once.

* * * * *

Almost two years after the Frenchman, Louis Bonard, made his bequest to the ASPCA, the money was finally granted—minus $30,000 in legal fees. Bergh applauded Elbridge Gerry for his tenacious pursuit of justice, and for his ability to convince the politicians that he represented an organization worthy of its attention and generosity.

Following his death, Bonard was buried in Greenwood Cemetery, in a plot purchased by the society. Over his grave was placed a granite headstone, adorned with a bronze medallion bearing the emblem of the ASPCA. The cost of the headstone was $2500, and Bergh sent an equal amount to St. Vincent's hospital for the care they gave Bonard up until his death.

The real estate bequeathed included two stores on Platt Street, two tenement houses on Mulberry Street, two more on East 12th Street, and another on Madison Street. All told, the combined value of the real property was estimated at approximately $125,000, the remainder being ready money, which came to roughly $10,000 after the legal fees were satisfied. The first thing Bergh did was to vacate the premises at 696 Broadway, and move the society to larger offices at the corner of Fourth Avenue and Twenty-second Street. This location was large enough to accommodate the growing staff and featured another of Bergh's innovations—a shelter for fifty or so small animals and stables to shelter five horses—in the back courtyard. Now the society could focus on the future, not merely its existence.

* * * * *

March 1873
Three Months Later

Margaret scrubbed the hall floor, her hands deep in the bucket of sullied, gray water when she saw her. "Mary, dear! How did you get out?"

Mary Ellen stood before her, barefoot and wearing only the same frayed beige dress she had worn the first day Margaret saw her. Despite the forty-six degree temperature outside, she didn't appear cold, or to be the slightest bit aware of the weather.

"I just runned out," she said, smiling. "What's your name?"

190

"You call me Miss Margaret. Where are your parents?"

"Well, Mama went out and she didn't lock the door, and Papa went out for beer and he didn't lock it, so I just runned out." She stared out the open front door of the building as though mesmerized by it, but made no move to go outside.

Margaret looked at the poor child, so small and thin. "Are you hungry?" she asked.

Mary Ellen nodded, and Margaret stood up, shaking her hands over the bucket. She glanced out the door for Mr. Connolly. He was nowhere in sight, but he could walk in at any moment. So could his wife, for that matter. "Come quickly, let me get you something. You take it and eat it while you're running back to your room."

Inside, she had some cookies Jenny had made the day before. They were coated with sugar, perfect for a hungry little girl. She put three of them in Mary Ellen's hand. "Go, now. Hurry and run back up."

Just then the front door opened, and Francis Connolly walked into the hall carrying a package. Margaret stepped quickly in front of Mary Ellen and pushed her door closed. The child would get such a beating! She must think of something fast!

She knelt down and whispered, "Your father just came in, Mary. Listen to me very closely. When I open this door, you stand behind it and don't make a peep. When I get your father inside, you sneak into the hall as quiet as a little mouse and run home, do you understand?"

Mary Ellen's hands trembled. The cookies she held dropped to the floor.

"Here," Margaret said. She picked them up and put them on the table. "I'll save the cookies for you, okay? You just be brave, and hurry behind the door now!"

Mary Ellen hid behind the door as Margaret opened it and rushed into the hall. Francis Connolly was just reaching the door that led to the courtyard. Beyond that was the rear house.

"Mr. Connolly!" Margaret tried not to look too panicked.

He turned and looked at her. "Mrs. Bingham . . . What's wrong?"

Margaret put a hand on her back. "Mr. Connolly, I'd certainly appreciate it if you would be so kind as to help me move my stove away from the wall. I only need it moved a few inches."

Francis Connolly rolled his eyes and groaned, then put his package down and started back down the hall.

Margaret let out a sigh of relief. If he had gone to the room and found the child gone, she would surely have been beaten senseless. And it would have been her fault!

"Thank you so much, Mr. Connolly. I know it's a bother, but I must clean behind it and my back won't allow it. It will be nothing for you to move."

"Let's make it quick."

"Of course, Mr. Connolly. These are the times I miss my husband, Daniel, the most. He was a strong man in his day."

She led the way inside as Connolly followed, mumbling to himself.

* * * * *

Mary Ellen waited behind the door. She wasn't sure she understood what Miss Margaret wanted her to do, but it sounded scary! She wasn't supposed to be outside of her apartment, and now Miss Margaret was inviting Papa inside her hiding place!

Miss Margaret said to sneak out when Papa came in, like a little mouse, real quiet so he didn't hear her. Mary Ellen lifted her feet one by one and put them back on the floor. She must practice sneaking so she didn't make a mistake. She heard Papa's voice! He was coming! She squeezed herself back behind the door and waited.

Miss Margaret walked in first, with Papa close behind her. She walked straight into the kitchen, and Papa followed, without looking back.

Now was her chance. Mary Ellen looked once more just to be sure, then stepped out from behind the door and spotted the cookies. They looked so yummy, and they were right there on the table, just three feet away!

She stopped and listened. She could hear Papa grunting from the next room as he helped Miss Margaret in the kitchen. She could get to the cookies and then sneak out before they came back! She tiptoed quietly to the table and scooped them into her hands.

Mary Ellen looked over just in time to see the panicked face of Miss

Margaret.

* * * * *

Margaret's heart stopped when she saw the little girl standing in her living room, just visible around the corner. She saw that the cookies were no longer on the table. The poor child had wanted so badly to take them! Margaret screamed and whirled around to face Francis Connolly, who nearly plowed into her on his way out.

"What the hell's wrong, Mrs. Bingham!"

"Oh, my Lord! I'm quite sure I just saw a rat run across my dining table!" shouted Margaret. Her heart thumped in her chest again. He hadn't seen the child, and now she was gone.

"You're as white as a ghost. Seems you'd be used to rats by now, living where we do."

She laughed a nervous laugh and put her hand over her heart. "I'll never get used to the filthy creatures," she said. "I apologize, Mr. Connolly, for my foolish reaction." She walked him back into the hallway.

"Don't worry about it," he said, heading once more toward the rear door. "Mary can't stand 'em either."

* * * * *

The door behind Mary Ellen had just latched when she heard Papa's voice in the hall. She took one quick glance around the courtyard, then ran to the rear building door. Scurrying down the short hallway and into the room, Mary Ellen closed the door behind her as quietly as she could. Her mind kept returning to the day that she'd sneaked out to go to the water closet and had been whipped by Mama. It had been one of the worst beatings she could remember. She had been luckier this time.

Once inside, she looked at the wonderful cookies in her hand. She must eat them quickly before her papa came in! She stuffed two of them in her mouth and chewed as fast as she could, her taste buds singing from the sweetness.

When the door opened half a minute later, she sat beneath the window in

193

the kitchen, wiping the last crumbs from her mouth and watching the little boy and girl who had just entered the courtyard. It was Richie and Martha.

"Ellie!"

"Yes, Papa."

"Just making sure you're here."

"Yes, Papa. I'm looking out the window."

"You've been looking out there long enough. And you *know* how your Mama feels about it. Close the blind and get away."

"But—"

"You heard me! If I tell your mama she'll tan you."

Mary Ellen lowered the blind and looked at her papa as he sank into his chair. She had been so happy during her short time with Miss Margaret. And the cookies she'd given her were almost better than the candy that nice man Stuart brought her sometimes, only the cookies were kind of like bread, too. Sweet bread.

She decided she would have to go and see Miss Margaret again, and ask if she would give her some more cookies.

* * * * *

December 1873
Nine Months Later

Bergh was in Cincinnati, speaking to nearly one thousand at Pike's Opera House. He shared a favorite story of his, one he often used to entertain and draw his guests into his message.

"I dreamed that I was dead," Bergh began, "and that I had been transported to a place that seemed to me to be a paradise of animals. When I knocked on the gate, the door was opened by a mule. I took off my hat, bowed respectfully, and said: 'Pray, Mr. Mule, will you allow a man to enter?' The mule but looked at me for a moment, then replied, 'This is a singular request. I perceive that you are one of those that we, in former life, were wont to consider superior animals. This is no place for you—however, you may come in.'"

Bergh said, "I entered, but had hardly done so when a great number of animals crowded around me. After a thorough inspection of my appearance, each animal commenced a great noise. The horse snorted furiously, the sheep bleated, the oxen bellowed, and the dogs howled. The turtles turned over on their backs, all these actions meant to show their feelings. But as they were about to bite and kick me, a beautiful white horse rose up, pawing the air with majestic hoofs and thus spoke:

'Fellow animals! We must have mercy. Let us show a good example and return good for the evils that have been inflicted upon us when we were inferior animals. The being now before us I recognize as one who befriended us much on earth, and who has labored in New York and elsewhere for the benefit of our entire race.'

"Then," Bergh said, his hands gesturing wondrously, "the animals all crowded around me to share with me their earthly histories. An ox approached me, a horn broken from his head and his body covered with ulcers. 'I was born in Texas and roamed about the wild plains until I was five years old. I was then captured by some two-legged villains who drove me and my family off to the pens. I was transferred to a box on wheels, and during fourteen days of motion I was crushed and suffocated with twenty other animals, receiving little water or food. We arrived in Weehawken and I stumbled as I jumped from the cart to solid earth, and was goaded and struck with a heavy rod that broke my horns. I was allowed to rest a few days, then fed with dry, salted food that enraged my thirst. After drinking many gallons of water to quench this unnatural thirst, I appeared quite full-bodied. This was intended, as I was then led to the slaughterhouse, where I was finally sold, then cruelly butchered, finding in death a happy release.'

Bergh hung his head for a moment to allow the crowd time to reflect, then continued. "Next, a dilapidated old horse, blind in one eye, and with a sore shoulder and ribs showing like circles 'round a cask approached me. 'Sir, my sight is dim, but you remind me of one who has often befriended me in the streets of New York. With your permission, I will relate my history. I sprang from pureblooded stock, and was a favorite with my master, having, as the jockeys say, almost annihilated time; but time has annihilated me now. My sister makes her living on a tow-path, my aunt died of the horse plague, and my uncle died afflicted with ringbone and springhalt. In my younger days, I was provided the best of food and water, a careful groom, and a stable fitted

195

up as luxuriously as a lady's boudoir. That's all past now, for I won one race, but by just half a length, coming up to the stand more dead than alive. Even now the roar of the assembled multitude rings in my ears. I was carried off, and my master, disappointed, sold me. Suffering from cramp and cough, I was put to work on a streetcar, to draw one of those ponderous, overloaded vehicles eighteen miles a day. From this toil I became lame, and was sold again to the driver of a night hack; even he tired of me, and sold me to a man who peddled stale fish and kindling wood. One day my old master happened to pass by where I stood, half dead and trembling with fatigue. He recognized me by the white spot on my head, and his eyes met mine. I tried to move and fell forward at his feet—dead.'"

Bergh paused another moment, then said, "Next, I heard a terrible bellowing. An emaciated cow approached me with some difficulty, her fevered mouth showing several rotted teeth. Her bones could all be counted through her skin, which resembled the leather covering of a trunk; and her tail hung, or rather dragged behind, like an icicle in the winter sun. Her appearance oppressed me as with a nightmare. Tottering before the captivated audience, she sank down upon her haunches and said, 'For eighteen months I have been secured, with other unfortunates, in a pen where there was scarcely room to stand, and where, twice a day, rough hands extracted from my udder a poisonous scum, falsely called milk. Before our noses, in a trough, ran the swill from which we strove to gain nourishment necessary to enable us to furnish fluid sustenance for the children of superior animals. In the yard, daily, stood a cart ready to receive the dead, who were turned over to a butcher who sold the putrid carcasses for food.'"

Bergh looked out over the audience, now silent in reverent respect for the images he painted with his words.

"I often have dreams such as the one I've related to you tonight," he said. "They probably invade my restfulness to remind me, when I grow unsure, of the good things our society has done for mankind. No, I did not misspeak. I said *mankind*. For in treating animals thoughtfully, our children reap the benefits of that kindness with healthier milk and meat. Our horses do not fall sick, and they live longer under this kind treatment; and most of all, our children grow up with a reverence for all living things, and that is consequential. Remember, as the twig is bent, so the tree is inclined. Teach our children

196

kindness, and in generations to come, cruelty might be erased from our existence."

Bergh finished his speech that evening with the spirited plaudits of the audience and several hundred dollars in donations as his reward. Upon his return to New York, he bundled up against the bone-chilling cold and walked the familiar path along Water Street. As he passed a building, some words painted on a window caught his eye. The sign read: Water Street Home For Women.

Bergh laughed out loud. He stopped and tipped his hat to the sign, saying, "I tip my hat to you, Kit Burns! It doesn't matter how it was done, only that it was!" But Bergh knew how it was done, for the building at 273 Water Street was once known as Kit Burn's Sportsmen's Hall. In its heyday, there were often two hundred men gathered around the tiny dirt ring, cheering wildly as rat baiting, dog fights, cock fights, and brutal battles between two bare-fisted men took place. Many would wager their week's pay while their families hungered for food in dilapidated tenement buildings.

Over the years, Bergh and his men had been persistent in their efforts to put an end to the inhumane spectacles that went on there, just as Bergh had solemnly promised himself during the days just prior to the inception of the SPCA. Now the building housed an organization for the rehabilitation of repentant prostitutes, a noble and worthy cause. Bergh, with a new spring in his step, hurried home to share the news with his beloved Matilda.

* * * * *

Charlotte Fiehling sat on the bench in the courtyard, knitting a new blanket to get her through the remainder of winter. It was forty degrees out, but there had been steady rain for nearly an entire week, and she did not enjoy being cooped up inside. Now that there was an evening without rain, she put on heavy clothing and took advantage of it.

The door of the front building opened and Mary Connolly entered the courtyard. There was no way to get from 41st Street to the rear building without passing through the yard unless you entered through the alley, but that was sometimes dangerous with the young thugs who prowled there.

Charlotte's first instinct was to bury her head in her knitting and ignore the Connolly woman. Why, though? It was her duty as a Christian to appeal to her about the bruises she saw on Mary Ellen's body. If she didn't, she was as guilty of cruelty as Mary Connolly was. She put her knitting down and prepared herself. Connolly was just passing the bench when she stood up. "Excuse me, Mrs. Connolly."

Connolly stopped and looked at her, eyebrows raised. "I beg your pardon."

"Uh . . . you don't know me, Mrs. Connolly, but I must take exception to the treatment of your child."

"What do *you* know of *my* child?" she asked.

Charlotte fingered her knitting, preparing her words carefully. This was too important to back down. "I know . . . what I saw, madam. I saw her poor legs black and blue from the beatings you give her."

"It is none of your business, whoever you are. You will do quite well to keep your nose out of our family's affairs." She turned to leave, and Charlotte reached out and put a hand on her shoulder.

Connolly turned, her eyes flashing anger. "Unhand me this instant, you busybody, or I shall have you arrested!"

Charlotte immediately released Connolly's shoulder and tried to still her shaking hand against the other. Her mind recalling the vicious marks on the child's legs and arms, Charlotte's eyes narrowed and she moved close to Mary Connolly. "If it were put to the law, you would be punished, Mrs. Connolly. That poor child is never allowed outside, she's beaten regularly. I know this, for many times I've cried along with her as her screams of pain echo through the halls of this building. I'm not the only one who hears her torture, and you had better heed my warning and put an abrupt end to your cruel treatment!"

Connolly appeared to be without words, and Charlotte was glad of it. She had never told anyone her feelings so directly before, and perhaps it would make a difference in the child's life.

Connolly stormed toward the door, and Charlotte dropped onto the bench. She picked up her knitting and tried to calm herself when she heard the woman's voice behind her.

"If anybody tries to interfere with my family," Connolly said, "I will go through the highest law with them. Is that clear?"

Charlotte had no chance to answer, nor did she know what she would have said. Instead, she said a prayer for Mary Ellen. Mary Connolly disappeared into the hallway beyond the door.

The unfortunate child would have her next.

* * * * *

"Mary, there's a woman," Margaret said, "who visits with you occasionally. She's from St. Luke's Mission, I believe. If you don't mind me asking, what is her name?"

Mary Litzbeney smiled and nodded. She and Margaret Bingham sat on her small sofa inside her living room. Her furniture was old but well-kept, and being inside her apartment made Margaret wish all her tenants were as pleasant and orderly as Mary was.

"Well, her name is Etta Wheeler," Mary said. "She's a good Christian and a generous lady as well. What is your interest in her?"

"I was wondering if you would mind telling her about poor Mary Ellen next door."

Mary shook her head and took a sip of the tea she'd prepared for their visit. "I can't bear the beatings," Mary said. "I told the Connolly woman just yesterday that if I hear her beating that child again I shall call the police to come and put her in jail."

"You said that?"

Mary looked indignant. "Yes I did. And I meant it, too."

"How did she respond?"

"She said go right ahead, as she was moving out this Saturday, and they would never get her."

Margaret's mouth dropped open. "She's moving *this* Saturday? Are you sure, Mary?"

"That's what she said, Margaret. That poor little one will disappear into the city, and who knows what her fate will be."

After leaving Mary's apartment, Margaret went to her daughter's rooms. She paced back and forth as Jenny stood at the basin washing the breakfast dishes.

"How will we stop them?" she asked.

"You intend to try to stop them from moving? Mother, don't be ridicu-

199

lous!"

"We've got to stop them from taking that pitiful thing away, Jenny! If she's taken from here, she might never be saved from the wrath of that ungodly woman!"

"Mother, I didn't realize we were in the business of saving anyone. Just how do you expect to do that?"

Margaret wrung her hands together in frustration. "That's why I'm here, talking to you, Jenny. You must help me think of a way."

Jenny was silent for a time, her expression pensive as she finished the last dish. She picked up a towel and dried them. When she was almost finished, she looked at her mother. "They're leaving this Saturday?"

"That's what Mary Litzbeney says."

"It's simple then," Jenny said. "We'll just have Stuart follow them when they leave."

Margaret slapped a hand to her forehead. "That is simple, Jenny!" she said. A split second later, her face drooped again. "Ah, but what if they go too far? How long can he follow? I mean, what if they go out of the state?"

"Well, Mother. If that happens, we can only say we've done our best, and leave it at that. What else would you propose?"

"I know, I know. You're right. I've already asked Mary to tell her friend from St. Luke's Mission about the child's treatment. Perhaps there's something she can do to help her."

"That's all you can do, Mother."

Margaret walked to her daughter and hugged her. Jenny put the pot she was drying down and wrapped her arms around her. "Mother, you've always been so good to me. If only little Mary Ellen had a mother like you."

Margaret smiled. "They can't all be mine, can they? However unfortunate for them."

Jenny laughed. "Remember your modesty, Mother."

17

Stuart crouched behind the corner of the building, his horse tied a few feet behind him, out of sight. The Connolly family was on the move before sunrise, but Stuart was ready. He watched the street until the wagon in front of Margaret's building was completely loaded, then prepared to follow them. Mary Ellen wore the same clothing he had seen on her during his brief visits. She wore no wrap though the temperature was just above freezing. Stuart was saddened and angered at the sight of the child exposed to such bitter cold. It was hard to believe she never became deathly ill, being neglected in every conceivable way. Such a tiny, frail thing, too. She must be so strong in spirit.

He led his horse to the mouth of the alley beside the building as the cart pulled away, fighting the urge to go to her and cover her with his coat. He had no logical reason to approach them beforehand, as their rent payments were not delinquent; if they had been trying to dodge payment, he might have been able to arrest one or both of the Connollys and take the child as a secondary result. Once he had the battered girl in police custody, he had only to present her before a judge to prove the abuse inflicted on her, and perhaps then her parents would be deemed unfit to raise her in a safe environment. Unfortunately, they were only leaving because of the complaints against them over

Mary Ellen's abuse. They must have seen it would not be tolerated much longer, their signal to part present company and neighbors.

The sun was just coming up now, the clouds obscuring its rays and keeping a blanket of cold over the city. Many of the shopkeepers were already opening their doors and preparing their wares for the day's business as Stuart watched from his hiding place, waiting patiently. When the Connollys' cart was far enough up the street, Stuart guided his horse from the alley into the street a good distance behind them. A moment after he started after them, they stopped and pulled their wagon to the same side of the street as his mother-in-law's building. They had probably forgotten something inside their old apartment and Mr. Connolly was coming back to get it.

Stuart guided his horse back into the alley. Tucked behind the corner of the building, he watched once more as Connolly dismounted, reached up and pulled a basket of clothing from the wagon, then carried it up the stairs of the building directly in front of the cart.

The Connollys were unloading! A smile spread across Stuart's face as he realized why they had chosen to leave so early in the morning. Their obvious intention was to disappear into the throng of the city around them without a trace. Even on the same street, especially 41st, it would be possible to vanish. The street was crowded enough that the Connollys could have gone on with their lives indefinitely without being noticed by anyone from Margaret's building, even though it was located in the same block. Now there was no chance that would happen.

Stuart watched as Mary Connolly and little Mary Ellen climbed down from the wagon and up the steps of the building, disappearing inside. That was good. At least the poor thing didn't have to spend hours in the blistering cold before reaching her new home. He observed Connolly unloading for fifteen more minutes to make sure it wasn't a trick of some kind; perhaps he had known they would follow. It might be silly, but Stuart felt better waiting until he was absolutely sure they were there for good.

Stuart tied Abe, his horse, to the hitching rail in the alley and ran inside to tell Jenny and her mother the good news. Ordinarily he would not leave his horse in such a place, for the youth gangs would surely steal it. The thieves were creatures of relative comfort, though, and it was still far too early and much too cold for them to be about.

* * * * *

"They've moved just up the street?" asked Margaret.

"Yep. Five buildings away," Stuart said.

"But why?" asked Jenny. "Why, when they could leave this area and destroy any chance of being interfered with?"

"Maybe they don't think we will," Stuart said.

"They had *better* think again," Margaret said. "Something must be done. I know from Mary Litzbeney that Mrs. Wheeler will be coming around sometime this week."

"Where's she from again?"

"She's a missionary from St. Luke's. She helps those who live here that can't support themselves. Church money."

"The churches have plenty of that, I'll tell you," Stuart said, shaking his head. "More than the rest of us."

"Yes, and they need every penny," Margaret snapped. "If you needed it yourself you wouldn't be so cheeky."

"Cheeky?"

"You know what I mean, smart man. The Connollys are the scoundrels, not the good people who work to help others."

"Enough of that, you two. It's a matter of waiting now," Jenny said. "There's nothing we can do except keep our eyes on number three-fifteen."

Margaret's eyes narrowed. "I think I'll be spending quite a bit more time outside, sweeping the front stoop."

* * * * *

"Put those things over there," Mary ordered, as Mary Ellen struggled with the heavy basket full of knickknacks. "Drop it and you'll get another spanking!"

Mary Ellen looked at her mama, knowing in her heart that she would not be able to put the basket down right. Mama was tired now; she could see it by the lines in her face, especially around her eyes. She must put the basket down very quietly so Mama wouldn't get angry with her.

Mary Ellen trembled at the prospect of getting whipped yet another time when she was already so sad. She had lost her precious, colorful strings, her only toys. She had tried to bring them with her, but when she dipped into the closet to retrieve them, Mama wanted to know what she was doing. In her surprise, she had blurted out she was just getting her strings, and then Mama wanted to see them.

Why didn't she just say she was looking for anything Mama might have missed? She was so stupid sometimes she couldn't stand it! Instead, she had pulled them out and held them up for Mama to see. Her hands were shaking, she remembered, and they felt clammy as Mama plucked the tiny, colorful threads out of them. A tear rolled down her cheek when Mama took them away.

"Stop crying, Mary Ellen."

"Mama, I love my little strings. I play with them." She said the words, knowing it was useless.

"That's stupid. These aren't toys, child. They're garbage and should be in the garbage can for the ragpickers to gather."

"No, Mama!" she had shouted in her panic. "Please, please let me keep them. I'll never ask for anything else, I promise."

Mama laughed, and the sound of it frightened her. "Why . . . you may ask if you like, Mary Ellen. You know what you'll get for it, don't you?"

Mary Ellen didn't remember seeing the rawhide whip in the boxes yet, but it was kept high in the kitchen cupboard. She watched her mama storm into the kitchen, and Mary Ellen slumped to the floor and cried. It would never stop. Even when she just wanted to help, she did the wrong thing. "Mama, please," she remembered crying, "Don't hurt me!" There was the squeak of the cupboard as it opened, the sound so slow and terrifying to her ears. "No, Mama! Please . . . I'll be good, I promise! I don't want the strings!"

Mama walked toward her with the whip in her hand. Her knuckles were white from gripping the handle, her mouth set in a thin line. "Get up!"

Mary Ellen didn't even try. There was no strength left in her legs, no strength in her mind.

"I said get up!" Mama said, lashing at her with the leather crop.

Mary Ellen didn't move or cover her exposed flesh with her hands. Instead, she tried hard to drift into her safe place. As she received the beating, she remained motionless, staring straight ahead. Mary Ellen looked not at the bunch of colorful threads Mama had dropped on the floor, but at something beyond them, somewhere deep in the warmest, safest parts of her mind.

But that was last night. No beatings had been given today, since Mama and Papa were busy moving their things. Right now, Mary Ellen needed to put this heavy basket down without making noise. Concentrating, she bent her knees and lowered the heavy basket to the floor in the corner where her mother had said. As it touched the ground, she heard the clank of the items inside as they rattled against one another, and looked instinctively at her mama.

She didn't look up, or notice the sound. Mary Ellen breathed a sigh of relief and rejoiced inside. Maybe here, in this new house, everything would be better. Mary Ellen hoped so, with all her heart.

* * * * *

The sun pierced through the clouds more than an hour earlier, but the day was still quite cold, and nearly everyone she passed on the street wore extra layers of clothing to stay warm. Etta buttoned her heavy overcoat all the way to the collar as she walked down the steps of 325 West 41st Street, and turned left toward the building at 315.

Etta knew the building well. Along with Margaret's building, it had been one she visited regularly before Pastor Jameson changed her route. The building at 315 wasn't so nice as Margaret Bingham's, for though it was the same size, the rooms had been divided in two by flimsy walls built much later. This was to allow a maximum number of people to be housed within the structure, and as a result the rooms were smaller, and the conditions from the overcrowding, ghastly.

Etta approached the steps of the building and started up. The front door was splintered and cracked, and the windows she could see were either filthy from oil smoke, or broken out entirely. It was typical of these tenements; the landlords filled them with people desperate to escape the winter cold or the summer heat, and put little money into them. There was no profit in repairs, and that was their common philosophy. Occasionally, Etta's appeals to them would result in a minor repair here and there, but overall, the condition of the tenements would decline until something was done on a government level.

The church, even when appealing to one's sense of compassion, could be ignored if that person's conscience allowed it. The government, however, could make that same landlord's pocketbook suffer, rather than just their soul.

"Hello," Etta said to a carpenter repairing a floorboard just inside the front door. Etta looked around the building. The gentleman with the tools had plenty to keep him busy for a long time. Etta almost said exactly that, but decided against it. At least he was making repairs.

"Uh-huh," he replied.

"Do the Connollys live here?"

"Who?"

"The Connollys. They would have moved in only about a week ago."

"Oh, yeah . . . the Connollys. I remember them now. Yeah, they live here." He pointed up the stairs. "All the way up, first door on the right at the top of the stairs."

"Thank you, sir. And may I add, that's a fine job you're doing on that floorboard."

"What do you know about it?"

Etta laughed politely. By the looks of it, she knew a bit more than him about repairing floorboards. She'd fixed more of them than she cared to remember, in tenements far more dilapidated than this. "Not very much," Etta answered, as she started up the stairs.

At the top of the stairs she paused outside the door to the Connollys' apartment and listened. No sound. She tried the knob. Locked. Was the child in there? Maybe she would knock and welcome them to the neighborhood. She unbuttoned her coat and brushed her dress down flat, then poised her hand to knock.

No, a voice inside told her. If she did anything wrong, Mrs. Connolly may become suspicious about a stranger knocking. The woman might have seen her before, in Margaret Bingham's building.

Etta turned toward the door across the hall from the Connollys' and knocked softly. She waited a moment, then knocked again. A faint voice came from within the room. It was almost a whisper, and Etta might have missed it had there been any noise whatsoever. "Herein," the voice said.

Etta opened the door, and was welcomed by a neat and orderly room, the floors swept and the single window crystal clear. She saw no one immediately, but heard a feeble voice call, "Here, Madam."

Etta saw a woman lying in bed in the rear room. She went to her. "I'm sorry to intrude, dear, but I'm from St. Luke's Mission. Are you all right?"

"I'm as well as one could expect. Would you mind terribly getting me a cup of water, please?"

"Of course, dear." Etta filled a cup from the basin in the kitchen. "My name is Etta Wheeler," she said.

"Welcome, Etta. My name is Mary Smitt. My husband is Charles, but he isn't due to be home for some time yet."

The woman's heavy accent sounded German, but Etta could make out her words with some effort. "Then it's good I've come, Mary," Etta said. "I also have a husband named Charles, so it appears we have something in common to begin with."

The woman smiled and Etta held her head while she took a sip of the cool water. Etta noticed her skin was quite pale, and her face gaunt. She would be as light as a feather to carry, so slight was her frame. "Are you ill?" Etta asked, stroking her hair away from her face.

"Oh, yes. I am dying—or so the doctors have told me."

"You have a warm, clean home, Mary. Cleanliness and faith in God will help cure you." Etta studied her face. Mary's features were those of a woman no more than fifty years old, but the illness seemed to have deepened each wrinkle, making her appear much older. A silvery-gray had overtaken what might have been brown hair in her earlier years. Still, There had to be hope that she would live. Blue eyes sparkled from a tired face. "Do you have a neighbor who comes to see you, Mary? To help you?"

"I did for a time," Mary said. "She's recently moved away though."

"Do you know if a little girl lives in the apartment across the hall from you?"

"I know one does, though I've not seen her. I hear her crying almost every day." Mary put a hand on Etta's arm, her expression worried. "Perhaps she's sick, too. Have you looked in on her?"

"No," Etta said, shaking her head. "I will, though. If she proves to be healthy and fit, I'll speak to her mother about having the child come over occasionally to help you. If you make friends with her, she may be a great comfort through the winter months."

"You are a blessed woman," Mary said, holding weakly to Etta's wrist. "I'd very much like to talk a while if you don't mind. I know that may sound odd, but . . . I seldom have a lady friend to chat with."

Etta sat next to her on the thin mattress. "That would be wonderful. Are you feeling well enough?"

"I never feel much better than I do at present," the woman said with a smile.

Etta and Mary Smitt spoke for nearly an hour about Mary's homeland and her longing to be there again. Mary lamented about leaving a sister in Germany who later married and had two children that Mary was sure she would never have the chance to meet. Etta told her about St. Luke's, describing the beautiful church in great detail. Mary seemed to enjoy it.

When Etta was ready to leave, she promised to return to see Mary a few times each week, then left her apartment when she was sure she was resting peacefully. Two steps across the hall, and she stood in front of the Connollys' door again. Etta knocked, and a moment later, the door opened about eighteen inches. A tall, stern-looking woman peered out of the rooms.

"What may I do for you."

It was more of a curt statement than a question. Stepping forward in an attempt to force the door open further, Etta said, "Hello, madam. My name is Etta Wheeler, and I work—"

"I'm busy," the woman interrupted, stepping back despite her words. Etta took another step inside the room, smiling the entire time.

"What is your errand, Mrs. Wheeler?"

"May I ask your name Mrs. . . . ?"

"I'm Mary Connolly, but as I told—"

"It is a pleasure to meet you, Mary. As I said, my name is Etta Wheeler, and I'm from St. Luke's Mission." Etta was now three feet inside the room, speaking animatedly. "Do you know you have a sick neighbor across the hall? Her name is Mary Smitt, and it's a horrible pity, what she's going through."

With chatter as her distraction, Etta stepped completely away from the door, nonchalantly forcing Mary Connolly to move back out of her way. Once inside, she spotted the child standing on a little keg, washing dishes from a large pan. Mary Litzbeney had told her the child was supposed to be around eight or nine, but this frail thing could be no more than five years. Her arms and legs were covered with vicious welts and bruises, but her little face told her harrowing tale with more poignancy. Her eyes were empty, her expression one of fear. She bore the face of one who knew only the fearsome side of life, where good behavior was rewarded by silence, and anything else, real or imagined, by brutality.

The child did not look at Etta. She slowly picked dishes up from the table beside her and washed them.

Trying not to stare at Mary Ellen, Etta spoke constantly, telling Connolly that Mary Smitt was a sweet woman who just needed a little assistance. "I believe it would be an extraordinary help if you let your little girl see to her sometime." Etta made her way across the room and sat in one of the wood chairs around a small table, putting her purse down as though she expected to stay for a bit.

Unable to interrupt, Mary Connolly closed the door in a huff and sat in the chair opposite Etta. "What is her sickness? I will not send my child over to be dirtied and made sick."

"Oh, it's not a contagious disease," Etta said. "The poor woman has been ill for several months." It was at that moment Etta spotted a rawhide horsewhip on the table beside the child. She had not seen it before because dishes had been stacked in front of it. It was nearly three feet long, and made of twisted leather strands. Dangling from the end of it were several strips of thinner material, and at the handle was a strap that might accommodate one's hand.

Etta found herself staring at it as she spoke, then tore her eyes away and back to Mary Connolly before she noticed the source of her distraction. "The poor woman's doctors are certain she won't recover, so it would be an act of generous mercy on your part." Mary Ellen still didn't appear to be aware Etta was even in the room. She had probably been punished for acknowledging guests in the past.

"I have nothing to give her," Connolly said. "We live meager lives, and every morsel of food is important."

"Oh, no!" laughed Etta. "I'll bring food from the church for you to give her; perhaps some things that should remain uncooked, or broth that you could warm for her. Would that be acceptable?"

"I . . . I suppose so," Connolly said. "Though I don't really have the time for such—"

Etta interrupted again. "Poor Mary's husband is away at work most of the day. She's entirely alone." Etta was more than satisfied that the reports of the girl's abuse were true. "I do appreciate your help, Mrs. Connolly, and I know Mary Smitt will, too." Etta stood. "I look forward to meeting your husband on my next visit."

Mary stood and walked immediately to the door. She pulled it open, an invitation for Etta to depart.

"Thank you so much," Etta said, walking through the door. She turned just in time to catch a last glimpse of the child, and said a quick prayer for her.

The door closed and she hurried away, leaving behind her the sinful place where a demon named Connolly was allowed to rein terror on an innocent child. She would not rest until the girl was taken out of that place.

* * * * *

The temperature had taken a downward plunge, and the streets and alleys were covered by a blanket of white from the heavy snowfall throughout the day.

It was now late in the evening and only a light snow fell. A horse pulling an overloaded dray had come upon an alleyway blocked by a high drift of snow. The narrow path ran between two buildings, and the snow had piled up as a result of a sharp downhill grade that preceded the entrance by twenty feet.

A large load of firewood was stacked in the back of the wagon, and the driver, Willie Elberton, was in no mood for a delay. The horse he normally would have harnessed for such a task had fallen ill, and the one he had been forced to use was not accustomed to pulling a cart. The gentle, white horse was a favorite of Josh and Jeremy, his two sons, and the boys had named it Whitey, after its flawless white coat.

Naming an animal was ridiculous. It was as ludicrous as naming your wagon, or a pair of boots. Willie took a swig from his flask of whiskey, praised the warmth as it ran down his throat, then pressed the horse forward, unwilling to bypass the alley for another two blocks of harsh travel through what could develop into another heavy snow. The unblanketed horse snorted puffs of warm steam from its nose and mouth as Willie snapped the reigns, driving him further forward into the alley. Finally the horse stopped again, unable to take another step. He stood still, awaiting his master's next command.

"Move! Git in there!" shouted Willie. Whitey didn't move. The horse's front feet were pressed up against a packed drift of icy snow. "Son of a bitch!" Willie jumped off the seat and his feet sank into eight inches of slushy ice. He realized he would not be able to drive the horse forward. His usual horse could have driven through it, but this worthless child's toy didn't have the strength. There wasn't enough room between the horse's feet and the snowdrift to maneuver the cart to the right or the left; his only option was to drive him backward, away from the blocked alley.

Willie stomped through the snow, his boots filling with it, his feet freezing. He cursed aloud as he stood beside the horse and pulled on the reins, trying to guide him backward. The horse barely moved the cart two feet up the path before he weakened, allowing the heavy dray to roll forward again. The downhill that caused the snow to build up in the first place now prevented their withdrawal as well. The exhausted horse bellowed and whinnied, the puffs of steam coming more rapidly as the horse labored in vain.

Willie had had enough. He trudged back to get his whip. It was brand new, with a heavy wood handle that might come in handy with a gutless horse such as this one. He cursed the cold again, then took another pull from his flask of whiskey before making his way back to where the horse stood.

"Back, goddamnit!" he shouted, bringing the thick handle into the horse's nose. The horse could not escape, and whinnied in pain at the blow. It began anew to press backward, and again it failed when the forces of gravity prevailed.

Willie hit the horse again. This time he laid the butt of the whip against the side of the horse's head. Blood erupted from the point of contact, and the horse's front legs folded, the animal crumpling to its knees. Whitey's nose and mouth were beneath the snow as he fell into the drift and choked. He coughed and sputtered, struggling for a long moment, eventually getting his feet back under him. He now panted like a steam engine and his eyes darted back and forth, frantic.

Willie drew back the whip once more.

"Stop that this instant!" shouted someone from behind him.

He turned to see a man in a top hat approaching on foot. He carried a fashionable cane, and wore a heavy coat that covered him to his shins. Willie knew who he was, of course. Henry Bergh.

"Get outta here, Bergh! That is unless you plan on helping me get this horse moving!"

The tall man said no more; he simply walked up to Willie and stood face to face with him.

"What do you want, Bergh?"

"I don't believe we've met, sir. What is your name?"

"I ain't got time for chat, Mister. Either help or back off!"

Willie raised his whip again, and Bergh pulled it from his hand and threw it to another man who stood beside his carriage, fifteen feet away.

"What the devil are you doing? Give that back!"

Bergh withdrew his badge. "As you've already surmised, I'm Henry Bergh, of the American Society for the Prevention of Cruelty to Animals, and that gentleman over there is agent Alonzo Evans. What, sir, is your name?"

"Willie Elberton," he answered, starting toward the man who held his whip.

Bergh caught hold of his coatsleeve. "Come back here, sir. I will now show you the proper way to get the horse turned the other direction, then you'll be under arrest for cruel treatment of this animal."

"How?" Willie shouted. "How in the devil are you gonna get this horse out of here without the whip? *He won't move*, damnit!"

"Well, now. I suppose you aren't as smart as you'd like to think." Bergh grabbed his collar and pulled him to the rear of the cart. "Did you ever consider lightening the load? Removing some of this firewood? Like this?"

Bergh pulled a piece of wood from the cart and tossed it into the snow. He pulled several more out and did the same.

"What the—?"

"You'll unload the rest, sir, as I stand here and supervise the process. You'll keep unloading until this horse can manage to back the cart away from the snowdrift without assistance from you or your whip!" Bergh turned to Evans, who was examining the whip. "Alonzo! Get a blanket from our carriage, quickly!"

Willie looked at him. "Well, at least you have *some* compassion for men," he said.

Bergh erupted into laughter. "Oh, you are a buffoon! Certainly you didn't believe for one moment the blanket was for you!"

The other man laughed too, and walked around them to toss the blanket over his horse. He tied it around the horse's midsection and turned to Bergh. "His nose is bleeding, and there's a nasty wound beneath his left eye, but he should be all right."

"That's fortunate for our friend, here. Keep unloading, Mr. Elberton."

Willie grunted as he lifted another heavy piece of frozen wood from the cart. It was half empty now.

"Just a few more pieces," Bergh told him, "and your horse should be able to manage quite well."

Alonzo escorted Willie to the ASPCA carriage as Bergh guided Whitey backward, the cart rolling easily up the incline and out of the blockade. When the horse was safely back on level ground, Bergh walked back to his carriage. "Alonzo, will you drive Mr. Elberton's cart to the police station? I'll be happy to lecture him on the abuse of animals as we make our way there."

"I'm sure he'll find it all quite interesting, Mr. Bergh. I'll check over the horse again, see whether we need to take him to the shelter."

18

January 1874

The gentleman Etta Wheeler awaited now approached her, his horse only a few buildings down. Etta glanced once more toward the front door of 315 West 41st Street, hoping one of the Connollys would not make an appearance now. A few moments later, the postman reached the building and dismounted his horse.

"Good afternoon, sir," Etta said, smiling.

"Hello, madam. I saw you lingering from down the street," he said. "Awaiting an important letter?"

"No," Etta replied. "My name is Etta Wheeler, and I'm investigating a severe case of child beating going on in this building. I would like your assistance in a most important, though paltry way."

"Ah, detective work, eh? I've always found that sort of thing fascinating," the postman said.

"Missionary work, more precisely. I'm with St. Luke's, and the poor child I'm speaking of lives on the third floor of this building— under the name Connolly."

The postman scratched his chin in thought. "Hmm. Connolly you say?" He flipped through the letters in his hand and looked at her. "How long have they been here?"

"Only a little less than a month."

He slapped his forehead. "Oh, yes! I have good reason to remember them," he said. "Didn't they live just up the street? In . . . hmm . . . the building just over there?" He turned and pointed at Margaret Bingham's building.

"Yes! They did at that!"

"Well, I haven't delivered very much mail here yet, but a registered letter did come. That's what made me remember them. They often received registered letters at the other building. I've had to go up and have them sign for them."

Etta was intrigued. Registered letters usually meant government payments, possibly for keeping the child. According to Mrs. Bingham, Mrs. Connolly had indicated that little Mary Ellen was not her natural daughter. "Do you remember seeing a pitiful looking child in the rooms? A little girl?" Etta asked.

"Ma'am, I see so many people, but I seem to recall that sometimes as I came up the hall in the other place, a little girl would run from the hall into the room."

"It was probably her. She's a timid one."

"I don't know how much that helps, but I do have to get on my way now," the postman said. "I wish you luck, Mrs. Wheeler. I promise to be your eyes when I can, but I've my job to think about."

"You've done more than enough. Thank you so much."

* * * * *

"I'm reasonably sure she was adopted by the Connollys somehow or another," Etta said, her brown hair wrapped up in a knot the way she normally kept it.

Her niece, Gabrielle, had stopped by to visit, but Etta could think only of Mary Ellen. Her sister's daughter, sat quietly and listened. The girl was nineteen years old and very intelligent. Though Etta would never admit it to any-

215

one, she was the favorite among her nieces and nephews.

They sat in Etta's small but comfortable living room, with Charles still at work. It was Saturday, but that meant little to a newspaper man. He worked seven days a week, and it was one of the reasons St. Luke's was Etta's salvation. It occupied her hours, and gave her tremendous inner satisfaction.

Etta sipped her tea, her mind reeling over the things she'd learned. "When I spoke to Margaret Bingham, she said Mary Connolly made a comment about having a *good fortune* for taking care of the child, and that she intended to keep it."

"When was she able to speak to the Connolly woman about the child?"

"Apparently, Margaret confronted her about a disturbance between her and her husband one evening. She commented on the treatment of the child, and Mrs. Connolly said something about her husband always pressing her to put the child in an asylum."

"The poor child," Gabrielle said. "Have you spoken to Pastor Jameson about her?"

Etta shook her head. "No, not yet, not in any detail. I'm sure I've mentioned her in passing. God knows, it's all I ever speak of anymore."

"Why not see if there is anything he can do, Auntie. It couldn't hurt."

* * * * *

The next day, Etta visited with Pastor Jameson. He wore his casual clothes, but to Etta, he still looked like a holy man. He was quite modest, seeming not to notice her admiration. Pastor Jameson was nearly fifty, very tall and thin, but quite handsome. He was, in the truest sense of the phrase, married to the church. Etta respected him for his dedication, it was so rare to find a truly good man so devoted to his God in every way.

As Etta spoke, he listened with an expression of concern. "So you see, Pastor, the Connollys have already relocated once, and I fear if they're confronted again, they'll simply whisk that poor girl away where she'll never be saved from her treatment."

Frank Jameson shook his head. "Etta, we see countless sad situations in our service to the Lord, but we cannot help every one of them. Now, I know you have the best intentions in that blessed heart of yours, and it truly sounds as though this child needs help. Unfortunately, between our good intentions and the harsh treatment of this child, therein lies a sea of difficulty." The pastor stood from the pew and looked around the meager church, then back at Etta. "We're speaking of intervention of the church between guardian and child, something that will not be embraced by anyone."

"But Pastor, there's no one else who—"

Jameson held up a hand. "Now, I'm not finished yet, Etta. I will agree to make a single appeal to their sense of what is Godly and just. If you like, I'll go see the Connollys personally. In fact, it may even be best if I do. But as I said, only *one* appeal. Any more than that, and we may drive them off, just as you fear."

"People capable of these evils aren't normally receptive to the pleas of the church," Etta said, worried. "How will you state your purpose, how will you say you came to know of the situation?" Etta rose from the hard, wooden pew and paced back and forth. "The more I think of it, the more sure I become that what is needed is some sort of police involvement."

Pastor Jameson laughed softly and said, "You see? This is one reason you're so valuable to the church, Etta. You're wise. You don't try to convince yourself you can do the impossible, but still you have faith." He smiled and touched Etta's shoulder. "While we do have God on our side, we have to be realistic, and you're absolutely right. How shall I do it so the Connollys don't become alarmed? I'm not sure myself."

"Perhaps I should appeal to the police first," conceded Etta. "If I compose a letter to them detailing the situation, maybe they'll act upon it. If that fails, then you're our last hope. Maybe our best." She shrugged.

"That's reasonable, Etta. I'll act upon your word."

* * * * *

April 1st, 1874
Four Months later

Mary Ellen sat quietly on the stool watching as her mother glided the hot iron over the clothes on the board. Ironing was one task her mama would not let her do, since the last time she dropped the iron on the floor. It was too

217

heavy, and now she was afraid of hot things.

The child's hands moved unconsciously over the burns on her arms where Mama had touched the iron on her skin.

"What are you thinking, child? I asked you to hold this!" Mama had been talking to her and she was daydreaming again. "I'm sorry, Mama . . . I was watching you real careful."

"Well, try listening, too! Now pick up the legs of these trousers and help me."

Mary Ellen took the pant leg, and tried to control her shaking. She pulled the leg taut and watched her mama, waiting for instructions. As the iron slid down the leg of the trousers toward her she could feel the heat on her skin. Her arm instinctively twitched, and her mama snatched her wrist in her hand. Mary Ellen tried to pull away, but Mama held her much too tightly.

"What did I tell you, stupid child?"

"You said to hold it still!"

"And did you? Did you? *Quit fighting me and answer!*"

"Mama, no! I tried to—" Mary Ellen screamed.

In a flash, Mary touched the tip of the iron to Mary Ellen's arm, then pulled it back and pushed her from the stool. Mary Ellen toppled to the floor and screamed in agony.

"You shut your mouth! I'm doing my best to teach you housework, you idiot! No man will ever have you if you refuse to learn anything! Not that I think anyone will want you anyway. Look at yourself, you scrawny, pitiful creature."

Mary Ellen gently touched the place where her skin had turned a fiery red, the pain so intense she couldn't even take a breath. Her cheek was flat against the floorboards as she stayed curled up, cowering. Mama was screaming something that she could not understand at the moment. To her horror, she felt something happening between her legs and could do nothing to stop it.

The warm liquid spread over her legs and soaked into her dress. No matter how she concentrated, it kept coming. She was relieving herself on the floor. Tears welled in her eyes as she squeezed her legs together, but it was no use. Now she couldn't get up or Mama would see. It didn't matter. The pool spread across the floor beyond her dress, and Mama would surely see it soon.

She had to do something, or risk another burn. Mary Ellen scrambled to her feet as fast as she could and ran toward the kitchen. Before she made it there, Mama's hand reached out and caught her hair.

Mary Ellen felt her head snap back and before she knew what happened, she was blinking her eyes, trying to clear away the black spots that danced all around her head. The spots blocked out the ceiling that spun around and around. She wasn't sure exactly what had happened until she felt the wetness of her petticoat and dress. She remembered now—she had peed herself, and Mama was angry.

"You're awake. Good. Now get up and clean up this mess. After that, you can get what you deserve for such disgusting behavior."

She closed her eyes and sat up, cupping her hand over the painful burn. Mama stood over her with the rawhide whip in her hand. She brought it down on her back and Mary Ellen jumped to her feet and ran.

"Stop!" Mama shouted, but Mary Ellen was afraid. Mama came after her, the whip raised over her head.

"Mama! Please, don't hurt me, Mama!" she screamed as she ran from one end of the room to the other. Another wave of dizziness came over her and she fell into the wall with a loud thud, then collapsed onto the floor.

Mama whipped her until she fell asleep.

* * * * *

April 5th, 1874
Easter Sunday

For Charles Wheeler, Easter represented not only the resurrection of Christ, but also another day of work. Etta was accustomed to this, for Charles had worked for the *New York Daily News* for almost twelve years, and keeping abreast of developments in a city the size of New York was no simple task. All the small paper's reporters were taxed to their limits, but Charles found the work fascinating and never complained about the constant work schedule or the long hours.

For Etta, however, Easter was a day of worship and a day of remembrance. The evening would give her and Charles time to celebrate Easter with a pleasant supper and quiet prayer. She went to St. Luke's early that day, as

Charles had left the house before sunup, hoping to make it back home before dark. As she approached the beautiful church building, she marveled at its beauty for the hundredth time.

It had been built in 1810 by missionaries who had used Sing Sing convicts to quarry the white marble from which it was constructed. Eighteen years later, when the church finally reaped the benefits of a financially healthy fellowship, the beautiful Greek Revival steeple was added. This was followed by an Italianate cast-iron portico, which kept the church abreast of the latest architectural fashions of the 1850s. While all these things were lovely, Etta knew Pastor Jameson would choose a simple structure without the ornate additions to better serve the poor. He was proud of his church, though, and he had a right to be. It was, after all, a lovely, holy place where less fortunate parishioners could leave behind the terrible conditions of their tenements for an hour or two of splendor. Many of them did this regularly.

The day was bright with sunshine, and as Etta walked up the two steps that led to the doors of the church, she smiled and nodded hello to those she passed. Some she knew, others she didn't, but they all smiled and wished one another a happy Easter. Stepping into the church, Etta breathed in the light, sweet scent of lilies, dozens and dozens of them that decorated the church. Beautiful palms accompanied them, and angled yellow rays of sunshine streamed through the windows, touching the brilliant mosaic and adding to the splendor.

Many were seated in the pews, and Etta took a seat in the very rear, alone. She looked around the church once more, saw Pastor Jameson at the front of the church, not quite ready to begin his sermon, but preparing all the tools of his trade. The beauty here, while inviting and peaceful, was something Etta could enjoy any day she chose. Today she must try to brighten another person's life. Mary Smitt came immediately to mind. She rose from the pew, genuflected, and started up the aisle. "Pastor Jameson," she whispered, "Happy Easter to you."

"Happy Easter to you, Etta. Could we have had a more beautiful day to celebrate His resurrection?"

Etta turned and looked over the church. It *was* most beautiful. "No, Pastor. It is a lovely day."

"I get the notion you won't be staying." He smiled at her. "Have something else in mind?"

Etta nodded. "It's just that I feel . . . well, a bit indulgent being here."

"You'll be going to the tenements?"

"Yes, I believe so. There's a woman there, Mary Smitt. She's not long for this Earth, and her husband is working today, just as Charles is. Do you mind if I take her some lilies, and perhaps a palm or two?"

"You're perfectly welcome, take as many as you like, Etta. Offer her my best wishes, if you will."

* * * * *

"You didn't actually believe I'd let you spend Easter Sunday alone, did you?" asked Etta, cutting the stems of the lilies to fit the vase.

"They're beautiful, Etta. So are the palms. I don't get outside to enjoy the spring anymore."

"Well, then," she said, walking to the window, "let's at least open the window to let some spring inside." Etta slid the window open. It opened up to a view of the building next door, but still the air could be felt within the room, and it was a gentle, warm breeze.

"It's lovely," Mary said.

"Yes, it is."

Mary sighed. "She's alone today, you know."

Etta looked at her, her heart aching. "You mean Mary Ellen."

"Yes. Not an hour ago I heard Mr. and Mrs. Connolly go out. These walls are as thin as paper, as you well know." A tear slid down her cheek and she wiped it away.

Etta put a hand on Mary's shoulder, soothing her. "Come now, Mary. I made a promise to myself that I'll get her out of there, and I will."

Mary shook her head, the tears flowing unchecked now. "Etta, as tired as I am, as ready to meet the Lord as I am, I *refuse* to die until that child has been taken from her horrible home and that woman punished! My life is over, I know and accept that, but this child! I've seen her only twice, but it seems as though we're together—connected—somehow."

Etta stared at her, wondering how such a wonderful woman could be made to suffer so.

"When she is released from her misery, so will I be. Not until then."

"It's wonderful that you hold such strength in your heart for that child, Mary," Etta said, "but you have to hold some for yourself as well. Just as you won't give up hope that she'll be rescued, you shouldn't give up hope that you'll recover."

Etta spoke the words, but any person with two eyes could see that Mary was not wrong about her own fate. She was, though a relatively young woman, a near skeleton, so emaciated was her body. Whatever had stricken Mary was consuming her from the inside out.

"Yes, I know, Etta. You're saying I should keep my faith. I shall tell you here and now that I have never lost it—I just replaced a longing to be back in my homeland with a longing to be in the land where sickness is not. In the land of God. All things considered . . . that would be a blessing."

As the gentle breezes of spring danced through the small tenement room, the two women talked about their lives. Mary told Etta how she and her young husband traveled across what seemed a vicious, endless sea on a grueling journey during which many had died. They had eventually arrived on these shores, a country of strangers and strange speech, a land where the values of the old country were almost meaningless. Though it was strange and wonderful, it was a place where hard work and endless toil did not ensure you would live a long and comfortable life.

"Mary," Etta said, after three hours had passed and the conversation had drifted into silence for a few moments. "Have you heard of an organization here in New York that serves to protect animals?"

Mary shook her head. "No, I'm certain I haven't. What are they being protected from?"

"Cruelty inflicted upon them by their owners, from what I've read in the newspapers. Horses mostly, but there have been times they've intervened in the treatment of dogs, cats—even dairy cows and pigeons."

"Well, just from my window I've seen men beating horses in such a terrible manner," Mary said. "I've always thought it was quite cruel."

"A gentleman called Bergh is the president of the society. I've . . . well, considered approaching him, but it seemed foolish. After all, she's a child, not an animal."

"What else have you done? Have you spoken with the police?"

"Yes, and they said they would see what could be done but that was months ago. Each time I go back, they put me off further."

"What of Pastor Jameson? Can he help her?" Mary asked.

"He's only waiting for me to give him the word, then he'll speak to them," Etta said. "I've spoken to Margaret Bingham, the owner of the building where the Connollys used to live. I'm going to see Mrs. Bingham's son-in-law tomorrow. He's a policeman too, and said he would speak with me."

"He knows of the child's situation then?"

"Yes. He's visited her on a few occasions, and he's the one who followed the family from there to this building," she said frowning. "The fact that he's a policeman doesn't encourage me. He knows the laws just as the police I've already spoken with. I may be wasting my time."

"Remember, Etta, to keep your faith, too. That little girl over there has an angel by her side, and her name is Etta."

* * * * *

Across the hall, alone for the day, Mary Ellen knew nothing of Easter or of its meaning, so on this day, she noticed only that it was a little quieter in the street than usual. She had, however, found an Easter friend. She lay on her stomach beneath the dirty window and put her finger on the floor. The tiny brown spider crawled onto it, and she lifted her finger to her eyes.

"I'll name you . . . Timmy! That was the name of the boy in my picture book. I liked him, and I like you, too. Timmy is your new name." She sat up, her legs dirty, her hair matted, but a new smile on her face. "Here," she said, putting her finger to the ground. "You . . . go . . . there! Walk along the floor, and I'll count how long it takes you to get to this spot right here."

She quickly wet the tip of her finger and put a spot on the wood floor. "One . . . two . . . three . . ." The spider crawled in the wrong direction, but Mary Ellen simply made another spot on the floor where the spider was headed.

She laughed out loud as the spider reached her mark. The sound of her own laughter was strange even to her ears, but it felt so good! She smiled as she watched Timmy make his way from spot to spot. "I'll remember to hide you before Mama and Papa get home," she said. "But where? Where can I keep a tiny thing like you where you won't run away?" She would think of something. She laughed again, enjoying the sound and the feeling of it. It was nice to have a friend.

Even a tiny one like Timmy.

19

April 6th, 1874
Monday, 10:00 A.M.

"So you see, Mrs. Wheeler, the law states the victim of a crime must step forward, and only then may the alleged perpetrator of the crime be charged. Our problem is, and always has been, there is no way we know of to get the child out of the Connollys' home and into court where an official evaluation of her physical condition can be made. If we were to simply go in and take her, it would be in violation of law."

Margaret, Stuart, Jenny, and Etta sat in the front room of Margaret's apartment. The identical quandary plagued all of them. "It's all very involved, isn't it?" Etta said. "Meanwhile, a little girl suffers."

Stuart nodded. "Yep. Not to mention, there has to be an admission by the child that she has been beaten or otherwise abused—or there must be sufficient evidence on her body to convince the judge of that fact."

"I don't think that would be too difficult, Mr. Slater," Etta said. "I've seen her, just as you have, and those marks won't disappear even after they've healed. My God, just thinking about it makes me shudder!"

Stuart shook his head in disgust. "Mary Ellen's a little sweetheart, too. I was almost caught up there three times, just for not wanting to leave her when I knew I was already pushing my luck. She looks like a guttersnipe, and she's never even been out on the street!"

Margaret wrung her hands together nervously, then looked at Etta. "Mrs. Wheeler, what can St. Luke's do to help her? Is there any hope, any chance of some offering there?"

Etta leaned forward, her wringing hands mirroring those of Margaret. "Pastor Jameson is willing to pay a visit to Mary Connolly. It's my fear the woman will smell a rat, so to speak, and if that occurs, who is to say she won't run again? According to some of your neighbors, Mrs. Connolly has indicated she'll battle tooth and nail to keep the child."

"Let's cover the details again," Stuart said. "Any appeals or complaints by outsiders have had no effect other than to cause them to flee. As a police officer, I know *we* can't do anything unless we can present the child in court. Beyond that, there's only the appeal of the church." Stuart shrugged. "That's the only thing that hasn't been done."

"I'll have Pastor Jameson speak to them as soon as he can," Etta said. "Maybe they'll show some concern for their own souls, if nothing else."

"I'll make you a promise Mrs. Wheeler," Stuart said. "If Pastor Jameson's appeal fails, I'll follow the Connollys for a hundred miles if I have to. Then, we'll just think of something else."

"That's what she needs, Stuart." Etta reached out and took the hands of Jenny and Margaret. "Thank you, all of you. For all your help."

* * * * *

1:00 P.M.

Pastor Frank Jameson knocked, then waited outside the door of the Connolly apartment. He heard noises from within, and knew someone was home. Finally, the door opened.

"I've no donation to offer you today, Father," Francis Connolly said. The man stood just inside the room, wearing loose fitting striped trousers, a clean, white shirt, and a low-crowned hat. All in all, Jameson thought he was dressed

226

extraordinarily well. He waved his hand. "That's not why I've come to see you today sir, and I'm sorry if I caught you on your way out . . . Mr. Connolly is it?"

"Uh . . . yeah. How do you know my name?"

"I'm with St. Luke's Mission—"

Mary Connolly hurried to the door and nudged her husband aside. "St. Luke's you say? If you're here in place of that Wheeler woman, we got no time to visit that sick woman or to cook her food—"

"I assure you I'm not here on behalf of Mrs. Smitt. May I come in?"

"State your business, Father," Mary said.

"It's Pastor, Mrs. Connolly. Pastor Franklin Jameson, and yes, Etta Wheeler does serve the poor for St. Luke's."

"Whatever you say, Pastor. I still won't let you in unless you state your business with us."

The woman kept the door against her, and Jameson couldn't see beyond it. He needed to catch a glimpse of the child, and unless he could get in, it would be impossible. "Please, allow me to come in for just a moment. I walked here from the church and my feet are in need of a rest. Please?"

"For Christ's sake, let him in Mary!" her husband ordered.

Jameson smiled. She opened the door and he stepped inside, his eyes searching for the child. He saw Mary Ellen instantly. With a large cloth she wiped the floor in the kitchen. She was barefoot, and the bottoms of her feet were filthy. Her tattered white dress was nearly in shreds, and her dark brown hair did not appear to have ever been combed. He stared at her as he made his way toward one of the wooden chairs, then sat. Jameson looked from the woman to the man, then at the child once more.

"That poor child is the reason I have come to see you," he said, having no desire to mince words.

"Get out!" Mary shouted.

He put his hands up in a calming gesture. "I only ask that you listen to me for a moment, then I'll go."

"Francis! Get him out if here. *Get him out of here right now!*"

"Mary, goddammit! Just shut up and let him speak his piece!"

Jameson's hands trembled with emotion. He felt he may well be the child's last chance.

Mrs. Connolly settled uneasily in the chair beside Jameson, but her position seemed tentative. She appeared ready to leap from her seat at any moment. Mr. Connolly leaned against the door, his arms folded as he listened.

"Look at that little child, Mrs. Connolly . . . look at her closely! She's pitiful! Is this how you think the innocent creatures of God should be treated? How in God's name can you look at the scars on her arms and legs and not think to yourself, *What have I done?*"

Pastor Jameson looked at the ragged child, but Mary Ellen didn't return his gaze. Instead, she kept her eyes on the floor, her expression blank as she wiped the dirty rag back and forth. Looking at her, Jameson knew he was out of control. He had to regain his composure or he would only succeed in infuriating the woman further. He took several slow breaths and spoke softly. "As a representative of the church, I've come to ask you to give up this child. I will make sure she is placed in a proper—"

Mary Connolly leapt to her feet. "Now! Francis, I want him out of here now!" Her fists were balled at her sides.

Jameson could take no more. He, too, rose from his chair and stood a foot from the despicable woman. He realized what a large woman she was then, as he was nearly six feet tall, yet she matched his height nearly to the inch. Jameson met her eyes as he spoke, his voice quivering. "You can dismiss me now, Mrs. Connolly, just as you have the others who have come to the defense of this poor innocent! But don't think you can escape the wrath of God, for he will punish you a thousand times for the evils you've done to this little one!"

He turned toward Francis. "And you, Mr. Connolly. Don't distance yourself from this for a moment, if that's what you intend to do. I imagine you've both taken your turns with the child, and in God's eyes, both of you will be held equally responsible for her treatment!"

Connolly stared at him for a moment, then said in a very calm voice, "I think it is time you go, Pastor." Connolly stood and opened the door.

Pastor Jameson hesitated, then walked toward it.

He turned toward Mary Ellen and stopped. "Mary Ellen, don't you worry, child. You've done nothing wrong. You'll be taken from here soon, I promise. Somehow." As he stepped into the hall, he paused as the door slammed behind him. He looked back at the closed door, knowing he failed in his mission. He prayed for the little girl locked within as he made his way back to St. Luke's, where Etta awaited his return.

* * * * *

"It was my fault, Etta. I laid eyes on that child and . . . well, you've seen her. I suppose I wasn't prepared for such a sight."

"Pastor Jameson, you needn't hold yourself responsible. You went there to ask that they give the child up voluntarily, and they wouldn't. We never expected them to, did we?"

He shook his head. "No, I suppose not."

"I believe I'll stay here a while and pray for her, pastor. Thank you for what you've done. I guess I'll just keep in contact with the police. Maybe they'll come up with something they haven't thought of before."

* * * * *

Etta arrived home around five o' clock that evening, happy to find that Gabrielle had come for another visit. She needed someone to talk with, and Gabrielle was always more than an open ear. Together, they prepared the evening's supper, and after it was gone, Charles went up to bed. He wasn't feeling well, so Etta put him to bed early. He worked hard, and tomorrow would be another busy day for him.

Etta washed and Gabrielle dried the dishes. By the light of a single lamp in the living room, they shared conversation over a cup of tea.

"So, there she remains, in that horrible home," Etta said. "Pastor Jameson was very upset when he returned, though I told him he could have done nothing more."

Gabrielle sat in the comfortable, overstuffed chair across from her, looking as though she wanted to say something, but hesitant to come out with it. Etta put her cup and saucer down and leaned over to touch her hand. "What are you thinking, child?"

"Auntie," Gabrielle said. "You're so troubled over that abused child, why not go to Mr. Bergh from the animal cruelty society? She's a little animal, surely."

229

"As you know, I've thought about it. I just . . . it's not really what he does, is it?"

"*What he does,* Auntie, is care for abused creatures. Is not Mary Ellen abused, and is she not a creature?"

Etta nodded. Yes, Mary Ellen was both of those things, and like a dumb animal, she probably didn't even realize her own plight. "Imagine, Gabby. A child who has never known love. What thoughts must she have? How does the world appear to her?" Etta picked up her cup and sipped the hot tea, deep in thought.

"Promise me you'll pay a visit to Mr. Bergh tomorrow, Auntie. You've nothing to lose."

"I will, Gabrielle. You're absolutely right. And little Mary Ellen has everything to gain."

* * * * *

April 7th, 1874
Tuesday, 9:00 A.M.

The brownstone and brick building at the corner of Fourth Avenue and Twenty-second Street was quite impressive. At the entrance of the structure was a beautiful fountain from which the city's horses could drink and refresh themselves. Crowning the twenty-five foot tall fountain was a majestic, life-size iron horse, free from bridle or saddle as it was before man dominated it.

As Etta rounded the corner of the building, she smiled as she heard the urgent sounds of several dogs of differing vocal abilities barking. She passed the ambulance Mr. Bergh had designed to pick up lame and sick horses, cows, and dogs from the streets, and wondered when such a service might become available to humans in dire need of medical attention. The animals had surely found a hero in this kind man.

As she stepped into the building, she smiled again. Mr. Bergh had turned the lower floor of the building into a makeshift shelter for the smaller animals. On one side were dogs, and on the opposite wall, cages for cats. All looked quite comfortable to Etta, though the dogs' vantage point of the cats was probably a bit too clear. Neither side could really relax, and that made for some

230

busy attendants. She had read in the newspaper that the horses were accommodated in a small stable in the rear courtyard of the building. Overall, quite an impressive operation.

After obtaining directions, she walked up one flight of stairs to Henry Bergh's office. He was in and agreed to see her.

"Mr. Bergh, thank you for allowing me in to speak with you without a prior appointment."

Bergh waved it off. "Much of what I do each day is quite unexpected, Mrs. . . ."

She held out her hand. "Wheeler. Mrs. Charles Wheeler."

"It's a pleasure, I'm sure, Mrs. Wheeler. Now how may I assist you?"

"It's difficult to know where to begin, Mr. Bergh," Etta said. "I haven't come to see you regarding the abuse of a typical animal."

Bergh's eyebrows rose. "Oh?"

"No. I've come to see you about a horribly abused child."

Bergh's expression seemed to change, his posture to stiffen. "Please, Mrs. Wheeler. Sit down and tell me about this . . . child."

Etta suddenly felt foolish. The gentleman behind the desk seemed to have an air of amusement on his face, and she wondered if she wasn't simply wasting both of their time. I'm already here, she thought. There can be no harm in telling him if he's willing to listen.

"The child is a little girl called Mary Ellen. I've seen her myself and would estimate her age at somewhere near six or seven years." She was relieved to see that Bergh took notes as she spoke.

When she finished telling him the story, some forty minutes later, Bergh remained silent for a long moment. Finally, he spoke. "Mrs. Wheeler, I'm sure you understand that very definite testimony is needed to warrant interference between a child and those claiming guardianship." He put his pen down on the pad upon which he had been writing.

Etta's heart deflated. So it would be the same story here—just as she had experienced with the police, the so-called shelters, and with the church.

But Bergh wasn't done. "Mrs. Wheeler, will you send me a written statement that, at my leisure, I may judge the weight of the evidence and may also have time to consider if this society should interfere? I promise to consider the case carefully."

"Are you actually . . . saying you'll consider helping her?"

"I believe that's what I'm saying, Mrs. Wheeler. Animals and children are both innocent victims at the mercy of adult men and women. It may be more difficult to rescue abused children than abused animals, but before success or failure in any form may be realized, a task must first be undertaken."

Wiping the tears from her eyes, Etta stood, anxious to follow his instructions. "I'll prepare the statement today, sir. You shall have it first thing in the morning, at the very latest. God bless you, sir."

Bergh stood and smiled, extending his hand. "Good day, Mrs. Wheeler. I shall be anticipating its arrival."

* * * * *

After Etta Wheeler left his office, Bergh reviewed the notes he had taken as the woman told her story. Gerry had come in for a few moments following her visit but had to attend court shortly thereafter, so could not stay. Bergh made short mention of Mrs. Wheeler and the case, to which his attorney replied, "Shades of Emily Thompson." Then he walked out the door.

As the words met his ears, Bergh's thoughts drifted back to June of 1871, when a strange woman entered his office on Broadway and first introduced him to the plight of eight-year-old Emily Thompson. Intrigued, Bergh set aside his work for animals and listened to her appeal. It had been very much like this one.

The woman had approached the society to intervene "Because," she said, "a man who shows so much mercy to animals cannot be but equally kind to men." She told Bergh that from her window she could see into the yard next door. There, she frequently watched a woman brutally beat and whip a little girl, sometimes for up to an hour at a time.

With some reluctance, Bergh sent agents to investigate. They returned with reports that little Emily was black and blue from the inhumane treatment. Upon further questioning, several neighbors came forward to testify that they, too, had witnessed the beatings almost daily. Shortly after, following some clever legal finagling by Gerry, little Emily Thompson was removed from the abusive home and presented before Judge Barnard in the Court of Special Sessions. In court, the child's face and neck were severely bruised, showing clear evidence of malicious abuse.

Mary Ann Larkin, the child's keeper, testified that Emily's parents, who had lived in Philadelphia, were both dead. During the trial, she further testified that Emily's grandmother, Violet Bickom, was deceased. Larkin testified before the court that she had taken Emily into her home out of the kindness of her heart, an arrangement she made with Mrs. Bickom just prior to her death. She denied ever beating Emily.

Bergh was excited about the achievement of such a feat—rescuing an innocent, abused child—until Emily stood before the judge and denied ever having been beaten by the woman. She also refused to be separated from the woman she thought of as her only mother.

Despite the child's denial of the charges, Judge Barnard found Larkin guilty as charged, using the testimony of the many witnesses and the terrible condition of the girl as evidence. But just as Bergh prepared to celebrate victory, Judge Barnard suspended Larkin's sentence and sent the girl back to live with her, stating that Emily had no living relatives, and since she wanted to return, it was the only thing for him to do.

If a miracle hadn't occurred that same week, the child might have remained with the cruel woman for years to come, and today, Bergh would have told Etta Wheeler he was quite sorry, but there was nothing of any consequence that he could do to help poor Mary Ellen.

But within the week, a "dead" woman showed up on his doorstep. Violet Bickom was Emily's grandmother, and quite animated for a woman in her grave for better than six months. Mrs. Bickom had been living in New Jersey when she read about the case in the newspapers. She took the first ferry she could catch to New York City, and tracked down Bergh. She told him she had allowed Larkin to raise her granddaughter, but only on the solemn promise that she would be treated as her own child.

What Larkin had testified about Emily's parents was true; they had been killed, and Mrs. Bickom felt she was much too old to care for the little girl. Unfortunately, shortly after Larkin took the child in, she told Mrs. Bickom that Emily died, telling Emily the same of her grandmother.

And that was that. The little girl was put back with her grandmother, and the two returned to New Jersey. It was a happy conclusion to a case that at first appeared to end badly. Now here was little Mary Ellen. A child kept in close confinement and cruelly beaten for not mere months, as was Emily Thompson, but years.

Bergh couldn't wait for Etta Wheeler to return.

* * * * *

Etta began her task by going directly to Margaret's building, where she interviewed each and every person she could find, taking pages of notes on their recollections. She then took a walk to both neighboring buildings and asked questions of some of the tenants there, concentrating primarily on those who lived in the rooms in close proximity to Margaret's building. Mary Ellen's punishment and cries of pain had been heard by some; every witness would probably be of assistance to Mr. Bergh. Etta found no need to go to the building at 315; the things told to her by Mary Smitt were etched in her memory.

As the bell tower of St. Luke's Mission rang out six times, Etta sat down to consolidate her notes into the statement she wanted Henry Bergh to read. A long day it had been, but the rescue of the child was closer than she ever dared dream. She would deliver the message herself tomorrow morning.

20

April 8th, 1874
Wednesday, 9:15 A.M.

Bergh opened the letter, hand-delivered by Mrs. Wheeler just moments before. She had the poor to attend to, and he understood, assuring her he would give the case his first attention. The statement was written on four pages of white, lined paper. Her handwriting was quite neat, and Bergh had no trouble at all making out the content:

Mr. Henry Bergh:

Dear Sir,

    Fearing that the notes of evidence in the Connolly case that I left with you yesterday were not very clearly stated, I repeat the same here, also adding what I obtained in the way of testimony after our interview in your office. The case is as follows:

A girl, about seven years old, called Mary Ellen, is being held by a man and woman named Connolly of 315 West 41st Street, rear house, top floor, right hand room. The evidence of unjust and cruel treatment of the girl on the part of Connolly and his wife is from the following named persons:

Mr. and Mrs. Smitt, a German couple living in the adjoining rooms, assert that through the partition dividing their living rooms, they can hear very clearly the child being severely whipped every day, sometimes more than once. They also say that during the four months the Connollys have occupied these rooms, the child is kept within them, having been seen outside only once, and just for a moment, in the yard.

Each time she has been seen, she has been without shoes or stockings—this includes the coldest winter months. Whenever the Connollys are away, she is locked in the bedroom, the window nailed shut, and the outer door being also locked. Mr. Smitt is ready to swear to the above facts, as is his wife.

Up until four months ago, the Connollys had lived for two years in the rear house of 325 West 41st Street. The landlord of this house, Mrs. Margaret Bingham, lives in the front house, same number. She asserts that Mrs. Connolly told her at different times that the little girl Mary Ellen was neither her child nor her husband's. She explained that at one time she, Mrs. Connolly, stated in the presence of her husband that she had a good fortune for keeping the child, and keep her she would—whatever trouble Mr. Connolly might make about it.

Mrs. Bingham also testifies that during the two years the Connollys lived in her house, the child was kept in close confinement. The child was locked alone in the room and left entire days both in summer and winter; and not dressed with either shoes or stockings or other sufficient clothing during the winter. She also states that the child's cruel treatment was notorious among the neighbors. Mrs. Bingham's daughter, Jane Slater, who lives in the same building, corroborates the preceding statements.

In the rear house of 325 where the Connollys lived is a Mrs. Catherine Kemp, who can testify to the above. Also in the same house is a Mrs. Fiehling, who also testifies to all the above facts, and to having once met the little girl in the water closet and saw her body to be black and blue from what were evidently blows with a whip. Where the child's limbs were not covered with clothing, they were covered with discolorations. Mrs. Studor, a woman in 317 West 41st Street has asserted that the child was constantly cruelly whipped when the Connollys lived next door to her building.

If the information will help, the name of the physician in attendance upon Mrs. Smitt in the room adjoining the Connollys present rooms is Dr. Raefle. His address is East 10th Street. near Third Avenue between Second and Third Avenues.

I am hoping that something may be done speedily in this case, as the matter has now been spoken of to so many persons that there is a great danger of its coming to the Connollys. They may then relieve themselves by either removing the child, or calling to their aid the influence and money of the parties to whom the child belongs. (Whoever they may be.)

I remain yours truly,
Mrs. Charles C. Wheeler
122 West 45th Street

Bergh read the entire statement over again, then pulled a clean sheet of ASPCA letterhead from the desk drawer, dipped his pen and wrote:

New York, April 8, 1874

Dear Mr. Gerry,

The enclosed letter from the lady to whom I alluded this morning speaks for itself. No time is to be lost—instruct me how to proceed. Shall I make the complaint myself on information and beliefs, then produce the witness, or how?

Messenger will await your answer.

Yours in haste,
Henry Bergh

I shall be at the Veterinary College at 4:00 P.M.

He folded it along with Wheeler's statement and gave it to his office messenger, saying, "Son, this must be delivered to Mr. Gerry with unqualified swiftness. It is most urgent and I want you to wait there for a reply."

The boy snatched the papers from his hand and hurried across the room to the appointment board to verify Gerry's location. The large posting board was there for times such as these—it had been Gerry's idea, as he and Bergh were often departing only moments after checking in, and it helped them keep track of one another, as well as the many agents. Bergh watched the messenger descend the stairs, then leaned back in his chair, a million thoughts and ideas whirling through his mind. He had many items that needed his attention, but suddenly, in the single turn of a clock's hour hand, he could no longer concentrate on them.

The minutes passed like hours as he awaited the messenger's return.

* * * * *

3:00 P.M.

"I'm telling you now, Mary, that was no census taker!" Francis stormed back and forth across the room as Mary Ellen cowered in the corner, staying out of the middle of things.

"Nonsense! He came in and asked us nothing but typical census questions! He counted us, one, two, three, and that was it! What on earth are you worried about?"

"I didn't hear him go across the hall, did you? They're after us—no, they're after *you* for beating that kid, Mary. I told you to get rid of her a long time ago, but no! You had to have your little slave!"

Mary stormed toward her husband, who now stood at the window, his back to her. He pulled the curtains aside and peered down into the alley. Mary spoke to his back. "Don't you dare tell me to give her up again, Francis. It's out of the question!"

"Oh, I don't intend to, Mary," he said, turning to face her. "I know it'd be a waste of breath!"

Mary folded her arms across her chest. "You don't *intend* to because you want her here. Don't think I don't know about you and her. Don't you think for one minute that I haven't made her confess to me what you've been doing." She turned to Mary Ellen and screamed, "You're the devil's child, just like I've told you! The devil's child!"

Mary Ellen cringed, hiding her face in her arms. Mary then circled Francis, whose eyes would not meet hers. Instead, he turned and walked away from her. She followed. "You want her for your sick little purposes."

Francis stopped, turned around suddenly, and backhanded Mary across the face. She reeled away from him, falling on top of Mary Ellen, who cried out in frightened surprise. He stared down at them, his hands clenched into fists, sweat seeping from the pores on his face. "I'm leaving today, woman! Right now! Whatever happens with you, whoever comes to take you away, I won't be anywhere near!"

Mary climbed to her feet. "Get the devil out of here, but don't think I won't tell them what you did to her. I'll tell them every last thing!"

"You won't," he said. "You won't because you'll want them to believe she had a normal life here, just like any child. The only problem is, look at her! You've beaten the hell out of her, you've kept her locked in the goddamned house—*in the closet*—for half her life!"

Mary Ellen burst into tears and ran to the back room. Neither Mary nor Francis paid any attention.

"Oh, and you really felt sorry for her, didn't you, Francis! That's why you took pity on her and used her for your little plaything! You were doing her a favor, were you?"

"Just shut up Mary, I'm warning you!"

Mary watched in silence as Frances reached beneath the mattress and withdrew a canvas duffel bag. Without a word more, he stuffed his belongings inside it, and when he was finished, he slung it over his shoulder and looked at his wife.

"You won't be seeing me again, Mary. It's been coming for a long time, now. Whatever reason I stayed with you is so far gone, I can't even remember it." He opened the door and stepped into the hall, pulling the door closed behind him.

Mary watched the door close. Moments later, she fell to the floor, sobbing.

In the eerie silence that followed, broken only by her mother's cries, Mary Ellen became terribly, terribly frightened.

* * * * *

Etta had been standing just down the hall when the young man—a survey taker, by all appearances—left the Connollys' rooms. After he made his way down the stairs, she had moved a bit closer to the door to listen to the terrible fighting that ensued. As she stood there, her ear practically pressed against the wall, the door flew open again, and Mr. Connolly stormed from the

240

room, his haversack over his shoulder. He went directly down the stairs, never even glancing back.

Etta's heart pounded through her chest as Connolly disappeared down the steps. If she were a criminal, she would no doubt be in prison, and if she were an inspector, she would be in need of work! Not very sly at all! When the hall was clear, she knocked on Charles and Mary Smitt's door, then went inside.

"Hello, Mrs. Wheeler," the nurse said as she stepped into the room.

Etta sighed with relief, her hand to her chest, her breathing labored. "Hello, Libby. How's she feeling today?" The young nurse, Libby Tyler, worked alongside Mary's doctor, and came by herself to check on Mary every couple of days. Etta was glad of it—she couldn't be there as much as she wanted to. There were still others who desperately needed her attention, too.

"I'm the same," chimed in Mary. "You didn't expect a full recovery, did you?"

"Don't you be funny with me," Etta joked. "The Lord works in mysterious ways, Mary. There is nothing out of His reach—including you."

"Yes, yes, I know," Mary said. "Are you well? You look ever so pale."

"It will pass. I heard the Connollys fighting, and almost ran squarely into the husband in the hall."

A knock came upon the door and Etta opened it. A young man stood in the hall with a large, official looking book tucked underneath his arm. He tipped his hat. "Hello, Ma'am. My name is Evans, and I'm with the Census Bureau, and I've been sent to take a census of this house. May I come in?"

"Of course, but I don't live here so it would be wise not to count me," Etta said, stepping aside.

Libby stood and closed her bag. "Etta, if you'll be here a bit there's no need for me to stay. I'll be back on Friday morning. Will that be all right, Mary?"

Mary took the nurse's hand in hers and patted it. "Thank you, Libby dear. You've been so kind to me."

"It's my pleasure, Mary. You're a perfectly wonderful patient. I'll see you Friday then." She left, closing the door behind her.

"Mary, this gentleman is from the Bureau of the Census. I imagine he wants to count you."

"You'd better count me while I'm still alive to be counted, young man."

The man appeared uncomfortable with Mary's morbid humor, but looked at Etta and said, "I've been in every room."

Etta asked, "Have you been across the hall?"

"Yes, I have," he said, then looked at Mary. "I take it you're Mrs. Mary Smitt, wife of Charles Smitt?"

"I am," she said, her voice weak. "But I suddenly feel very sleepy, young man, so if you're finished, would you please allow me privacy? I'd like to nap for a while." She turned to Etta. "Etta, dear? Could you get me a glass of water?"

The census taker seemed to perk at the mention of Etta's name. "I'm finished here," he said. "Thank you for letting me perform my duties unhindered, ladies." He made his way slowly to the door as he wrote something in his notepad, and Etta opened it for him. He stepped through and pointed to the front of the building, slipping an ASPCA badge from under his coat.

Etta's heart missed a beat. She touched him on the shoulder and whispered, "Wait for me in front of the building."

He smiled and nodded. When he left, Etta knelt next to the sick woman. "Mary! That young man was from Mr. Bergh's office! He's here about Mary Ellen! This is what we prayed for!"

Mary's eyes opened wide. "You hurry and go see him, Etta. I want to hear everything he says, you must promise me!"

Etta had never seen her so excited. "Yes, of course. You relax here and have your nap. I'll be back up as soon as I can." As she stood to leave, Mary took her hand again and held it tightly.

"Etta," she said. *"They must save her."* Her voice was barely a whisper, but the despair could be heard in her words.

"I know I say it a lot, but have faith, Mary." She smiled and left the room.

On the sidewalk in front of the building, the tall, blonde man waved as Etta came down the steps. "Alonzo Evans, Mrs. Wheeler. I'm with the ASPCA. You knew who I was immediately, didn't you?" he said.

"Almost," replied Etta. "I was so hopeful somebody would come, I might have suspected a stranger in the building had been sent by Mr. Bergh. Are you here to take her away, Mr. Evans?"

He shook his head. "Oh, no. I came to verify what you said in your statement, and I'm quite satisfied, having seen her. She's in a pitiful state.

The poor thing cowered in the corner when I went in. She must have thought I was going to harm her."

"And she's been like that for so long," Etta said. "A little captive."

"Don't worry, Mrs. Wheeler. I'll take what I've seen back to Mr. Bergh. I'm sure it will be enough to put him to action on her behalf."

21

"What's your feeling, Elbridge? Will the Act apply here as it did in Emily Thompson's case?"

Gerry patted the stack of documents from the earlier court case. "Henry, I studied long and hard to find Section 65," he said. "My arms were sore from lifting those damned legal volumes! For all that trouble, it should hold up well enough to save at least two children!"

Gerry opened one heavy volume he had hand-labeled *Habeas Corpus*, and marked a place with his finger. "To refresh your memory, it says, 'Whenever it shall appear by satisfactory proof that anyone is held in illegal confinement or custody, and that there is good reason to believe that he will be carried out of the state or suffer some irreparable injury before he can be relieved by the issuing of a Habeas corpus or certiorari, any court or officer authorized to issue such writs may issue a warrant under his hand and seal reciting the facts and directed to any sheriff, constable, or other person, and commanding such officer or person to take such prisoner and forthwith to bring him before such court or office to be dealt with according to law.'" Gerry looked at Bergh again and smiled. "What do *you* think?"

Bergh smiled. "It's in *your* language, Elbridge, but I gather most of it.

When do we act? Which judge do we see?"

"I've got a man in mind . . . you know him, Henry. Judge Abraham Lawrence, Court of Special Sessions. He's a good man and a friend, and I'm sure he'll issue the proper order. After all, we've got the Thompson case as a precedent for her removal."

Bergh stood. "I won't sleep tonight, Elbridge. I know that."

"Nor shall I, Henry. Nor shall I. I'll prepare the petition and deliver it to Judge Lawrence today. If he grants the order, the earlier we take the child the better."

* * * * *

Using the notes and information from Bergh and others, Gerry penned the petition. It read:

> The petition of Henry Bergh respectfully shows that a little girl, age about 7 years and called Mary Ellen, is held in illegal confinement and custody by a man and woman named Connolly, at and within the premises No. 315 West Forty-first Street, in the City of New York; that said child is not the child of said man and said woman or either of them, nor are they its lawful guardians or entitled to its custody; that such child is now kept in rigid confinement within said premises by the said man and woman, and is unlawfully and illegally restrained of its liberty, and is sad, has been by them daily, and frequently during each day, severely whipped, beaten, struck, and bruised, without any provocation or cause therefor; and that the marks of said beatings and bruises will appear plainly visible upon the body and limbs of the child at the present time upon inspection thereof; that such child has been kept without shoes or stockings during the entire winter; and that the said man and woman have been for a long time past in the constant and usual habit of leaving the child alone locked up in said premises and allowed to remain there crying for a long time, without

any other person whatever therein.

Deponent further states that he has received information from those who reside immediately adjacent to said premises, and in the house in which the child is confined, and whom deponent is ready to produce as witnesses to substantiate the statement by him herein above made, that the said man and woman have repeatedly stated that they had a good fortune for keeping the child, and keep her they would, whatever trouble might be made about it, and that such child was not the child of either of them.

Deponent further saith that the said man and woman have resided only recently in the premises in question, and that he is informed and is able to show by the persons aforesaid, and deponent verily believes, that the said man and woman will carry out of the State, or inflict upon the child aforesaid, or that such child will suffer some irreparable injury, and be further cruelly beaten, and, perhaps maimed, by the said man and woman, before such child can be relieved by the issuing of a Habeas corpus or certiorari.

Your petitioner, therefore, prays that a warrant may be immediately issued, pursuant to the statute in such case made and provided, and directed to such sheriff, constable, or other person as it may be deemed proper, and commanding such officer or person to take such child and forthwith to bring her before you to be dealt with according to law. And further, to arrest and bring before you the said man and woman having such child in his, her, or their custody, to be dealt with according to law, pursuant to the statute in such case made and provided.

Gerry finished it and delivered it himself, waiting with his heart thundering in his ears as Judge Lawrence read the petition. To his great relief, an order was immediately issued to remove the child from the Connolly residence.

Elbridge T. Gerry left the building with the order in hand and sent word to Bergh by messenger. As predicted, neither man slept through the night. The rescue would be attempted on April 9th, the next day.

* * * * *

Mary took Mary Ellen by the shoulders and spun the child around to face her. "You've done it, you little demon. You've driven away my husband, by giving yourself to him like a whore!"

"Mama, please don't hit me! I'm not a . . . whore, I promise!" Mary Ellen didn't know what the word meant, but Mama said it with such anger, it hurt her. Mama slapped her across the face and she stumbled backward.

"You are what I say you are. You're a child of sin, and you've sinned all your life. You lied plenty, and did things to make my husband want you, and hate me!" She took Mary Ellen's hair on both sides and jerked her head back and forth. "I can't stand the sight of you!"

Mary Ellen cried out, her eyes squeezed closed, tears running down her face. Papa was gone, and though he had done things that made her sad, his attentions never seemed as bad as this.

"Now, Mary Ellen, quit that screaming and listen to me. I want you to pack the things I've put on the mattress into these sacks, and pack them quickly. Only take the things I've put here. I haven't the time nor the means to take everything."

Mary Ellen waited until Mama released her hair, then walked silently to the mattress and started putting the clothing into the sacks she had laid out. She knew the routine from the last time. They would be loading up and moving again, this time without Papa. Mary Ellen couldn't help but wonder who would be there to help her the next time Mama got mad.

It wouldn't be God. Mama had told her lots of times that she was the devil's child, and even though she didn't know very much about God, she knew He hated the devil. Mama said her father was once her husband, too, and it made Mary Ellen wonder why Mama had ever married the devil. It frightened her to think the devil was her father, or that Mama would marry him, knowing it.

247

* * * * *

"Mary Ellen! What is this I've found beneath your rug?"

Mary Ellen felt an icy finger run down her spine. Mama had Timmy.

"Oh, Mama, you've found Timmy! He's my little friend the spider, and we play together when you and Papa aren't home."

Why had she told the truth? Mary Ellen cursed her stupidity.

"You know what I've told you about sneaking around behind my back!"

"Yes, Ellie," Papa said.

It was just his voice, coming from somewhere beyond the room.

"Papa? Where are you? I can't see you!"

Since you've lied to your mama I'm going to leave you, Ellie. Now your mama will beat you whenever she pleases. I'm afraid you've brought it on yourself."

She could see him now, but he was by the door, his bag thrown over his shoulder.

"No, Papa! Don't leave me! Put me on your lap, Papa! I'll do whatever you want me to!"

The door closed behind him.

"Shut up Mary Ellen!" Mama said. "The devil's child only speaks when she's told to speak! The devil's child is a liar, and that is how I know you are his child!"

"I haven't lied, Mama! You never asked me if I had a little spider! That's why you didn't know! I would have told you!" As the words left her lips she knew they were not true. Perhaps she really was the devil's child.

"Pick him up and bring him to me now, Mary Ellen."

"No, Mama . . ."

"Now!"

She lifted the tiny brown spider from the rug and let him crawl up her finger. She cried as she stood by the window, watching him.

"Now, Mary Ellen! Now!"

Mary Ellen looked up to see the heavy iron in Mama's hand.

"Mama, don't kill him! Please don't kill him!"

"Bring the insect here! Now!"

248

"No, I won't let you! I won't let you!" Mary Ellen turned back toward the window and clenched her fist. She ran toward it and slammed her hand through the dirty pane. Clear shards of sharp glass cut her hand and arm, but she was smiling! As the blood flowed from her cuts, she was actually laughing!

She slipped her other hand through the broken window and watched as Timmy crawled to the tip of her finger, then dropped off to the ledge below, walking away from her where he would be safe.

As she waved good-bye, she felt hands grip her shoulders from behind and shake her.

"What have you done! Mary Ellen! Mary Ellen . . ."

" . . . Mary Ellen!"

Mary Ellen's eyes flew open as she sat up, her heart pounding. Mama was shaking her, but she soon realized it was only to awaken her from her sleep. She'd been dreaming! Thank goodness!

"Finally, child! Now, get up and help me with this sewing. It's nearly six o' clock, and I wanted to be gone before sunrise!"

Two lamps burned in the room giving it a soft glow, but the warm, yellow light of the sun had not yet crested the rooftops of the big buildings across the street. Mary Ellen's thoughts were still on her spider, Timmy, whom she had released yesterday through the crack in the window. She had known it was the right thing, even though she would miss him. Her dream proved that.

She sat up and stretched.

"Hurry along, Mary Ellen! I've gone and torn my dress in my haste to get everything ready."

"Get your sewing stool and put it right there," Mama said.

Mary Ellen put the stool down in front of the chair where Mama sat.

"Now, you hold my dress out while I sew it. Keep it still."

Mary Ellen held the dress as Mama pulled the thread and cut it, her mind drifting back to her dream. She had saved Timmy in the dream, but it was harder than in real life. In real life, Mama had never known about him. Did Papa know? Is that why he left them?

Mary Ellen's tired eyes grew heavier with each passing second and she felt her fingers slipping . . . slipping. . . .

"Mary Ellen! See what you've done!"

Her eyes sprung back open. A flash of metal came toward her face, and she felt a sharp pain from her forehead to her chin. Her left eye filled with water and she became dizzy, the room twirling in circles. She felt herself falling from the low stool, but she could not catch herself. Her head knocked into the floor and the ceiling above her spun around in circles.

"Get up!"

Her mama's face was blurry but . . . no, there she was, spinning above her, holding the shears. Around . . . around . . . Mary Ellen closed her eyes and tried to escape the world of things that twirled too fast. Maybe if she didn't look at the ceiling. It was beginning to slow down a little now. She felt warmth trickling down her face as Mama took her shoulders and shook her again.

"Get up and hold this dress right, girl! If you'd listen instead of day-dream!"

Mama's voice faded in and out. The spinning world slowed now. Mary Ellen saw the scissors on the floor beside Mama's knee. Red liquid oozed from the tip onto the floor, and Mary Ellen's shaking hand instinctively moved to where the pain was. She touched it and pinpricks ran from her eye all the way down to her neck. Screaming, she pulled her hand back and saw the blood running down the very finger upon which little Timmy used to walk. More of the thick, warm stuff ran from her face onto the floor.

"I see you're not going to be in any shape to help with my sewing. Get up and press this rag to your face. We've wasted so much time we have to go now. Move!"

* * * * *

April 9, 1874
Thursday, 7:20 A.M.

"I thought it would be a good idea to send messengers to the newspapers to tell them we're up to something they won't want to miss," Bergh said. "If history is any indicator, there's already a score of reporters at the courthouse waiting for her. There's no reason we shouldn't get some publicity out of this."

"Good idea, Henry," Gerry said. "I expect the ASPCA rescuing another child shall cause quite a stir."

"That's exactly what I hope for," Bergh said. "By the way, I sent for Mrs. Wheeler to meet us at the courthouse as well. I thought she should be present."

Alonzo Evans approached with a quick step and animated expression. "We're ready, Mr. Bergh. The messengers we sent will have the men from the newspapers there within twenty minutes, and Judge Lawrence will await our arrival. He's even agreed to let the reporters wait inside the courthouse."

"Excellent, Alonzo. Do you have the order?"

"Here," Evans said. "I'm proud to carry it, sir, but I was wondering . . ." He hesitated, and seemed unsure.

"What is it, Alonzo? Feel free to speak. You've been with me a long time."

"Well, sir, I know you weren't happy with how little Emily's case came out, and I'm surprised . . . why are you doing this?"

Bergh smiled. "I regard a helpless child in the same light as a dumb animal, Alonzo. Both are God's creatures, and my duty is imperative to aid them."

A broad smile crossed Alonzo's face. He held up the writ and shook it in the air triumphantly. "I'm leaving in a few moments, gentlemen. Mary Ellen and I shall see you at the courthouse."

* * * * *

April 9th, 1874
7:45 A.M.

"Mary Ellen! I told you to bring me the bags and *I'll* take them down! You stay here and don't you dare leave the room until I tell you to!"

Mary Ellen struggled with the bag of clothes, dragging it just to the door where she released it. "Is that all, Mama?"

"Yes . . . God, I can't stand to look at you! Couldn't you wipe your face better than that? You look terrible!"

Mary Ellen's eyes fell to the floor as she touched the cut on her face with her fingers. She ran them along the ridge of the cut, and sucked in her breath.

251

It was swollen and hurt more than she wanted to think about. As Mama carried the load down the steps, Mary Ellen slid down the wall to the floor, exhausted from head to toe. Mama said they didn't have anywhere to go, and that was scary. They might go to her Aunt Peg's house in some place called Pennsylvania, but Mama wasn't sure. She couldn't stop her tears when Mama came back.

"Shut up, you idiot! Some men are coming down the hall and I don't want them to hear you crying like that!" Mama slammed the door and locked it

"Stop it!" Mama screamed, slapping her again.

Mary Ellen fell onto her back, the world beginning to spin again. Mama grabbed her arm and pulled her back up. Moments later, a pounding came on the door.

Mama let go of her arm and stood very still.

* * * * *

"The door's locked," Officer McDougal said, trying to turn the knob.

"Break it in," Alonzo said. "You're a big fellow."

"I'm also an officer of the law. I might try knocking first." He smiled and rapped hard on the door.

No response. McDougal frowned. "Did you see the carriage down below?"

"Yeah," Alonzo said. "Looks loaded with belongings and ready to move. Think it belongs to the Connollys?"

"That would be my guess, especially if they suspected we'd come. It's a bit early for ordinary folks to be moving, wouldn't you say?"

"I'm surprised they aren't already gone. Here, try this."

"The key?"

Alonzo shrugged. "I got it from the landlord. Very cooperative."

"You could have told me before. You ready?"

"I think so," Alonzo said, taking a deep breath. "Open it."

McDougal put the key in the lock and turned it. He pushed the door open and walked in quickly, followed by Alonzo.

The woman was waiting behind the door. As Officer McDougal stepped in, Alonzo saw her.

"She's behind you!"

McDougal whirled around, but she simply stood there, a sly smirk on her face. "Who are you and what is your business here?" she asked, calmly.

"Here's our warrant. Are you Mrs. Francis Connolly?"

"I am."

"Where's Mr. Connolly? Is he at home?"

"No, he isn't. It seems you've missed him."

"We've come to take a little girl named Mary Ellen from your custody."

"Take her if you want," Connolly said. "Do whatever you want with her. I only want to know why. She's not worth anything to anyone."

"That will be explained to you later, Mrs. Connolly. We're only here to remove her."

"There she is," Alonzo said, pointing to the opposite side of the room. "Poor thing."

The child was huddled in the corner, her arms criss-crossed over her head. As he approached her, she jumped up and ran into the bedroom, screaming. McDougal followed her back, finding her pressed against the wall as though she could escape through it with enough effort. She was crying as the policeman leaned over and gently picked her up.

A soft whimper escaped her as he lifted her into his arms, but she didn't struggle. Instead, she sobbed in relative silence, resting her head against McDougal's chest as he carried her to where Alonzo waited.

Mary Connolly gave no fight. An odd smile spread across her face as Officer McDougal carried Mary Ellen into the room.

"Let's go," McDougal said. "I want to get her out of here." He put her in a chair, removed his coat, and wrapped it around Mary Ellen.

"We'll be in contact, Mrs. Connolly. You and Mr. Connolly should unload the carriage outside, as you'll be under constant watch until you're required in court. Leaving town is out of the question."

"Well, you'll just have to be satisfied with me," she said. "My husband's gone already, and he ain't coming back, thanks to her!" She jabbed a finger toward Mary Ellen, who did not notice her accusation. McDougal immediately took the little girl outside.

"We'll be back," Alonzo said, closing the door behind him.

253

It was still early morning and just below fifty degrees outside. With his coat wrapped around the child, McDougal was quite cold.

"Alonzo, might you run back up and see if she has a wrap for the child?"

Alonzo looked at him, a smile on his face. "You do mean for *you*, don't you?"

"To be perfectly honest, yes."

"I'll try but I don't guarantee anything. She's an odd woman."

Alonzo returned to the apartment and knocked twice before opening the unlocked door. Mary Connolly stood in the same place as when they left.

"Do you have a cloak or blanket to put around the child?"

Her strange smile returned. "Nothing."

"She has absolutely nothing to wear? What about in the carriage down below?"

"I told you, she has nothing!"

"You are despicable, madam!" Alonzo spat. "You'll pay for your sins before long!" He stormed out of the room and returned to the coach.

"She says the child has nothing," he told McDougal, reaching inside the Connollys' carriage. He removed a folded horse blanket. "This ought to keep her warm. It appears to be clean, anyway." McDougal took his coat from over her and Alonzo wrapped Mary Ellen in the blanket. She remained quiet as he did so.

As Alonzo drove the carriage, McDougal focused his attention on the child. "What's that mark on your face, little one?"

"Mama done it."

"She struck you?"

"Yes, sir."

"With what?"

"A scissors." Her eyes welled with tears.

"Why did she strike you, darling?"

Mary Ellen struggled through her crying to tell him the story of helping her mama with the sewing. "I didn't hold it right," she said. "I was still sleepy."

"My God, child. How about that bruise on the other side of your face?"

"Mama whips me with a cowhide. It's from that, I think."

"Shh, now. You close your eyes and rest, and we'll take you someplace warm and safe."

No more words were spoken until they reached the police station. They brought Mary Ellen inside, and sat her on top of a desk where several sympathetic faces gazed upon her.

Chief of Police Matsell looked at Mary Ellen, his eyes running up and down the horrible gashes on her bare legs. "Where are her clothes? Did you bring any with you?"

"We only took the child and asked very quickly for clothes, which she denied having," McDougal said.

"I think we should go back," Alonzo said. "and look for that rawhide the child spoke of. Not to mention the shears."

"I'll accompany you, Alonzo," McDougal said.

"I'd also like to go," another young police officer, Thomas Dusenbury, said.

"Good," Chief Matsell said. "You three go and get all her clothes and see if you can't come up with the rawhide whip and the shears. Once we have those items, we'll take her immediately over to the courthouse. I imagine there's quite a crowd waiting for her by now."

22

"We've come back for all of her clothing, Mrs. Connolly."

"She has nothing, like I told you before. Now, get out!"

"She must have something, now produce them!"

Connolly, her fists clenched, stormed into the bedroom. A moment later she returned with two flimsy articles of clothing. A worn-through petticoat and another dress, obviously old and too small for the child now.

"This is it?" Officer McDougal asked.

"That is all. She's not my child and I had my husband to take care of."

"How long has she been here?"

"Perhaps it's . . . six years now."

"Six years? And this is all she has?" He was stunned. "I can't stand the sight of you, madam. You sicken me."

Officer Dusenbury was in the process of searching the kitchen cupboards. They were mostly empty. "There's not much here," he said. "Maybe Alonzo will find something down in the carriage to use in the case against this monster."

"We'll need these," McDougal said, bending over and retrieving a large pair of scissors from the floor. He held them up before Connolly. "Are these one of the items you're in the habit of beating her with? Perhaps a rawhide whip or a poker?"

She laughed. "I often whip her with my hand, sir. If I get her back, I'll whip her again, as often as I please!"

Alonzo Evans walked through the door. "I didn't find anything in the cart of any significance," he reported. "No sign of the whip. Are those the shears?"

"I suppose they are, but it appears everything else has been gotten rid of."

Mary Connolly seemed not to hear the men. She walked slowly toward Alonzo and touched his chest with her hand. He took a step back, revulsion on his face.

"My, my, you are a pretty man," she said. "Perhaps you'd like to come and stay with me sometime. Quietly, of course."

Evans turned away and the men left the apartment as Mary Connolly erupted into laughter again. They took their findings back to police headquarters and prepared to transport Mary Ellen to court.

* * * * *

"But she's filthy," Chief Matsell said. "Look at her hair."

"She'll have more impact with Judge Lawrence if she's taken in as she is now," McDougal said. "As much as I detest leaving her in this condition, we'll have a much better chance of having that woman brought in to face charges."

"You may be right, Mac," Matsell said. "As she is, then. Are you boys ready to go?"

Alonzo and McDougal nodded. "I'll wrap her in the blanket again," McDougal said. "It will add a certain drama to the predicament."

"Mary Ellen, we'll be taking you to the courthouse now," said Matsell. "When we get there, a nice man named Judge Lawrence will want to ask you some questions about how your mama treated you."

Mary Ellen's big brown eyes had cleared considerably from when she was first brought in. Since then, friendly faces and soothing voices had surrounded her. The fact that they were all strangers did not seem to have an effect on her.

"Mama whipped me a lot," she said, matter-of-factly.

"Yes, we know that," Matsell said. "I have something to show you before we go over to see Judge Lawrence, okay?"

She nodded, and he produced a large pair of scissors.

She cringed.

"Do you recognize these?"

Another nod. "Them are the scissors Mama cut me with this morning."

Matsell looked at the other men. "It was just this morning?"

"Yes. I wasn't holding her sewing the way she wanted me to. She got mad." She reached out to take them, and Matsell pulled the shears back.

"No, Mary Ellen, this is what we call evidence. I'll need to give them to Judge Lawrence. Okay?"

"Okay. Mama never let me touch them neither."

"Are you ready?"

Mary Ellen nodded.

"Let's go, gentlemen."

* * * * *

Five minutes after the carriage carrying Mary Ellen, Alonzo, and Christian McDougal left the police station for Chatham Square, Mary Ellen started to cry. McDougal now drove and Alonzo rode inside with the little girl. He put an arm over her shoulder to comfort her, but she pulled away, her wails growing louder. Alonzo frowned. He understood why she was frightened; her life had suddenly changed forever and she was smart enough to figure that out. He leaned his head out the window. "Hey Mac, our little girl in here's crying. Any ideas?"

"She seemed all right at the station."

"I know," he said, then sat back in his seat again, thinking. Nothing came to him, so he said, "Why are you crying, Mary Ellen? I promised you your mama won't be at the courthouse. You don't have to worry about that."

"I'm . . . scared," she cried. "I'm scared because when she does see me, she's gonna give me a good beating for running away like I done!"

"Just let her try," Alonzo said bravely. "I'll stand in front of you myself, and she'll have to get through me. Besides, you didn't run away. We took you away from there, and that's a big difference."

258

Her tears told him she didn't believe those things would matter to her mama. Alonzo had another idea. He leaned out the window again. "Mac, will you make a quick stop at the confectioner's on Beekman? I know how to make a sad child happy."

After a short stop, the trip resumed. Five minutes later, the black police carriage pulled up to the courthouse, McDougal guiding the official coach through the heavy carriage and foot traffic at the base of the courthouse steps. Alonzo looked at Mary Ellen, rejoicing at her dry cheeks. His trick had worked.

When he glanced out the window, he couldn't believe his eyes! Newsmen everywhere! More than Alonzo had ever seen before! He leaned over to Mary Ellen. "You ready, honey? We're going to have to go by a lot of people." She nodded. "I think so."

Alonzo opened the door of the carriage and held it for McDougal, who reached in to scoop up Mary Ellen. He had so fallen for the little waif that he would have liked to carry her himself, but she had grown accustomed to the policeman, and to help her feel at ease meant a lot to him. She needn't be frightened anymore.

As Alonzo turned back toward the courthouse, he saw Etta.

She stood at the top of the steps, her hand resting against one of the marble pillars. At the sight of Alonzo she lifted her hand to wave, then hurried down the steps toward them, nudging through the crowd of boisterous reporters. Ten feet away now, Alonzo knew the exact moment Etta spotted Mary Ellen in Christian McDougal's arms. She slowed to a stop, put one white-gloved hand to her mouth, and wept. Instinctively, he reached into his coat for a handkerchief.

"It's done," she said as they approached. "My dear God, it's finally done." Her watery eyes dropped to the child and remained there for a long moment. She hugged Alonzo.

He held her for a few moments, then pulled back. "Here," he said, holding out the handkerchief. "You don't need to cry now, Mrs. Wheeler."

Alonzo felt something run down his face, then realized that his cheeks were wet, too. He swiped a hand over the tears, embarrassed, but not sure why. Having seen the expression of love and thankfulness on the woman's face, the dam that had held his own flood of emotions crumbled. It felt good, he decided. Wonderful, in fact. Alonzo nodded at the policeman, and together they ascended the steps that would hopefully lead to justice for a little, abused girl—and perhaps many to follow.

* * * * *

New York Tribune reporter Jacob Riis looked at the child in the large officer's arms as he placed her on the bench in the rear of the courtroom. Wrapped in a horse blanket, her damaged legs barely showed from beneath it. In her hand was a large lollipop—a sharp contrast to her frightened face.

Seated on the bench next to her was Henry Bergh. He sat straight up, his expression soft, his eyes droopy and distant. He did not turn his head to survey the busy courtroom; did not listen to testimony given by attorneys pleading their cases; he sat quietly, occasionally glancing at the child. A woman whom Jacob did not recognize sat on the other side of the child, dressed in black, her expression serene and loving. The child's mother, perhaps, or an aunt.

In the bench directly in front of the pair was Elbridge Gerry, Bergh's attorney. His face, too, was somehow different than Jacob remembered it. He took no notes, nor did he review any notes taken earlier. He held his materials squarely on his lap and looked straight ahead. Jacob watched as a newsman from the *Times* approached Gerry.

"What is the meaning of all this?" the reporter asked.

Gerry looked at him, his eyes narrowed into slits. "Something that will make your blood boil, when you hear the facts."

He said no more, and Jacob looked once more at the pitiful child, her face so pale and marred with cuts and bruises. Moments later, Gerry rose and approached the judge's bench, stopping behind the railing in front of it. Jacob listened and jotted down the words as Gerry spoke.

* * * * *

"Your Honor, pursuant to the writ issued by you, we hereby present the child before you at this time," Gerry said. "Her cruel treatment has been recited in the petition presented by Mr. Bergh. If it pleases the court, I will explain the situation as we currently understand it."

Lawrence nodded. "Proceed, sir."

Gerry cleared his throat and glanced back at Bergh with a nod. "A woman, Mrs. Charles G. Wheeler, who is present here today, was visiting a dying woman in a tenement house at number 315 West Forty-first Street. This woman reported hearing the most agonizing shrieks of a child being beaten from the adjoining room."

Gerry walked back and forth before the railing, occasionally gesturing toward Mary Ellen, who sometimes smiled as Etta whispered to her. "Mrs. Wheeler acted upon this information by interviewing several neighbors in the building, and, upon doing so, learned that Francis and Mary Connolly, with whom the child lived, had mentioned that she was not their child. Furthermore, it was reported to her that the child had been habitually locked in the room, had been beaten cruelly, and had been left without shoes or stockings and almost no clothing during the entire winter." Gerry folded his arms behind him and awaited Judge Lawrence's reply.

"Are Francis and Mary Connolly in court?"

"They are not," replied Gerry. "I did not think it necessary to have them here at this stage of the proceeding."

Judge Lawrence frowned, his bushy gray eyebrows drawn together, his forehead creased. "Should not the parents of the child be notified?"

Gerry shrugged his shoulders. "Your Honor, from what I have been able to learn in the limited time available, it is evident that the parents do not wish to be known. Mr. Kellock of the Commissioners of Charities and Correction Bureau, placed the child with these people some years ago."

The judge straightened his spectacles and looked at some papers before him. A moment later he looked at Gerry. "Testimony will have to be taken in the case," he said. "to verify the allegations set forth in Mr. Bergh's statement."

Gerry swept his hand toward the small group accompanying him. "I have present only Mrs. Wheeler and the child," he said. "I ask that both be sworn."

Judge Lawrence waved them forward, and Alonzo lifted Mary Ellen from her seat and carried her to the front of the courtroom.

* * * * *

Jacob Riis watched as the child was carried forward, his heart pounding and sadness welling up within him. Mary Ellen's ragged, calico dress and tattered chemise hung down like the wilted flag of a losing army, and faces throughout the court saddened as she passed them by. The unfortunate child had no idea of just how pitiful her appearance was.

She had obviously been calmed somewhat by the woman who sat by her, Mrs. Wheeler, and now she simply gazed about the courtroom with wonderment and curiosity typical of any normal child. If the things Mr. Gerry said were proven to be true, this child had scarcely ever been out of her tenement rooms. This courthouse must be nothing less than another world to her!

The ASPCA officer named Evans lowered the tiny waif to the floor and gave her some quiet instruction along with a little nudge. She glanced nervously back at Mrs. Wheeler, who supplied an encouraging nod and a smile, and Mary Ellen walked toward the black-robed judge as he knelt down to one knee.

"Hello, Mary Ellen," he said. "I see you've got yourself a lollipop."

She looked down at it as though it had slipped her mind, then smiled. "Yes," she said, taking another lick.

"Officer McDougal, might you remove the blanket from her? I don't believe she'll be cold in here." He looked at Mary Ellen. "You just let us know if you get a chill, won't you?"

"Yes, sir."

Jacob watched as the blanket was taken from her. He wouldn't be able to restrain his tears, but he wasn't alone. Others wept and sobbed as Mary Ellen stood before the courtroom.

Her legs were filthy, covered not only with bruises, but fresh cuts from some instrument of torture he dared not think about. There were scars from cuts long healed, and bruises from beatings perhaps only hours before. A cut on her face ran from her eyebrow to her chin, and worst of all, her years of confinement were evident in her tiny, underdeveloped body.

She was rumored to be eight or nine, and indeed, her face and head resembled a child that age or much older. Her body, however, did not. A prisoner locked inside four walls for what probably was most of her life, she did not grow properly, her body stunted and small, no larger than that of a five or six-year-old.

Riis listened as Judge Lawrence continued. "Mary Ellen, I have to ask you some questions about your mother, and I must have you swear to God that you will tell the truth here today. Do you understand that?"

"Swear?"

"Yes, child. That means . . . promise to God. Have you been taught about Him?"

She shook her head. "No . . . not so that I remember."

Lawrence fingered his white beard and thought for a moment, then said, "God is the creator and ruler of everything in the universe. He is the Almighty Father. Do you understand?"

"I don't know what you mean. Mama told me the devil was my father."

Judge Lawrence stood, his face compassionate. "No, Mary Ellen, that's not true. Your father is a man, just as any other. We are all children of God, and of goodness." Lawrence waved Gerry forward.

In a low voice that Jacob had to strain to hear, the judge said, "This poor thing has been terribly misled by someone. I find the child unusually bright, but through lack of religious teaching, she does not understand the nature of an oath. I cannot swear her."

"What shall be done?" Gerry asked.

"I'll take her unsworn statement in my chambers. Would you, Mr. Bergh, Mr. Monell, and Mrs. Wheeler like to be present?"

"Give me a moment to gather everyone."

Jacob Riis watched them leave the courtroom, longing to follow but content to wait it out. He wasn't going to miss one minute of this case unless the Tribune editor himself came to drag him away.

* * * * *

Mary Ellen sat in a big, soft chair and took another lick of her lollipop. Mr. Evans was very nice to give it to her, and it made her stop crying right away. She looked around the big room, and marveled at the polished wood that gleamed like some of the carriages she had seen passing by her window. The wood was shiny and decorated with smooth shapes, and Mary Ellen knew without any doubt that this was some kind of palace, built for a king. She bounced up and down, enjoying the softness of the cushion beneath her. She noticed them all smile when she did this.

Now these people were going to ask her questions about Mama, and she decided she would tell them the truth. She didn't want these nice people to beat her like Mama did.

"Mary Ellen, will you give me your entire name?"

"Mary Ellen."

"How old are you?"

"I don't know," she replied.

"Are your real mother and father alive?"

She thought about this. Mama had told her a lot of times her real mother was dead. Sometimes she said the devil was her father, and other times she said he was dead. She shook her head no. "Mama told me they were dead."

"Where did you live before you lived with the Connollys?"

"I don't remember."

"How do you address Mrs. Connolly . . . what do you call her?"

"I've always called her mama."

"Do you have any shoes that you wear?"

She wiggled her toes. "I've never had any shoes on."

"So you've had no shoes on this winter?"

"No, sir."

"Stockings? Do you have any stockings?"

She shook her head. Mama had stockings, but she dared not put them on or she would get beat. "No, sir. Mama said shoes and things were for going out, and I have never been allowed to go out of the rooms where we live, except in the night time, and only in the yard to the water closet."

"Did you put on any flannel before going out in the cold?"

"Flannel?"

"Heavy material . . . to keep you warm."

"This is all I have to wear." She touched her outfit again. "I never wore anything else." She watched as the grownups looked at one another, shaking their heads. Was she saying something wrong? They all looked so sad! Just like she felt when she was taken away from home. One man didn't look sad. He just kept writing as fast as he could on a piece of paper.

"Where do you sleep, Mary Ellen?"

"On a piece of carpet by the window."

"On the floor?"

She nodded. "Yes, on a piece of carpet, though. I have a little quilt I put over me."

"In what do you sleep? What garment?"

"This," she said, touching her dress.

"Only that?"

She nodded. So many questions, but they were all so nice to her she didn't mind.

"Do you have any friends that you play with?"

"Oh, no. Mama never lets me play with other children. Mama says they will make me sick."

"You've never had any children in to see you?"

"No."

The man in the robe looked worried, then his face became very kind. "Mary Ellen, I want to ask you some questions regarding how Mrs. Connolly—your mama—treated you. Is that all right?"

Mary Ellen thought that would be just fine. She nodded.

"Did your mama beat you?"

"She would whip and beat me when she was mad."

"Everyday?"

Mary Ellen was not sure, but it seemed hardly a day passed that she wasn't punished. "Yes, sir. I think everyday."

"With her hand?"

"No," Mary Ellen said. "Well, sometimes. Other times she beat me with a twisted whip . . . she called it a rawhide."

"Did the marks now on your body come from that rawhide?"

Mary Ellen looked at her arms and legs. "It always left black and blue marks on me." She touched her head. "I must have a mark here, don't I? It hurts, and Mama hit me there yesterday."

She noticed the woman, Mrs. Wheeler, beginning to cry. It made her cry, too. She felt her lip begin to shake, and she couldn't stop it.

"Mrs. Wheeler," the man in the black robe said, "I believe you may be upsetting the child."

"I'm sorry," she said. "I'll try to control my emotions. Don't cry, Mary Ellen. You're safe now. I'll be brave if you will."

"Okay," said the child. "But don't go away, please?" She liked the lady named Mrs. Wheeler. She had given her some tea and bread cakes earlier, and they filled her tummy good.

"I'm not going anywhere, I promise. Now you listen to Judge Lawrence." The man smiled and continued. "How did you get that cut on your face, Mary Ellen? Right there." He pointed to it.

Mary Ellen told them again about the scissors.

"Did your mama ever kiss you?"

"I don't think I have ever been kissed by Mama."

She never took you on her lap to hold you?"

"No. If I was on her lap it was for a spanking."

"Have you ever spoken to anybody outside your rooms?"

Mary Ellen had, but if she told them, perhaps Mama would find out. She had spoken to Mrs. Bingham and some other ladies, as well as that nice man, Stuart. No, she decided. She had better say no. "I never spoke to anyone . . . if Mama found out I would get whipped."

"Do you have any other clothes? Other than what you have on?"

"I don't remember having anything more than what I have on now," she said. "I've seen clothes in the rooms, but I would get a beating if I put them on. Stockings, too."

"Did your mama and papa often leave you alone?"

"Yes, sir. They would lock me in the bedroom when they went out. It was dark, but I made up games to play or went to sleep. I liked to play with some little strings I found. Mama threw them away."

Just then Alonzo opened the door, and in his hand were the scissors. He presented them to Judge Lawrence.

"Mary Ellen, do you recognize these?" Judge Lawrence asked.

"Yes."

"Are these the shears that cut you this morning?"

"Yes, sir."

"Do you know the reasons your mama beat you? Did she ever tell you anything?"

"No," Mary Ellen said. "I could tell when she was getting angry. She never said why she beat me, she just did."

"Have you ever been allowed in the street?"

Mary Ellen thought about the children she had come to know from her window, and the games they used to play. She had so longed to join them, and she wouldn't even mind always being the one to search for the others when they played hide and seek. She shook her head. "No. I've never been in the street."

"Do you want to go back and live with your mama?"

Mary Ellen didn't expect the question. She thought she would be sent back to Mama, because she never lived anywhere else. Tears slipped from her eyes at the thought. "No, sir . . . I don't want to go back to live with Mama, because she beats me so." Her tears fell; it was no use to try to hold them back. When she cried in front of Mama, she just beat her harder. These people were so nice to her! "I'd like to live with Mrs. Wheeler," she said, watching their eyes.

"We'll see how things progress, but don't worry, child. If you don't wish to go back there, everything will be done to see that you don't."

The man in the robe sat up straight and Mary Ellen took another lick from her now tiny lollipop. She stared at their faces, licked and smiled.

"I believe the child's statement is adequate," Lawrence said.

Bergh stood and said, "Your Honor, would you allow her statement to be released to the press now? Perhaps we can draw out her parents, if indeed they are still alive and want to be found."

"I see no reason why not," he said. "Her name may stir recognition in someone who knows who they are."

23

April 10, 1874

"There will be order in my court," Lawrence said, pounding the gavel. "We shall be taking testimony in the matter of the custody of the child called Mary Ellen. Mr. Gerry, what witness do you call?"

When they arrived the next day, the courtroom was already filled to capacity with reporters and the public. Outside the building, a bevy of society ladies awaited Mary Ellen, who still wore the same scant clothes she had on the previous day. She had been washed and cleaned by the matron at the police station, but no new clothes had yet been supplied for her.

Henry Bergh sat upright, his eyes scanning the courtroom, carefully watching the melee of reporters and interested citizens. The morning's papers had been filled with plaudits to Henry Bergh and Elbridge Gerry for their brilliant use of Section 65 of the Habeas corpus writ. While some were torn between Bergh's new ability to come into their homes and remove their children, most saw that there had never before been a recognized way to remove a child from an unfit home, and it had perhaps opened the door for the rescue of more abused children.

Other articles simply attempted to nudge Bergh's organization more permanently toward the focus of child-saving, rather than animal-saving. 'Mr. Bergh Enlarging His Sphere Of Usefulness', one *New York Times* headline read. The *Tribune* reported: 'Terrible Cruelty To A Child; A case for charitable interference—Henry Bergh rescues a little girl from her inhuman parents—Proceedings in the Supreme Court.'

Mary Ellen's name spread over every newspaper in the city, and the story was picked up in newspapers throughout the nation. More than a dozen ladies wanting to adopt her came forward, but her parents had not yet materialized. It was early yet. Bergh held out hopes that they would.

The scene in the courtroom was nothing less than a circus, every bit worthy of P.T. Barnum's name. Gerry stood and motioned toward the seats in front. "I call Mary Connolly to the witness stand."

Connolly rose from her seat and approached the bench. She wore a long, striped overskirt with too many cheery ruffles for the occasion. Her spare figure more than filled the outfit, and she wore her hair up on her head with a few straggling curls hanging down. Connolly's face was set in a smug expression, and while she was being sworn in, she stared across the courtroom at Mary Ellen, who was involved with Etta and did not notice.

Elbridge Gerry stood before her. He felt a special malice toward the woman who now sat before him, and his tired eyes still had enough left in them to glare. He had no tolerance for her type, and knew he must try to control his emotions while questioning her.

"What is your name?"

"My name is Mrs. Mary Connolly at the present time."

"How old are you?"

"About thirty-eight years."

"Are you married or single?"

"I am a married woman at present."

"What is the name of your husband?"

"Francis Connolly."

"When were you married?"

"I was married some years ago, about five or six years."

"Have you any children?"

"I haven't got any living now."

"Did you ever have any children?"

"I did have children."

"How many?"

"I had three."

"What were they, boys or girls?"

"There was two girls and one boy."

"Where are they now?" questioned Gerry.

"In Heaven, I hope, where we will all be."

"I am not so certain about that," Gerry said, knowing it wasn't the place, but unable to stop himself.

Connolly, her face indignant, said, "Well, we expect to. We must not judge. There is another Judge, higher."

"When did your children die?"

"Well, it is a good many years. I cannot tell really the date."

"Have you been married more than once?"

"Yes, sir."

"When were you first married?"

"I was married in 1851."

"To whom?"

"Tom McCormick."

"When did he die?"

"He died the 15th—I am not really confident of the date, but in August 1866 with asthmatic cholera. I am sorry."

"Then the children that you have spoken of were his children, were they not?"

"Yes, sir."

"And all of them are dead?"

"The three of them was dead before him."

"So that you now have no children living?"

"So that I have none living."

"What is the occupation of your present husband?"

"He is a laborer."

"Where do you live?"

"I live in 315 West 41st Street. It is well known."

"What part of the house?"

"The upper part."

"How many stories up?" Connolly appeared to think about this, and Gerry rolled his eyes. How long to figure out on which floor one lives?

"I guess it is three stories. It is a four story building I believe."

"How many rooms do you occupy there?"

"I occupy two."

"What are they?" asked the attorney.

"They are dwelling rooms, of course. What do you suppose they would be? Two rooms!"

"I am examining you now, and I don't want any argument about it!"

"What should two rooms be?" asked Connolly, smirking.

"What is your particular occupation?" he asked, changing the subject.

"My *particular occupation* is housekeeping."

"Anything else?"

Connolly sat up in the seat and tossed her head back. "Well, I sleep with the boss."

Gerry stared at her for a moment. The woman was vile! He paced back toward the spectators, regaining his composure. He turned toward her once more. "Anything else?"

"Nothing else. I don't mind anything else."

"You don't work for your living in any manner, do you?"

"I do housekeeping so as to mend and make clean for my husband."

"Is that all?"

Connolly stood up and spoke in a loud voice. "I do that, and that is a great deal for a woman to do. If she does it in a proper manner, it is a great deal for a housekeeper, if she does her own work. Not everybody does it!"

"Please be seated," Judge Lawrence said.

She looked at him, but didn't move.

"Now," Lawrence warned, "or I'll have you taken from the court."

She returned to her seat, and Gerry shook his head. "Do you know this child in court, this Mary Ellen?"

"Certainly," she said. "I should know her."

"She has been in your possession for some time, hasn't she?"

"Since the second day of January, 1866."

"Where did you get her?"

"I got her from Mr. Kellock."

"Who is he?"

"Don't you know the gentleman?"

Gerry glared at her. "I am asking you the question. Who is he? I don't want any question put to me. Answer the question!"

"Mr. Kellock—don't you know him? I don't know who he is if he ain't one of the Commissioners."

"What is his first name?"

"George Kellock. I have it on this paper."

"Did you know him before you went to see him about the child?"

"Well, I hadn't known him ever in my life until I went to him about her."

"Did you apply for this particular child?"

"I did. I applied for her."

"How did you come to apply for this particular child?"

"I wanted to keep her as my own, of course."

"Did you know anything about the child prior to applying to Mr. Kellock?"

"Well, I did know she was there. I had knowledge that the child was there, left as an orphan."

Gerry was intrigued. "From whom did you learn that?"

"I learned that from my first husband."

"Was the child a relative of your first husband?"

She folded her arms in front of her. "Sometimes he said she was, and sometimes he said she wasn't. I felt bad for the child when I heard him say that. I told him we ought to just take her out."

"What relative did your first husband say she was?"

"I understood that she was his."

"*His* child?" It was beginning to make sense to Gerry. If she married her first husband, McCormick, in 1851, then the child was obviously the product of adultery. Mary Connolly might naturally hate the child.

"Yes, sir. His child."

"Did your first husband ever tell you who the mother was?"

"No. He wouldn't tell me. I often wanted him to. He said she was around, but that she was a good-for-nothing. He said it wasn't worth making mention of her, and she is living yet."

"Do you know who she is?"

"No, I wish I did. I would have given the child to her long, long ago. I am sorry I hadn't left her with Mr. Kellock and let him find the mother, for of course he knows who she is."

Gerry wrote notes on his pad. He would give the items to his other attorney, Ambrose Monell, to investigate. "When did your first husband tell you about the child?"

"He told me in 1855."

Gerry hesitated at the date given. "What did he say then, as near as you can remember it?"

"He says, 'I have a young one over in the home and as we have nary one, I wish you would see after it and get it out.'"

"How long after you were married was that?"

"It was a good long time. I cannot tell how many years. I never reckoned it up."

Gerry was perplexed. Mary Ellen would not have even been born until around ten years later. Perhaps she meant 1865.

"He told you in 1855, you say?"

"Yes, sir."

And what year were you married to him?"

"1851."

"And he told you this in 1855?"

"Yes, sir."

No matter how much he tried to make her see the error in the year she gave, Connolly did not catch on. "When were you married the second time?"

"I guess around six years last August. About the latter end of August or the commencement of September."

"About 1867, then?"

"Yes, sir. Somewhere about that."

"When did you say you got the child?" Gerry intended to find out if the incorrect dates she gave were attributed to a poor perception of the passing of years, or if they were outright lies.

"I got her the second day of January, 1866."

"When did your first husband die?"

"He died in August of 1866.

"So . . . you got the child before your husband died? You got it in his

273

lifetime, did you?"

"No, I did not get it in his lifetime."

Gerry scratched his head. She got the child in January 1866, and her husband died in August, 1866. He looked at her. One more try.

"You got it before your husband died, didn't you?"

"I got it before my husband died. I guess there was more than her to be had—there is two more. He said there was three of them."

"Where?"

"They must be there."

"How do you know that?"

"Well, he told me he had three."

"Did he give you their names?"

"He did not. I wanted to know if he had a boy there. He said, 'It makes no difference to you.' So this time, he got that one out."

"Did he get this child out and give it to you?"

"He helped get it out. He signed his hand to it. I have his paper here today. He signed his hand to it, and Mr. Kellock signed it."

Gerry wondered if she thought the paper she now presented would justify her right to treat the child so cruelly. "Let me have the paper, will you?"

He read over the paper. It was the official document stating the terms of the indenture of Mary Ellen to the McCormicks. At the bottom of the document was the official seal of the State of New York, and the signatures of Thomas McCormick, Mary McCormick, and George Kellock. When he was finished, he looked at Connolly once more. "It was your first husband, Thomas McCormick's suggestion that you should take the child, if I understand you right?"

"Yes, sir."

"And you agreed to do it?"

"I agreed to do it."

"And you knew at the time it was his illegitimate child, did you?"

"Well, he told me so."

"You hadn't any doubt about it then, had you?"

"I hadn't quite knowledge of it. I always believed what he said, be it right or wrong in regard to such a thing as that. I thought my husband was earnest, for I had heard him say that before. I didn't mind if he had ten illegitimate children."

"Do you know whether the child is named after her mother?"

Well, Mr. Kellock of course has it on the books. He says it is Wilson, and that she put her in there and that he listed the child after her name."

"Were you present when your husband applied for the child?"

"Yes."

"What did he tell Mr. Kellock at that time?"

"He stated that there was a child there and he would like to get it out."

"Did he tell Mr. Kellock that the child was his?"

"No, sir. He did not."

"What did he say to Mr. Kellock about it?"

"He did not want to let on anything about it, and he let me do all that was necessary."

Gerry shook his head. None of it made sense. If it was McCormick's child, it might have been easier—not harder—to claim her. Why would the man hide that truth unless there was never any proof it was his child to begin with?

"What did you do to get the child?"

"Mr. Kellock said, 'Well, does any neighbors know who you are? Are you able to give support to the child?' I told him yes, he could speak to our family doctor."

"Who is the doctor to whom he spoke?"

"Dr. McLaughlin, but he never spoke to him. We just brought in a statement signed by him."

"Did Mr. Kellock make any inquiries as to your connection with the child in any way? As to the child being a relative of yours?"

"No. I didn't let on about it."

"Do you know if the other children were named Wilson as well?"

"I suppose she named them all when she put them in. If she named one she must have named them all. Likely she might."

"Did your husband ever give you any possible clue as to where this woman called Wilson lived?"

"No, sir. He never told me. I often asked him."

"Did he say whether she was in New York or not?"

"Sometimes he would say she was in the city, others he would say she was not."

"Was the child delivered to you immediately upon signing this paper? This is your signature, isn't it?" He held the paper out so she could see it.

"Yes, sir."

"And your husband's?"

"Yes, sir."

"When did you get the child?"

"We had the child from the second of January. This paper wasn't ready then, but we returned on the fifteenth to sign it. You can see the date is there."

Gerry stared at her long and hard. The child was removed without so much as a paper being signed! He bore down on Connolly. "So you had the child on the second of January and the paper was not executed until the fifteenth?"

"Not until the fifteenth."

"Did you have any paper given to you with the child when you took it on the second day of January?"

"No, sir."

"No receipt given for the child?"

"No receipt nor nothing."

"And when you eventually signed, this was the only paper you were required to sign?"

"That is the only one. They thought that was enough, I suppose."

"About how old is this child?"

"Well, I've had her since 1866. I suppose it is over seven years. Maybe past seven years, isn't it?"

"Do you believe the age of the child on the statement from Mr. Kellock to be correct?"

"I believe it must be nearly correct."

"Do you know whether this child has any relatives in the world?"

"Well, I don't know if that woman didn't die since."

"You say you don't know her?"

"I don't know her, and she may be living. I understand from many people that the mother is living."

"Who are those persons who tell you that?"

"I cannot give you names. Boys or young men or people when they would get drinking together. They would say, 'Well, don't be foolish, Mary. You know McCormick has got a lot of children. Don't give up your sense for it.' I'd just tell them, 'I don't care if he has ten or twenty! Let him fire away!'"

"Where were they drinking?"

"In our own house."

"Were you drinking?"

"I took a glass of lager."

"Anything else."

"No, sir."

"What were they drinking?"

"They were drinking lager, too."

"Who were the other young men?"

"I cannot say. He used to be working along with them and used to come home with them from the market."

"Can't you tell a single word that they told you about the mother of this child?"

"No. They only said, 'Don't you fool with McCormick. He has enough of them!'"

"Who were they?"

"I don't know their names. I didn't make no harm of it. It was only for play and joke's sake, as people do joke and play when drinking and in company. They can say many pleasant words and I don't mind what they say."

"Have you seen any of those persons since?"

"No, sir."

It was time to change the subject. Connolly wasn't giving the information Gerry was looking for. She had, however, admitted she drank with strange men; that should put the judge slightly more in opposition to her, for the child must have been present at the time.

"Have you ever received anything from any person for the support of the child?"

"Not one cent."

"Ever been promised anything for it?"

"Never one cent, though today they have me scandaled in the papers for it. I am thankful to the gentlemen for their scandal about me."

"At the time you took the child, was your husband, Thomas McCormick, then a butcher?"

"Yes, sir."

"Did you take the child as an apprentice or as an adopted child?"

"I took it as an adopted child. I could not get it out in any other way, as long as the mother left it in there and she was living."

Gerry referred to the indenture agreement now. "Did you ever teach or cause to be taught, or instruct this child in the trade and mystery of house-keeping and plain sewing?"

"Well, I understand as I read there that when she grows up of course I will do it. I teached her the alphabet and she can say it for you."

"Is that all you taught her?"

"I teached her the Lord's Prayer."

"Did you ever tell her that there was a God?"

"I did. I believe in God myself."

"I am not asking you about your own individual beliefs—"

"When you asked me about God I believe that there is a God. I understand that God created me."

"You do?" Gerry wondered if He would create such a beast.

"Yes, and all humans. I understand it. I thank Him for His mercy to all of us. I understand that there is a Lord God."

"Did you ever instruct that child that there is a God?"

"Yes, sir."

"Did you ever teach that child to pray?"

"I teached her the Lord's Prayer."

"Did you ever teach her what would become of her if she told a lie?"

"I did often, and she is first rate for it."

"Just answer the question," snapped Gerry. "Did you ever teach her the solemnity of an oath?"

"I believe I did not."

"Did you ever teach her what would become of her hereafter if she told a lie?"

"I told her she would go to the bad place if she told lies. I often teached her that."

Did you ever teach her what you meant by 'the bad place'?"

"Yes, that God wouldn't give her any place in Heaven."

"Did you so explain it to her?"

"I did, indeed."

"During the time she was with you—and I want you to answer me the question—did you actually teach her the trade and mystery of housekeeping and plain sewing?"

"Well, I couldn't, for the child is too young to learn housekeeping yet. She hasn't become a housekeeper yet."

"That is your idea, is it?"

"Well, a child of eight or nine years old wants her books more than she wants to do housekeeping."

"What books did you ever teach her?"

Connolly rolled her eyes back as if in thought. Gerry looked at Bergh, who smiled and nodded. Mary Ellen was still busy speaking to Etta Wheeler.

"I taught her the alphabet as far as to say small spelling and such as that. You can try her."

"What books did you ever teach her to spell from?"

"Nothing but a plain spelling book."

"What plain spelling book?"

"A child's reading book. I have paid five and ten and fifteen cents for books such as that."

"What clothing did that child have when she came to you?"

"She had just about as much as she has now."

"Nothing else?"

"Nothing else. What was on her was plain and simple clothing."

Officer Evans carried the extra calico dress and chemise up to the front of the courtroom and gave it to Gerry. He held it up for Mary Connolly to see. "Is this plain clothing? Just look at it and see whether that is the plain simple attire that you say she had when she came to you."

Connolly did not look at it. She simply nodded. "That is about the same. She had a petticoat such as that—not as good as that—when I got her at the place."

Gerry took a long look at the pitiful clothes he now held and said, "She had a petticoat when she came out of the asylum, did she?"

"Yes, sir," replied Connolly. "She has a clean one now. I am not ashamed of what I wash. I am but a very humble woman myself. I can't be a lady . . .

I can't play lady no how."

"You say when she came to you she had a flannel petticoat?"

"Yes, sir."

"What became of it?"

"I let her wear it out."

"Did you ever replace it?"

"Indeed I did. What would keep a child six or seven years? Have you been the father of a child and know what clothes you want for six years? I think you are man enough for that!"

The woman was babbling. Gerry needed to regain control before Judge Lawrence intervened the examination or questioned her competency to stand trial. "*I* am examining *you*, Mrs. Connolly," he said calmly.

Mary leapt to her feet again and pointed at Gerry. "You charge me with it and I ask you what would a child wear out in six years? I am the master over the child, and I keep her clean too! You are *not* to do that!"

"Please be seated, Mrs. Connolly, and I'll demand that you do not leave your seat further," ordered Judge Lawrence. He waited while she made up her mind. Glaring at Gerry, she dropped hard into the seat and folded her arms.

The judge looked at Gerry, his eyes serious. "Please proceed, Mr. Gerry."

"Thank you, Your Honor," he said. "Mrs. Connolly, has that child now a plain petticoat?"

"Yes. It is very plain and clean."

"Has the child any other clothing in your possession excepting what is now produced in court?"

"No, she hasn't got any more clothing."

Gerry turned and motioned for Mary Ellen to stand. She did so, her eyes on the floor.

"But you see that the child has on a fragment of a calico dress," he said, his voice rising and taking on an accusatory tone, "and a little worn out chemise under it and no shoes or stockings or bonnet, and these, with another shredded dress and chemise, were, you told the officers, all her clothes! Do you call this *dressing her well*?"

"This whole thing is a persecution," shouted Connolly. "by people who do not know what they are talking about!"

"You'll find out by and by whether they know anything about it," responded Gerry, a slightly bemused look on his face.

Lawrence pounded his gavel on the podium. "Mrs. Connolly! Please control yourself. Mr. Gerry, are you ready to proceed with a line of pertinent questioning?"

"Yes, Your Honor."

"Very well, then. Please do."

"Mrs. Connolly," Gerry said, smiling. "was the child ever sick during the time she was with you?"

"No," she answered. "the child was never sickly."

"Never was?"

"She never was sickly. She was a healthy kept child. I always kept her comfortable. She always got enough to eat and had a good warm fire, better than myself."

Gerry walked to the bench and picked up the paper she had given him earlier. "Mrs. Connolly, this paper contains the following clause. At the head of the paper it says, 'Go report to the said Commissioners of Public Charities and Correction once in each year the character and condition of said girl.'" He folded the paper and looked her in the eye. "Did you ever make any such report?"

"Yes, sir."

"How many times did you report the character and condition of the child to the CPCC after you got this paper?"

"I took her down there twice. That's all."

"Only twice? When was the first time you took her down?"

"I don't know exactly. I didn't put the date down."

"How long after you first got her?"

"I had her for nearly a year. When I brought her down there the man was very proud of her keeping indeed."

"When was the next time you brought her down?"

"In the next year. The month I can't recollect."

"Since that time you have not brought her down?"

Connolly huffed. "No. I didn't bring her down because I saw they paid no attention to her. They were satisfied I didn't need to bring her there anymore."

"Who paid no attention to her?"

"The gentleman said she seemed to be well enough off."

"Did they tell you that you need not come again?"

"No, they did not tell me that."

"You can read, can't you?"

"I can read."

"And you've read this paper through, haven't you?"

"I read it a couple of times."

Gerry folded the paper and gave it to Judge Lawrence. "Mrs. Connolly," Gerry said, exhaling a sigh, "what is the full name of your present husband?"

"Francis Connolly."

He turned away from her and looked at Bergh and Etta, shaking his head. "I have nothing further."

Lawrence looked at Connolly. "Mrs. Connolly, you may step down. I order you to remain within the City of New York until such time as this case is concluded."

"Yes, sir."

Mary Connolly stepped down from the stand and left the courtroom. She hurried out of the building without a glance toward Bergh, Etta, or Mary Ellen.

24

"I call Alonzo Evans to the stand," Gerry said.

Bergh sat quietly beside Mary Ellen and Etta, listening to his officer's testimony. Evans recounted his experience as a 'census man', and gave the details of the child's demeanor and condition when he went to retrieve her.

All in all, it was going very well. Bergh looked at Mary Ellen and leaned down to whisper, "Well? What do you think?"

She looked at him and whispered back, "I like him. He's very nice, you know. He gave me a lollipop."

"And quite a lollipop it was," he said. "It was nearly as big as you."

She laughed, and Bergh put a finger to his lips. "Shh, now. Mr. Gerry is asking some important questions up there."

"Like that man in the robe asked me?"

"Exactly. Very important things."

"I said the truth. I really did."

"I know, Mary Ellen. Let's listen now."

Gerry dispensed with Alonzo Evans' questioning quickly, then Ambrose Monell took over during the questioning of the police officers, Christian McDougal and Thomas Dusenbury.

Monell was a straightforward attorney who knew police department policies and procedures, and therefore handled all dealings with them. He presented his interrogation of police witnesses in such a stylized manner that its familiarity put them at ease; this allowed them to offer comfortable responses with little confusion as to the meaning of the questions.

McDougal told the details of Mary Connolly's advances toward Alonzo Evans only to the court reporter, who put it in the notes. Bergh was intrigued. Evans had done the same thing.

"Alonzo," he whispered behind him.

Evans leaned forward. "Yes, Mr. Bergh?"

"What on earth did Connolly say to you in there? You whispered it during your testimony, and now so has Officer McDougal."

Alonzo looked at Mary Ellen next to him, then moved around to Bergh's opposite ear. He told him about Connolly's offer to return to her rooms and Bergh laughed aloud. "Are you going to go?"

Monell, at the front of the court, glared at Bergh, his face tense. Bergh quit smiling and returned his attentions to the trial. Gerry sat in front of him on the bench until Monell finished with Thomas Dusenbury.

Before rising again, Gerry turned to Bergh and said, "Before I call my next witness I'll ask you to control yourself, Henry. I'm not as secure as Ambrose."

Bergh was still smiling as Gerry called Charlotte Fiehling to the stand. The poor woman was so nervous before the courtroom full of people, she chewed on her lip and kept brushing non-existent wrinkles from her dress. A merciful Gerry recognized her discomfort and made her appearance a short one. Fiehling recounted her meeting with Mary Ellen in the courtyard that cold winter evening, and later, her confrontation with Mary Connolly. Because of her meek voice and honest appearance, her time on the witness stand was effective. At least Bergh thought so.

The next two witnesses Gerry called were Catherine Kemp and a woman who lived in the building next to Margaret Bingham's, Marilyn Studor. Studor, who did not speak English, testified through an interpreter. She stated that she had often heard the sounds of a child receiving a beating through her window, which was positioned directly across from the Connollys' rooms.

Following their testimony, Gerry called Margaret Bingham. Bergh settled back for a longer testimony, as Margaret had been the one to make sure some-one else knew about Mary Ellen and her plight. She would have plenty to say, and Bergh wanted to hear it.

"Poor thing couldn't get the window up more than this." Margaret indi-cated with her thumb and forefinger.

"Not more than an inch?" asked Gerry.

"Not more than an inch. Mrs. Connolly would go away in the morning and seldom came back until after dark, and she left that child locked up. That was done repeatedly, not once or twice."

Margaret answered his questions thoroughly, elaborating when Gerry prompted it. She recounted the time Mary Ellen surprised her by appearing at her door, leaving out no detail.

"She had a cut across there." She said in conclusion, pointing to her face.

"A cut across the chin?"

"Yes, sir."

"How large a cut?"

"Well, as if it was made by the point of some scissors or the edge of a knife. It wasn't a whip."

"Could it have been made by such an instrument as this?" He lifted the pair of scissors from the table.

"Yes, sir. Something like that. I couldn't really say."

"That was some time ago? It's worn off?"

Margaret nodded. "Oh, yes. I imagine it was a year ago, at least."

The questioning continued, and Gerry looked embarrassed. "Mrs. Bingham, I'm afraid I omitted to ask you. You will pardon me, but I would like to know how old you are."

She laughed and said, "Next month I will be sixty-nine."

"Thank you, Mrs. Bingham. That will be all."

* * * * *

It had been a long day, and it was not to be over soon. Mr. Bergh had told Etta before the day's proceedings began that she might not be questioned to-day, but she wanted to be there with Mary Ellen nonetheless. She squeezed the little girl's hand, wishing the waif didn't have to wear those miserable, worn-out clothes. Several lovely dresses had been delivered to the courthouse this morning by various women of society, some of whom had hopes of adopting Mary Ellen, so glowing were the descriptions of her haunting beauty and innocence by the newspapers.

Etta held Mary Ellen's hand as Charles Smitt, Mary's husband, took the stand. He testified to having heard Mary Ellen running back and forth, screaming "Mama! Mama!" while being whipped. Hearing his testimony, Etta remembered sitting with him on several occasions when Mary was sleeping, and hearing him speak of the tears his wife had cried over the child. It had been a source of pain for Mary, and Charles believed that if the child was rescued, his wife might just recover from her illness. Etta wasn't so sure; Mary seemed to have deteriorated more each time she saw her. As Etta sat listening, deep in thought, she felt a tug on her sleeve.

"Mrs. Wheeler!" Mary Ellen whispered, louder than she meant to.

"Yes?"

"I have to go to the potty!"

"Now?"

"Yes, please. Will you take me?"

Etta smiled and stroked the child's now clean cheek. The cut looked much better since she had been cleaned up. She tapped Bergh on the shoulder. "Mr. Bergh, I'm taking Mary Ellen out for a moment. Is that okay?"

Bergh nodded. "Yes, but do hurry. I believe your testimony will be taken today after all."

"Very well. Back in two shakes of a lamb's tail, then."

"Two shakes of what?" asked Mary Ellen.

"I'll tell you later, child. Come on, now."

* * * * *

Jane Slater stepped down from the stand and Gerry said, "I'd like to call Mrs. Charles Wheeler, Your Honor."

Etta patted Mary Ellen on the hand and made her way to the stand.

After she was sworn in, Gerry began. "Would you state your name, please?"

"Etta Angell Wheeler."

"Mrs. Wheeler, you attended Mrs. Smitt, did you not?"

"I did occasionally."

"Will you state under what circumstances you attended her, and what you there learned in reference to this matter and what communication you made to Mr. Bergh about it?"

Etta took a deep breath. "Yes, of course," she began. "A woman, Mary Litzbeney, whom I used to call on and who lived in Mrs. Bingham's house, told me that Margaret Bingham asked her to tell me about a child who had been living there up to two weeks before, and had been very cruelly treated. The child had since been moved from 325 West 41st Street, Mrs. Bingham's building, to 315 West 41st Street. I was told substantially what has been given in evidence today about the confinement and beating and other things."

"Did you call on Mrs. Smitt?"

"I went to 315 West 41st Street and asked them on the first floor if a woman named Connolly was living in the house. I was told there was, and I was told the room where she lived—the top floor, on the right hand side. I went to the top floor and knocked on the door across the hall instead, but received no reply. I opened the door and saw a very neat, orderly room, perfectly clean. I went in and looked into the bedroom, which was a little to the left, and saw a woman lying in bed. I went in and spoke to her, as I had gone there hoping to get some excuse for going into the Connolly's room. The people at 325 had told me I would not gain admittance to the Connollys' room, being a stranger. I hoped to find some reason in this other room for going to their room. Instead, I found this sick woman. I talked with her and saw that she needed attention, and such attention that I could give her."

"What did you do then?"

"I told her that I would attempt to befriend her through the winter. I also told her she had a neighbor and asked if she ever came in to see her. She said she did, and the woman seemed very kind, so I asked her if there was a little girl there, and she said she thought there was, though she had not seen her. I then told her I would ask the woman across the hall to let the little girl come in and wait upon her. I suggested that if she made friends with the child, she could be a comfort to her, helping her through the winter."

"Did you subsequently attempt to see Mrs. Connolly?"

"I left the room then and went to Mrs. Connolly's room. She did not ask me to come in, but I went in uninvited and sat down. That was when I first saw Mrs. Connolly and this little child."

"The child now in court?"

"Yes, sir. The little one was washing dishes from a pan, standing upon a little keg turned before the table. She was taking the dishes up from the table and washing them. She paid no attention to me, no more, I think, than if I had not gone into the room. It was as though she wasn't aware of my presence. Across the table lay a whip, or what I call a rawhide."

"It was on the table?" asked Gerry.

"Yes, it lay across the table from which the child was taking the dishes. It was about three feet long, as I recall it."

"Three feet?"

"Yes, or about a yard, as I call it. It was leather twisted together, large at one end and small at the other, and painted green. The child acted in a very nervous manner. I did not speak to her, I ignored her presence entirely. I got into conversation with Mrs. Connolly about her sick neighbor and asked if she would go in and attend to her a little. I told her the husband was away at work and the woman was entirely alone through the day. After my brief conversation, I was satisfied the reports that I had heard about the child's treatment were true and I left the room."

"What reply did Mrs. Connolly make to this suggestion, this offer of yours?"

"It was not a frank reply. I judged that she wished me to understand that she would comply, but at the same time I did not think she meant it. She never spoke to me frankly."

"Did you have any further interviews?"

"I did. I can give no dates."

"Will you state anything that transpired at any of those interviews?"

"I went in again. The second time that I went in, the child was seated in the farthest part of the room and had evidently been sewing. She was sewing while I was there. I sat down for a few minutes uninvited and I talked with Mrs. Connolly. The rawhide at that time was lying across a chair that stood near the stool upon which the child was sitting. The only time I spoke to the child before I saw her yesterday, I said in an offhand manner, 'Come and see me, dear, will you?' The child started nervously toward me, then dropped again. I paid no attention to the matter and went away again. My talk with Mrs. Connolly was always confined to the care of the sick woman. I have visited Mrs. Smitt many times, and purposely on the coldest, bleakest days of the winter, fearing that the little girl might be alone, as she often was. I hoped at the same time that I might find the child more comfortably clothed, but she was always dressed as she is today, except the first time. Then she had on what I judge to be the little apron that was shown here this morning."

"How was this room of Mrs. Connolly's heated?"

"There is a stove, I believe. A common cooking stove."

"Is there a stove in the bedroom at all?"

"I have never seen the bedroom. I have looked into the bedroom, but I don't believe . . . no, there can be no stove in there."

"Did you see the child at any time outside of Mrs. Connolly's room?"

"Never. I have often seen the door a little ajar on my way up the stairs, perhaps just that much." Etta held her hands two feet apart. "The child always seemed to be on the guard and shut the door immediately. I've always looked at the windows of Mrs. Connolly's rooms and have never once seen the curtains raised."

"How large a room is this room that is occupied by the Connollys?"

Etta thought for a moment, then said, "I cannot say. If I should guess—it would be unreliable—but it may be sixteen feet square."

"I'd like to thank you, Mrs. Wheeler. Not only for your testimony, but for your kind heart."

"You're welcome, sir. Thank you."

Back in her seat, Etta stroked Mary Ellen's dark brown hair and said, "Will you be all right tonight, child?"

"I think so," she replied, her eyes tearing over.

"Be strong, Mary Ellen, please? I promise this will all be over soon."

"Will I be going back home?" she asked. "I miss Mama."

Mary Ellen's eyes filled with tears, and Etta felt powerless. She knelt down and put her arms around the weeping child. "Mary Ellen," she said, "I know you love your mama, but you must understand that she mistreated you. You're just . . . well, you're missing her a bit now."

Meara Webb, the police station matron, approached them.

"I don't know what Mama whipped me for. I always tried to be good."

289

"I know, honey. And you were, too. You were very good. Now I want you to go back with Mrs. Webb, and she's going to put you in a nice clean bed tonight. You know her. She took care of you last night."

"Hello, darling," the woman said. "We had fun last night, didn't we?"

"Yes ma'am," Mary Ellen said. "Are you going to give me another bath?"

"Do you want one?"

"It was fun. I've never had one like that before. Mama just made me wash my head in the sink."

"Your head?"

"Uh-huh."

"Sure, honey. I'll give you another bath if you like."

* * * * *

Etta went straight from the courtroom to Mary Smitt's building. Charles accompanied her from the courthouse, and as they reached the top of the stairs, they stepped quietly past Mary Connolly's room and went inside.

Harold Stetson, a representative of the court who had been sent to her bedside to record her sworn testimony, was interviewing Mary. The court reporter with whom Etta and Charles had become familiar accompanied him to write it all down.

Charles could not stay. He'd been away from the paper all day, and had to go off to work. Etta stood and hugged him good-bye, then sat nearby and listened as Stetson asked Mary the required questions.

"How old are you, Mrs. Smitt?"

"Pretty near forty-five."

"Have you been sick long?"

"Yes, sir. For eight months. I've been in the bed for three months steady."

"Are you very sick?"

"Yes. Eight doctors have given me up."

"Does the doctor come to see you anymore?"

"Oh yes, sir."

"Do you hope to get well?"

"No, sir. I'm satisfied I shall die."

Etta felt a knife pierce her heart. Poor Mary knew the truth, and still she

290

kept a positive, friendly disposition. Stetson, on the other hand, was unaffected by the words. He had seen and heard a lot in his years with the court.

"You expect to die?" he asked.

"Yes, sir."

"How long have you lived here?"

"Three years."

"Who lives in the next room?"

"Mrs. Connolly."

"How long has she lived there?"

"I guess about four months."

"Have you ever seen a little child named Mary Ellen here?"

"I saw her twice, but I didn't speak to her."

"What have you ever heard about that little child?"

"I have heard her when I have lain here. Mrs. Connolly licks her all the time . . . everyday. Mostly in the morning before she gets breakfast."

"About what time in the morning?"

"I don't know exactly. The man goes to work. He has got eight hours work. Sometimes she got licked before he went away and sometimes when he is gone. If she didn't get licked in the morning, she would get it through the day. She would get it sometimes twice in a day."

"Always every day?" asked Stetson.

"Always."

"Did you hear it anytime in the last week?"

"Yes, sir. I'm sure she got it during the last week."

"Has Mrs. Connolly ever said anything to you about it?"

"No, sir. And she daren't come out the door."

"Who?"

"Mary Ellen. She would see somebody and go and hide. I have seen her twice. Once she had the broom in her hand and when she saw me she went back in the door and locked it."

"Did you hear screaming?"

"I heard her scream. Mrs. Connolly licked her and the child ran back and forth from the corner to the bedroom crying 'Oh, Mama! Oh, Mama!'. I heard her being struck."

"Could you hear the blows?"

"Yes, sir. I could hear everything."

"Did you ever know of the man whipping her?"

"I never heard the man lick her. Never. I never heard a bad word from the man."

"Always from the woman?"

"Yes. It makes me so sick sometimes . . . I am so heartsick when I hear that little child."

Etta listened quietly until Mr. Stetson finished questioning Mary, then saw them to the door. She stayed with Mary for another hour, recounting the testimony of Connolly, Alonzo Evans, and the others. She told the sick woman about all the high society women that had shown up at the courthouse to try to claim Mary Ellen as their own, and how they longed to be near the poor thing.

Libby showed up an hour later, at which time Etta kissed Mary good-bye and left the room. Mary Connolly's door was shut tight as she passed, and she wondered if she was inside, and if so, what a woman such as she would be doing. She stepped onto the sidewalk of 41st Street and noticed an old soldier, his eight year-old uniform threadbare, the leg of the trousers knotted at the stub of his knee. He had only one arm as well, and the sleeve of his torn shirt was knotted at the elbow in a similar fashion. This was one of the last remaining street soldiers; men who once numbered in the hundreds and who had lost not only their limbs in the Brothers' War, but their spirits as well.

Etta leaned down and said, "Hello, sir. I've a bit to give you but that's all, I'm afraid." She dropped the coin into his tin cup and stood.

His eyes followed her. "That's almighty 'preciated, ma'am," he said, his voice cracked and dry. "If it wasn't for folks like yourself, I'd be cold as a wagon tire." His face was wrinkled and pitted far beyond his years, and one eye was clouded with cataracts as he looked up at her.

"God bless you, sir," she said, leaving him and continuing down the street. Her husband would be home now, and she missed him. It would be good to get there and tell him about her interesting, exhilarating day at the courthouse.

* * * * *

Long after Etta departed, somewhere around midnight, Charles Smitt awakened to a house thick with silence. He took slow, soft steps across the floor toward his wife's bed, knelt down, and rested his head on her chest. It was as he expected. There, within her body, he heard nothing, felt nothing except peace.

Finally, peace.

She had made a promise to herself that she would see the poor child across the hall rescued, and it had come to pass. Mary Ellen was now in the care of good people, and the evil Connolly woman would soon face justice. It must have been Mary's sign that it was okay to go to the Lord now.

Charles cried, there in the darkness of the New York City tenement room, for the woman he had loved for most of his life was now with the Lord.

The next morning, when Etta came to the door, a tired Charles Smitt told her the news. They embraced, mourning Mary's passing together, praying for her soul.

25

April 11, 1874

The reporters in attendance in the courtroom were understandably disappointed when Mary Ellen was not among them Saturday. She had, up until that point, been the main attraction, and Bergh knew it as well as anyone there. Today, he and Elbridge Gerry, along with Judge Lawrence and the bevy of reporters, listened to the testimony taken by Harold Stetson the day before.

Unaware Mrs. Smitt had passed away the night before, Gerry read her sworn statement and laughed, "No woman could possibly survive eight doctors!"

"It would, indeed, be a marvelous miracle," retorted Bergh, laughing along with the others who found the comment amusing. He realized many of the reporters were still so taken with the pitiable condition of Mary Ellen that they found very little humor in any part of the case. He choked back his remaining smile and listened to the remainder of Mary Smitt's heartfelt testimony.

Before leaving the court, Judge Lawrence called both men forward.

Bergh spoke first. "We've located George Kellock. He'll be in court on Monday."

"Is he your final witness?"

"We're still trying to locate the woman named Martha Score, who is named in Mr. Kellock's records as the woman who deposited the child with him. If fortune is on our side, we may find the mother yet."

Lawrence nodded. "Good. I'm going to order that Mary Connolly appear in court Monday," he said. "From what I've seen and heard thus far, I believe her arrest is the next logical step to take."

"Excellent, Your Honor," Bergh said. "The proof is extensive, and the witnesses credible."

"They are," Lawrence said. "I find that I'm looking forward to bringing her to justice."

"So are we all," Gerry said. "So are we all."

* * * * *

"How many do you think we'll receive?" Bergh asked, back at the ASPCA offices. "There must be hundreds here!"

Gerry spread the letters over the desk as Bergh sat opposite him. "Amazing, isn't it? Messages coming to the courthouse, more still to us. It seems the entire city of New York wants this little one."

"Not only that, the entire country!" Bergh said. "Ah, but the question is, where will she end up?"

"Let's see what Mr. Kellock knows first. He may set us upon Mrs. Score, and if we find her, I believe we'll find Mary Ellen's mother."

* * * * *

April 13, 1874

The courtroom was literally packed with spectators on Monday morning. The large, inquisitive crowd watched Mary Ellen, surrounded by a half dozen ladies, many of whom had brought the child new clothes.

And new clothes Mary Ellen wore. She pranced into the courthouse wearing a bright, plaid dress with a ruffled overskirt, the bodice adorned with a square ruffle-edged yoke. On her feet were comfortable shoes, worn over plain stockings, and atop her head sat a pretty, flower-covered bonnet. She hardly looked like the same child who sat beside Henry Bergh on Friday. A colorful picture book sat open on her lap, and she sat talking to the ladies, her mood happy, her facial expressions animated.

Mary Connolly walked into the courtroom and spotted her amidst her many admirers. Ignoring them, she approached Mary Ellen, her hand extended. "Hello, dear child," she said, smiling.

Mary Ellen looked at her, her face aglow, then took her tormentor's hand. "Good morning, Mama! I have got new clothes!"

"I see you do," said Connolly, finally heeding the glares from the ladies around her and taking her seat on the opposite side of the room. Mary Ellen returned to her chatter as if Mary Connolly were merely an old acquaintance who stopped by to offer her greetings.

The gavel sounded and proceedings got underway.

"Please state your name," Gerry said.

The heavyset woman in the witness stand smiled and stated, "Meara Webb."

"Where do you reside, Mrs. Webb?"

"Police Headquarters. I am the Matron of Police Headquarters."

"What is your connection with that establishment?"

"To see to the children that are brought in."

"Stray children found wandering about the city are brought by the police to headquarters where they are consigned to your care?"

"Yes, sir."

"Have you seen the child Mary Ellen?"

"I have, sir."

"When was she brought in?"

"The ninth of this month."

"I want you to state," Gerry said, "what the condition of the child was regarding clothing, cleanliness, and whether you saw any scars or marks on her. Just go on and describe what you saw."

Meara sighed. "Well, in the first place her clothing was in very bad condition and very dirty. I took them off of her and found her body to be in the same condition. It wasn't dirty from a week's standing, or a month, but I should suppose several months. The filth was crusted on like a child who had not been washed for months, the body of this child."

"Was this dirt plainly visible?"

"Yes, indeed. As it was washed off it left a thick scum over the bath."

"What did you use in order to get it off her?"

"Plenty of soap and water."

"How many washings did it require in order to remove the whole of this deposit of dirt upon the skin?"

"Three different waters were applied to the child."

"Was this universally the condition of the body beneath the clothing?"

"Yes, sir. The feet also. She had never run in the street with bare feet, but they were discolored like children who run in the house with bare feet. She also had three distinct bruises on her, and others."

"Where were they?"

"One was just above the hip, another just above the elbow, and another a little above the left knee. One was as if very recently done."

"Which was that?"

"The one above the elbow."

"How long have you been in charge of this department, Mrs. Webb?"

"Two years next August."

"How many children during that time have been brought to your notice within the department?"

"In warm weather we average three hundred a month. In the month of May we have had four hundred, but other months vary."

"You have had a large experience then with children?"

"Yes, sir."

"What was the condition of this child's hair?"

"It was very bad. I had it combed, and of course it had vermin in it."

"The hair was full of vermin, was it?"

"I cannot say exactly full, but it had too much for any child that has had any care."

"Did it appear to have been combed at any recent time?"

"I guess it got no combing or it would not have had vermin in it."

"Did you observe any scars or marks upon her face?"

"The first day I saw her she had a very dark purple spot right on the forehead and side, and a large scratch that was done with the scissors. There was another mark on her temple she said was made by a whip."

"And those marks were plainly visible when you first saw her?"

"When I got her they were plain, but now we have washed her and fussed with her until they have quite disappeared. They don't show much now."

"The clothes that she has on today when she was produced here in court are not the clothes with which she was clothed then?"

"No, sir. Not one article."

"Thank you, Mrs. Webb." Gerry turned to the judge. "No more questions, Your Honor. I'd like now to call George Kellock."

* * * * *

George Kellock couldn't believe it had come back to him. He told himself in 1866 that he would never forget the woman Connolly, and now he knew it was true. She was there, right in front of him. The attorney, Mr. Gerry was preparing to question him, and the sweat poured from his face. He didn't know what she had told them, but he prayed she never mentioned the "terms" of their transaction for the child.

"What official position do you hold, if any, in connection with any of our institutions?" Gerry awaited his answer.

"Superintendent of the Outdoor Poor."

"In what department?"

"Public Charities and Correction."

"How long?"

"Since 1848."

"Do you know this woman, Mary Connolly?"

This was it. Either he remained in control and lied, or he broke down and told the truth. He knew the only thing he could do. He had a family and a reputation. "I cannot say that I do know her, sir."

"Have you been able to find anything in regard to this child Mary Ellen, who is mentioned under the name of Mary Ellen Wilson in an indenture purporting to come from your office and signed by you as one of the parties to it?"

"Yes, sir." He produced a book from beneath his clammy hands and opened it.

"What book is that?"

298

"Nurse Book number fifteen," he replied. "Folio 58-1/2."

"What do you find there?" asked Gerry.

Kellock read from the book. "Mary Ellen Wilson, 18 months old, left in charge of deponent about the 21st of May, 1864. Has received eight dollars per month until three weeks since. Does not know where the mother lives. As per affidavit of Martha Score, number 235 Mulberry Street, July 7, 1865."

"I observe on the right hand of the entry, the words 'Almshouse Blackwell's Island, July 10, 1865'. What does that mean?"

"It means that she was sent up there to nurse at the time she was brought to the department."

"The words 'Mary Ellen Wilson, 18 mo.' Does that mean eighteen months at the time this entry was made?"

"Eighteen months old. Yes, sir."

"About what time was this entry made?"

"The date is there." Kellock pointed to it.

"July 7, 1865?"

"Yes, sir."

"Is that right?"

"Yes, sir."

"Have you been able to find any affidavit of Martha Score, who lived at 235 Mulberry Street?"

"We have not. We moved our office since that time and the affidavits previous to 1870 are perhaps somewhere about the building. We cannot lay our hands on them at present."

"I wish you would kindly make another diligent search if you will."

"I will." He glanced at Mary Connolly, the quickly averted his eyes. The woman made him feel sick.

"In regard to the mention here, 'has received eight dollars per month until three weeks since', have you any clue as to where that memorandum comes from, or to whom and by whom that eight dollars was paid?"

"That is paid by the party who placed the child in care of Martha Score but neglected to keep up paying for it I presume."

"Do you know who Martha Score is?"

"I do not."

"She is not a nurse or any person connected in any way with your department?"

"No, sir."

"After this affidavit was made, the child, as I understand it, was sent up to Blackwell's Island?"

"Yes, sir."

"And kept in the almshouse there until called out by these people?"

"Yes, sir." At the mention of the Connollys, he felt sweat break out on the back of his neck and begin to soak his shirt collar.

"In regard to the application by these people for this child," Gerry said, "Before making that application, were they bound either to give a bond or make an affidavit or enter into any undertaking?"

What had she told them! If he only knew, he could come up with some explanation that might cover his actions! "No, sir," he said, wiping away the sweat dripping from his nose. "They required only a reference in regard to their capability of taking care of the child."

"Do you remember the reference they gave you?"

"I do not remember, but I think it was a Dr. McLaughlin."

"She referred your department to this doctor?"

"He was her family physician at the time."

"Did you know him?"

"I think I did. I might be able to find him for you."

"Was the deposit of the child made on the representations of Dr. McLaughlin that the woman was a competent person?"

"Yes, sir. That the woman and man were both competent to take care of the child."

"They were both parties to the agreement?"

"Yes, sir."

"Do you remember how they came to select this particular child?"

"I do not, but the general way is they go and look among the children and pick out the one they think will suit. Then they come down to me to get an order for the child."

"Then the first thing they must have done before getting this child was to go to the almshouse at Blackwell's Island and ask to see the child Mary Ellen Wilson?"

"I don't think so. I believe they saw all the children."

"Could the Connollys have found out the child's name at the almshouse?"

"Yes, sir."

"Without seeing the child?"

"Yes, sir."

"At the almshouse do they permit people to see children without a permit?"

"No, sir."

"A permit from whom?"

"From me."

"Do you remember having given any permit to this couple to go and see the child?"

"I don't remember. I presume I did."

"After seeing the child up at Blackwell's Island, the next course is an application to you for an indenture, is it?"

"For an order to get the child."

"Is the child brought down first before the indenture is given?"

"No, if the child is one who can be placed, and the reference is satisfactory, the order is given to the party to obtain the child."

"Without any indenture being made?"

"The indenture is made after they have the child."

Gerry scratched his mutton chop whiskers with one hand. "Do you mean to say they are allowed to have the child first on the simple order?"

"Yes, sir."

"Is the application required to be fortified by any affidavit?"

"No affidavit, only the reference."

"On being satisfied of the capacity of the party to take the child?"

"If the reference is not satisfactory, we generally send a visitor to look into the standing of the parties."

"Your recollection is that in the present case, the reference was satisfactory?"

"I think the reference was satisfactory, he being a family physician."

"You relied on the statement of the family physician as knowing more about the person than other persons?"

"Yes, sir."

Gerry grunted as if to himself. "Did the husband—Mr. McCormick—

make any statement at the time about the child being his?"

"Nothing of the kind."

"Who is the person at the almshouse that would have charge of the child while there?"

George knew well who it was—Abigail Quigley. To his relief, she had left the facility four years ago, a welcomed departure. After the Connolly fiasco, she had watched him like a hawk, never letting him forget she knew what he'd done. "The person who was in charge of the children is not there now."

"Can you give me the name?"

"I don't remember. I think I can obtain it for you."

"The indenture requires that the Connollys report each year as to the condition of the child. I want to ask you first how the report is made. Is it a report in writing, or do they bring in the child?"

"They generally bring in the child and show it to the department."

"Who do they show it to?"

"To me, or to the commissioners if they're there."

"Do you remember her bringing in the child?"

He surely did. He also remembered seeing several bruises on the child, though she was dressed fairly well. When he pointed them out, the Connolly woman raved about the money she had paid for the child, and he wanted nothing more than to get rid of them before Abigail Quigley turned up. She had gone on an errand, and was due back any moment. "I think I saw her bring the child in once or twice."

"I want to ask you your recollection of the condition of that child; her manner of clothing and her physical condition in regard to cleanliness on the occasions when you think she produced the child before you. Can you bear in mind anything about it?"

"I don't remember any child being produced there that wasn't clothed pretty well and looked pretty well. I would have noticed the difference, of course."

"How many children do you have passing through your establishment each year?"

"Perhaps five or six hundred a year."

"Of course you don't bear in mind the appearance of any particular child?"

"No, sir."

"If you remember, was there anything in the child's appearance when she was produced before you that attracted your attention in any way?"

"No, sir."

"Did you ever have any conversation with this Dr. McLaughlin about this child?"

"No, sir."

"Do your rules require you to keep any particular memorandum in regard to the presentation of these children as required by that indenture?"

"Well, we don't do it. They generally bring the children to us and report. Some of the reports we have received in writing. Those reports are kept on file."

"Mr. Kellock, is there any . . . security required to be given on the indenture?"

Kellock froze. He found himself staring at Mary Connolly, and he thought he saw a slight smile touch her lips. "I . . . beg your pardon? Security?"

"Yes, sir. Payment of any kind."

He glanced again at Connolly, then back at Gerry and answered, "No, sir. No security, only character. That is all."

Gerry nodded. "Is there anything else that I can ask you?"

Kellock felt his breath release. It was over. "I don't know of anything else," he said. "I would be glad to give you any information I could."

"That will be all, Mr. Kellock."

* * * * *

As Mary Connolly rose to leave the courtroom upon adjournment, a police officer approached her.

"Mrs. Mary Connolly?"

"Yes, sir?"

"I am placing you under arrest, to be confined to the Tombs until such time as the Grand Jury reaches a decision on five charges of felony assault against the child, Mary Ellen Wilson."

Mary Connolly did not resist.

26

Over the following days, Mary Ellen healed, her skin becoming smooth and clear for the first time in years. The messages and letters poured in from people wanting to take her under their wing, and Bergh, Gerry, Monell, and Abraham Lawrence read each and every one. Many claimed to be relatives of the little waif, and others boasted that they would give her riches beyond belief, while still others had nothing at all except a desire to meet the now famous little girl.

* * * * *

Bergh pushed open the door of Gerry's offices and stopped, his eyes searching the room. He spotted Gerry by the file cabinet.

"Elbridge! We've found her!"

Gerry turned and stared for a moment, then a broad smile crossed his lips. "You mean Martha Score? Our lost witness?"

"Yes, and she's still living on Mulberry."

"My God, the same address listed on his paper?"

"Just across the street. It seems once you live in such a world it's difficult to remove yourself from it."

"When do you suppose she can be brought in for testimony?"

"How does this Tuesday next strike you?"

"I'll be more than ready. When it's confirmed, just send a messenger to let me know."

"Very well, Elbridge. You realize I couldn't have done this without you."

Gerry laughed. "I know that, Henry. Nor would the opportunity have been afforded me if not for you."

* * * * *

On the morning of April 21st, Martha was more than a little nervous at first sight of the courthouse. It was so enormous it overwhelmed her, especially when filled with gentlemen shouting questions at her regarding little Mary Ellen.

She had never forgotten the child—looking at her now, she saw Mary Ellen had grown into a lovely young lady. Her eyes were the same as she remembered, and her little mouth was no different than it had been. Her once wispy hair was now dark brown and as wavy as a field of tall grass. She appeared to be happy today, though from what Martha had been told, it wasn't always so. Apparently the woman she'd heard about, Connolly, had beaten and abused her for years.

Not a week had passed since giving her up that Martha didn't think of her, wondering where and with whom she lived. She'd been tempted to go and see Mr. Kellock at the Commissioner's office and ask after her, but never did. Martha sat quietly, having already sworn with her hand on the bible.

Mr. Gerry, the gentleman who spoke to her before she came in the courthouse, approached her. "What is your name?" he asked.

"Martha Score."

"Are you married or single?"

Martha hesitated for the first time. "Married, sir." She *was* married. She would be married until such time as she heard of the death of James Score, or until she saw divorce documents.

"What is the name of your husband?"

"James Score."

"What is his business?"

"Cigar maker."

"Where do you reside now?"

"195 Mulberry Street."

"Do you remember anything about a child called Mary Ellen Wilson that was delivered by you into the custody of the Commissioner of Charities and Corrections some years since?"

"Yes, sir. I took care of her for her mother. At least she told me she was her mother. I was paid two dollars per week."

"How did she come to you?"

"By an acquaintance."

"Had you known her previously?"

"No, sir. I never was acquainted with her."

"Who brought her to you?"

"A lady named Alanna Cavanagh."

"She lived in the same house with you?"

"No, sir. Not in the same house with me at that time, but she was a neighbor."

"She had previously lived in the same house?"

"Yes, sir."

"Were you married at that time?"

"Yes, sir. As I am today."

"Had you children of your own?"

The sides of Martha's mouth pulled downward, and she groped for a handkerchief. Her thoughts drifted backward in time to the day she watched James walk away with his children; all of whom she loved as her own.

"Yes, sir. I had three," she said, controlling her sadness.

"And this Mrs. Cavanagh, what did she say about this woman before she came to you?"

"She told me she was a servant in the St. Nicholas Hotel, and asked me if I would take care of this baby for her. She had no person to take care of it, and she would pay me. I took the child because . . . my husband was away, and it would help me along."

"What did she say the name of this woman was, the mother?"

"Fanny Wilson."

"Do you know whether she said anything about the parentage of the child?"

"No, sir."

"Did she say anything about Fanny Wilson being married or single?"

"She told me she was a married woman and her husband was in the war. He died and left her a widowed woman."

"Did she say anything whatever about this child being an illegitimate child?"

"It was her own child, she said."

"You saw Fanny Wilson?"

"I did."

"What sort of a person was she?"

"A good looking woman, with dark eyes and dark hair."

"Was she tall?"

"Medium size."

"She was a good looking woman?"

"Very good looking."

"How old a woman was she?" asked Gerry.

"I could not say."

"About how old?"

"About thirty years . . . well, perhaps from twenty-seven to thirty as near as I should judge."

"Have you any idea of what nationality she was, whether Irish or American?"

"She told me she was an English woman."

"Did she say what her husband's name was?"

Martha tried hard to remember, but it escaped her. Poor Fanny had been so distraught over his death, too. Why couldn't she remember?

"Mrs. Score?" Gerry prompted.

"She told me, but I forget."

"Did she say what position he occupied in the army?"

"No, sir."

"Did she give you any articles of clothing with the child?"

"A few little articles, not a great deal."

"How much a week did she give you?"

"Two dollars."

"Won't you fix the time—as near as you can—that she gave you the child?"

"I really could not say. I should think it was about a year after my husband . . . I could not say. I really could not say." Martha bit her lip. Why did everything dredge up memories of the life that slipped away from her? The child sitting fifteen feet away from her, thoughts of her husband, and children who left so many years ago. She wanted to leave.

Mr. Gerry was persistent. "Could you fix the date as near as possible?"

Martha shook her head. "I really could not say."

"About how old was the child when she was brought to you?"

"Perhaps between five and six months."

"Was it as long ago as ten years?"

"No, sir, it is not. I could not say exactly."

"Mrs. Score, you made an application when you resided at 235 Mulberry Street in 1865."

"Yes, sir."

"So it appears by the entries that have been produced here in evidence by the Commissioners of Charities and Corrections, Mr. Kellock. You know him personally, don't you?"

"Yes, sir." Martha listened as the attorney read the affidavit she made in George Kellock's office to her.

When he finished, he looked at her. "You made such an affidavit?"

"Yes, sir."

"How long did you keep the child before you took her to the Commissioners of Charities and Corrections?"

"About a year."

"And up until that time, was the money paid by that woman, the two dollars a week?"

"While she was at the St. Nicholas she paid me punctually. Then she went away and I couldn't get a trace of her for some time. When I did see her next, she gave me the ticket to draw the money to pay for the baby. The soldier's relief ticket."

"Do you recollect the soldier's name on that ticket?"

"No, sir. I do not."

"When was the last time you saw Mrs. Wilson?"

"I could not say."

"Have you got the ticket yet?"

"No, sir. The ticket was kept where the money was given." Martha would never forget that day. So many horrifying memories!

"Did Mrs. Wilson say what business her husband was in before he went to the war?"

"She told me he was an oyster man at the St. Nicholas."

"Did she say anything about the place where he was killed?"

"No, sir."

"Did Mrs. Wilson ever write to you or call on you afterwards?"

"I saw her once more . . . I told her about the child and she told me the child was all right where she was." Martha would never forget what she had actually told Fanny. How could anyone ever forget telling a woman her child was dead? She looked at Mary Ellen, thankful it had only been a lie, a terrible lie.

"Did she ever appear attached to the child?"

"She used to come and see her and then go away to work."

"Was the child a nursing child when you took it?"

"Oh, yes. A delicate . . ." Her voice trailed off as Martha became lost in memories.

"Mrs. Score? Was it a nursing child when you took it?"

"No, sir."

"Did the mother appear to exhibit any symptoms of affection when she came to see her?"

"Yes, sir. She kissed her often."

"Did she give any reason for stopping the payment of the money?"

"No, but I believe she left the St. Nicholas at that time."

"Have you any idea of any means by which we can ascertain the where-abouts of Fanny Wilson at this time?"

"No, sir."

"You've seen Mary Ellen, I presume."

Martha looked at her. "Yes, of course."

"Does she look like the same child?"

The question stung, as though he had asked if Martha could forget her own children's faces. She would never forget that child's face, not in a million years. "Yes, as near as I can tell," she answered, looking at the attorney. His eyes were sunken, encompassed by dark rings, and she knew he must have spent many long hours working on the case. She didn't know what might have happened if she had told the truth about Fanny Wilson, but it would probably have led them no further toward finding her.

Alanna Cavanagh was now in her grave, and knowing Fanny Wilson had committed herself to the bottle could not have helped the gentlemen. Even if she were to be found on the street or in an inebriate asylum, she still would not be awarded custody of the child in such condition. If she were anywhere else, living a respectable life, she would have heard of the case on the streets or seen it in the papers, and obviously did not want to be found. If that was the case, thought Martha, a foolish woman she was.

Mr. Gerry seemed disappointed at her answers. She probably hadn't given him as much as he had hoped for.

"The child was treated kindly so long as she remained with you?"

"I didn't treat her bad . . . only with kindness, sir."

"You treated her the same as your own children?"

"The very same as my own."

"Mr. Hawk kept the St. Nicholas at the time Mrs. Wilson worked there, didn't he?"

"I don't know who kept it."

"Do you know anyone who knows Fanny Wilson?"

"No, sir."

"Very well, Mrs. Score, I have only one more question. Do you know whether the ticket you were paid under had the name of Wilson on it?"

"I didn't take notice, and even if I had, it's so long ago I probably wouldn't remember it."

"I thank you for coming in, Mrs. Score. You'll be notified if you're required further."

Martha rose from the chair and stepped down from the stand. She walked slowly down the center aisle of the courtroom toward Mary Ellen, who sat beside a tall, thin man with a gaunt face. From his droopy eyes to the top hat on the bench beside him, she assumed it was Henry Bergh, whom she had seen mentioned so many times in the newspaper. She nodded to him and leaned toward the little girl.

Martha had supposed the words she wanted to say to Mary Ellen would simply come to her, but when the little girl turned her eyes to Martha, a cherubic smile on her tiny face, she reached out and stroked the child's cheek, instead, saying nothing. Her tears flowing, Martha hurried out of the courtroom, leaving the man to stare after her.

What had she needed so badly to say to Mary Ellen? As much as the child had once meant to her; after the enormous affect she had ultimately had on Mary Ellen's life, shouldn't the words have been clear in her mind? Should she have said she was sorry for leaving her with George Kellock? Sorry for saving her from a woman who might have killed her in a drunken stupor? Now, she supposed, it no longer made a difference anyway. Martha would never see her again.

But she had believed that many years ago, too.

* * * * *

April 27, 1874

In the Court of General Sessions, Recorder Hackett presided over the jury trial of Mary Connolly. Bergh, Gerry, and Etta were all in attendance the day the jury returned the verdict, and indeed, Gerry had not missed a day of testimony. The only other time Etta attended was when Mary Ellen took the stand. Her first time to be questioned before the crowd did not proceed without a hitch.

She did well in the beginning; Recorder Hackett explained the nature of an oath, then swore Mary Ellen in. The child took the stand and answered Recorder Hackett's questions readily, but before long she took quick glances at her former keeper, and soon gave way to tearful sobs. When she finally left the stand, Mary Ellen rushed toward Etta, her arms out and her eyes squirting tears.

The jury had been out only twenty minutes when the door opened and they filed back into the jury box. The slip was given to Hackett, and a few moments later he stood and looked directly at Mary Connolly, his face unreadable. "Would the defendant please rise," said Hackett.

Mary Connolly stood, looking straight ahead. Hackett stared at her.

"Mrs. Connolly, I have no doubt whatever of your guilt. You have been afforded every opportunity to prove your innocence, and this court is fully satisfied that you are guilty of gross and wanton cruelty." He looked for a moment at Mary Ellen, resting comfortably on Etta's lap, then continued. "This jury has found you guilty of felonious assault against Mary Ellen Wilson. Bear in mind, I would have been satisfied if the jury had found you guilty of the highest offense charged. As a punishment to you, but more as a warning to others, I shall sentence you to the extreme penalty of the law—one year in the penitentiary at hard labor."

Mary Connolly stood as erect as a stone pillar, her face set in an expression of hatred and repulsion. Her hands trembled, her body shuddered, but she showed no sorrow or regret over her punishment.

Etta looked at the evil woman, no pity whatsoever in her heart. Instead, she found herself wondering if one year of hard labor would be enough to teach Mary Connolly the error of her ways. She had been so cruel for so many years . . . at least she would have no children to mistreat upon her return to society.

Connolly had been surprisingly fortunate. Of the five counts against her—assault and battery, felonious assault, assault with intent to do bodily harm, assault with intent to kill, and assault with intent to maim—she had been convicted of only one. It was impossible, but it had happened. And so justice went, about as mysterious as God's ways sometimes were.

"This court is adjourned," said Recorder Hackett.

Etta rose, still holding the heavy child in her arms, and carried her to the police Matron, Meara Webb. "There you are, Mary Ellen," she said, putting her down. "I'll see you soon, I promise."

"You promise? Do you . . . *sweer*?"

"That word is *swear*, and yes, of course I do." Etta leaned down and kissed her, and she flung her arms around her neck.

"Oh, my! I said I'll see you soon, little one."

"I know," she replied. "I just wanted a big hug."

As they reached the door to the courthouse, Etta held out her hand to Bergh. "Mr. Bergh, thank you for all you've done to save this child, but may I ask you a final question before we part company?"

The bloodhound-faced gentleman smiled broadly and clasped her hand in both of his. "Of course, my dear woman, anything! Oh, wait just one moment." He reached into his pocket and drew forth his wallet. "Take this," he said, handing her twenty-five dollars in bills. "Buy the little girl some clothing—and some goodies, maybe."

Etta took the money, thanked him and said, "Mr. Bergh, you've done so much I hate to ask anything further, but couldn't there be a Society for the Prevention of Cruelty to Children that will do for children what is being so well done for animals?"

Bergh did not hesitate. "Mrs. Wheeler," he said excitedly, "I've already decided on that." He took her hands again. "There shall be one."

27

June 15, 1874

"But Mr. Bergh," Judge Lawrence said, "his testimony is very clearly stated, and all indications are that the child is John Connor's cousin. You gave me the letters sent to you and Mr. Gerry from Michael Connor as well. I'm reasonably sure, considering all this information, that Mary Ellen is Mr. Connor's grandchild." He wasn't about to budge.

"Be that as it may, Your Honor, he also clearly indicated they could hardly afford to care for themselves," Bergh insisted. "He wrote that he has been out of work for six years and they currently live from their life's earnings."

"Further investigation must be done. Mary Ellen shall remain in the Sheltering Arms until such time as I am satisfied where she does belong. Even if it is determined by me the child should go to her grandparents or her aunt, I have no confidence the State of New York will bear the financial burden of sending her to England, these persons as yet unseen—especially with so many others offering to take her in."

"You do realize that Mrs. Wheeler has requested the child be placed in the custody of her sister," Bergh said.

"Of course. I haven't excluded that possibility, Mr. Bergh. It's just that while there are two grandparents, two cousins, an uncle, and a sister who are willing to take her, I must review all pertinent information available before making a decision. Be they family or not, they must be financially able to care for her, and must also have the proper character." Judge Lawrence removed his spectacles and rubbed his eyes. "You are aware the entire nation is following the developments of this case, and I'll not rush into anything. To put her back into a difficult situation would hardly be fair to the child after what she's been through."

"I realize that, sir. I, too, am concerned with her placement, which is why I must offer my support to Mrs. Wheeler."

"Are you suggesting that Mrs. Wheeler's family would be the best guardian for the child, even over her own family?" Judge Lawrence sat in a dark brown wing-backed chair and puffed his pipe.

Bergh paced back and forth in front of him. "I understand you must exhaust all other possibilities of placement with those claiming to be family," Bergh said. "But after that is done, assuming they are not deemed to be legitimate or capable, yes, that's what I would recommend."

"I'll consider it, Mr. Bergh. I promise you that."

"If you don't mind, may I read the deposition of John Connor, the one who says he's the cousin of the child's mother?"

The judge had it by his side. The case was being given top priority, as Bergh believed it should. He gave it to Bergh, who took the chair opposite him and read it to himself:

I am a married man, 28 years old, and have no children. My uncle, Michael Connor, resides at 56 Marsham Street, Westminister, London, England. I knew my cousin Fanny Wilson before and at the time of her marriage. She was about five feet one inch high, dark hair and eyes, broad and somewhat projecting forehead, round face with fair complexion with a little color. She was weighing about 120 pounds. She was married to Thomas Wilson about 1862. He was an oyster opener in the St. Nicholas Hotel, and she was a laundress there. I saw Thomas Wilson once. He was an Irishman about five feet seven or eight inches high, with light red hair and no side-whiskers. I believe he went to the war and first enlisted in the 69th Regiment, then re-enlisting in the Hawkins Second Fire Zouaves. I met Fanny on Spring Street about this time with a child in her arms that was about three weeks old. She called it by the name Mary Ellen and said she had named after her mother, Mary Connor, and her sister, Ellen Connor, who is now Ellen Fitzgerald. The child had whitish hair then. I stood talking to my cousin Fanny about half an hour. This was about 1863.

About two years after this, the next time that I met Fanny Wilson, she said she had put the child to nurse with a woman who told her the child had died. I did not again see Fanny until 1871, when I met her on First Avenue near Twelfth Street. She then told me that her husband, Thomas Wilson, had died in the war, and that she had married a man named Gibbon, who had also enlisted and was then on Governors Island.

She appeared to be then under the influence of liquor. I met her once after that on First Avenue near Tenth Street. She then said she was living at 525 East Twelfth Street, and that she was going to move out. I went there frequently to inquire after her, and after some difficulty, ascertained that she died at the Hospital on Ward's Island, then somewhere about 34 years old. I learned that her remains had been sent to Bellevue Hospital in the expectation that her relatives might claim them, but this was not done and she was buried in the Potter's Field.

I have been written to more than once by my uncle, Michael Connor, and also by my cousin Ellen requesting me to make inquiries about Fanny Wilson, which I did without success. The last letter I so received and which I have was February 2, 1872. I wrote back and shared with them all I had ascertained by accidentally meeting her. About May last, after reading of this case in the newspapers, I cut them out and mailed the articles to Michael Connor. I called at the Police Headquarters shortly since and saw the child Mary Ellen. She bears a strong personal likeness to my cousin Fanny Wilson in her face and expression, the chief difference being in the lighter color of her hair.

Bergh looked at Judge Lawrence, his jaw dropping. "This is the most information we've seen, and yet it all seems to fit in with what we already know. How is Mr. Connor's financial condition?"

"That's the problem, Mr. Bergh," Lawrence said. "Neither he nor his wife has any source of income now except government relief. He says he can't afford to take the child. He only wants to see her placed with her own family."

Bergh stood and brushed off his coat, preparing to leave. "Your Honor, I've read nothing here to convince me that Mary Ellen should not be placed with Mrs. Wheeler's family. They have a nice farm just outside of Rochester, and her mother and sister are perfectly willing to take her in. Mary Ellen herself has expressed an interest in being with her. I realize you have more investigation to do, and I'll tell as much to Mrs. Wheeler, but when you decide it has become a task without hope, you know my opinion."

Lawrence puffed his pipe and stood. "Mr. Bergh, thank you for coming in. Sometimes it helps just to discuss the case aloud. Still, I can't promise you my decision will be made anytime soon or that it will be in your favor. England is far away, and communication is slow, I'm sure you understand. You'll be second to know as developments occur."

"Thank you, Your Honor. I'll bring you any information I receive as well."

* * * * *

December 1874
Six Months Later

"Meara Webb's care was perfectly acceptable as a temporary place for Mary Ellen, as I know her to be a fine lady," Etta told Bergh. "But the Shelter-

317

ing Arms is a home for wayward children who are near grown and is entirely inappropriate for a young child who has lived such a singular life as Mary Ellen. They're training them as service workers, for Heaven's sake."

"Have you visited there, Mrs. Wheeler?" Bergh asked.

"Well yes, of course I visited immediately upon hearing of Judge Lawrence's decision to place her there, and I must tell you I was not impressed with the cleanliness or with the overcrowded conditions. Surely you must have some influence with him, Mr. Bergh."

"I have tried before, as you know. I've been hesitant to press him to make his decision, as he is dutifully attempting to ascertain whether her alleged family has the proper means to care for her. From what I've read in letters from them, some aren't interested in obtaining her, and those who are might not be able to support her." The lanky gentleman twisted his mustache between his fingers. "Perhaps it's time to make another plea on your behalf."

"I would appreciate it, Mr. Bergh. I see her often, and each time she asks me when she can come and live with me. I've told her of the house in the country, and she wants so to be there. You know I've already spoken to Judge Lawrence many times. I suppose he's being quite thorough in his search for her family, if nothing else. I, however, believe the time has come to move forward, investigate other avenues."

"I'll see what I can do, Mrs. Wheeler," Bergh said. "From what I gather, the European possibilities are becoming less and less hopeful each day."

"Thank you, Mr. Bergh. You'll inform me of your progress?"

"Of course, Mrs. Wheeler. You'll be next to know after myself."

* * * * *

June 4, 1875
Six Months Later

The offices at the corner of Fourth Avenue and Twenty-second Street were busier than usual, as they were currently being shared with the Society for the Prevention of Cruelty to Children, the fledgling organization newly sprung from Mary Ellen's case. Letters came in from all parts of the city from citizens who were positive the humane gentleman, Henry Bergh, would now be

318

breaking down doors in his efforts to rescue children from parents who spanked them. Some, though not all or these concerns were diminished when it was learned that John Wright—not Henry Bergh—would be serving as president of the society.

Bergh sat at his desk and picked up his pen. It was time to see what could be done about the child responsible for the creation of the SPCC. Judge Lawrence was near his wit's end with the myriad of claims on Mary Ellen, and Mrs. Wheeler was badly frustrated after more than a year of delays. He wrote:

June 4th, 1875

Honorable Abraham R. Lawrence

Dear Sir,

Mrs. Wheeler, the excellent lady who was instrumental in aiding me in rescuing "little Mary Ellen" from the hands of a brutal woman, has called to see me in relation to procuring her a home with her sister, who resides near Rochester in this state.

I take the liberty to address you on the subject, for the purpose of assuring you that no better disposition of that child could possibly be made. Mrs. Wheeler is a most amiable, intelligent, and Christian lady, and her sister is like her. The Matron of the establishment where she is at present, and all others familiar with the locality and her surroundings, are unanimous in the opinion that she should be removed without delay.

With Mrs. Wheeler's sister, she would have a good home, and be returned to morality and usefulness aloof from the vices of a great city.

I earnestly and most sincerely hope that you will sanction this proposal on the part of these ladies and issue an

319

order to that effect so that she may accompany Mrs. Wheeler to the country on Monday next, when she is obliged to leave, owing to the illness of her mother. If possible will you please return a reply by the bearer?

And believe me,
Your most obedient Servant,
Henry Bergh

Bergh called for a messenger and sent him off, smiling as he watched the young man climb atop his horse in the street below his window. A feeling of confidence overcame Bergh; one that he had felt on many earlier occasions in his life; when he met Matilda; when he asked her to marry him; when he first decided to bring the protection of animals to the United States; when he first heard the story of the little abused child. He always knew, deep in his heart, how each situation would turn out. Somehow, they had.

He sat back in his chair, glancing occasionally down at the street as he went through the stacks of papers on his desk that never seemed to grow smaller. It was just a matter of time. Mrs. Wheeler and Mary Ellen deserved wonderful news.

* * * * *

June 7, 1875
Three Days Later

Mary Ellen looked out at the vast pastures and tiny farmhouses in the distance. Her brown eyes wide with excitement, the questions came one after another. "What's that, Mrs. Wheeler? Is that a cow, like in my picture books?" She looked at Etta, smiling.

"Yes, it is. And that over there . . . see? That's a goat. And those animals there, see the fluffy ones?"

"Sheep! Those are sheep!"

"That's right, dear! You have been studying those picture books, haven't you?"

A man walked through the car calling, "Spencerport! Next stop is Spencerport station!"

Etta's heart leapt. After twelve hours, they had reached what was once her home. The place she'd met Charles. Such memories for her as a young girl. Perhaps Mary Ellen would someday have fond memories of this place, too. She put her arm around the child. "Come, Mary Ellen. Let's get our things together. Before long, you'll be able to pet the animals you've seen along the way."

"Really? I really could?"

"Of course."

"Won't they bite me?"

"Not if I show you how. Why, you'll learn to milk cows, and you'll get to feed the animals if you want, too. Oh, by the way . . . I hear Annabelle had a litter of puppies just a few weeks ago."

"A litter? Who's Annabelle?" asked Mary Ellen.

"She's a very sweet dog, Mary Ellen. She loves children. You'll see."

"I've never touched a dog," she said. "I saw one outside the window in the street, but it was a real mean dog. I saw it bite a little boy one time."

"Puppies love everyone, Mary Ellen. Perhaps, if you like, you can have one of your own."

"A puppy? For me?"

The locomotive slowed as it approached the station, but Etta's heart never beat faster than the moment the train pulled to a screeching stop. From that day on, the sound of a train whistle would take her back to Mary Ellen's first day of true freedom.

* * * * *

Mary Ellen ran as fast as she could across the flat pasture, feeling the warm wind kiss her face, the tall grass tickling her bare feet. The pretty yellow flowers scattered through the grass were so beautiful she picked handfuls of them. She would bring them to Mrs. Wheeler, because she loved her so. Aunt

Liz was nice, too. Maybe she should bring them both a bunch of the pretty flowers.

When she had two bundles, she brought them to her face, breathing in the wonderful aroma.

Mary Ellen stopped for a moment, looked up at the cloud dotted blue sky, and spun around and around, making herself dizzy. She watched the bunches of flowers in each of her hands, and soon she could no longer stand, and felt herself falling down. She landed on her back atop the cool grass and closed her eyes, enjoying the feeling of freedom. She could pick more flowers any-time—there were so many of them!

Then she saw them, charging across the pasture after her. She could see their teeth as they ran, their wet tongues hanging over them, and they were coming at her as fast as they could. Mary Ellen, still dizzy, jumped back to her feet, knowing she could not outrun them in this condition. Still, she must try however useless it was. She screamed as they approached her and continued running but knew she was losing ground. They were behind her already, the first one already nipping at her heels.

* * * * *

Etta watched from the kitchen door, laughing as Annabelle's six puppies charged across the field toward the little girl whom they had come to love. Mary Ellen fell into the tall grass and disappeared for a moment, and for just that moment, worry tugged at Etta's heart. She took two steps toward the fence dividing her from the field, then saw Mary Ellen sit up, all six pups jumping and licking and frolicking around her.

Mary Ellen had named her puppy Timmy, and as Etta looked on, the tiny, white puppy was clearly her favorite. She held him under his little legs and lowered him just enough so he could give her tiny, wet kisses. It had taken some time, but the larger animals were less frightening to her than at first.

How Etta hated to say good-bye to Mary Ellen for even a day, but there was no choice. Charles couldn't join her at the farm and he needed her by now. So, too, did the poor people living within the tenements. After all, things were done here for now; Mother had passed away and been buried two weeks ago, and Etta had stayed solely for the benefit of Mary Ellen and her sister Elizabeth, who had taken their mother's death to heart.

Etta looked to God for His wisdom, and thanked Him. Mother had been in her eighties, and not in the best of health. She was, she professed, ready for death. God took her much in the same way He took Mary Smitt; in her sleep, and gently.

Etta would say good-bye to Mary Ellen tomorrow.

* * * * *

New York, June 24, 1875

My Dear Mr. Bergh,

I returned to the city yesterday, leaving Mary Ellen very contentedly domiciled with my sister.

The child bears the freedom and variety of her new life with much good sense, but with a very keen enjoyment. For the first time in her life, she is unrestrained by bolts and locks, and she enjoys being out-of-doors as an escaped soul would Paradise. She is still a bit shy of all the household pets, the babies excepted, but they were all making love to her, insisting upon being friends, and she was fast losing her terror. She was greatly troubled by my coming away, but seems already quite attached to my sister and her family. She is a helpful, kindhearted little creature and is making friends for herself.

Her ignorance of the ordinary affairs of home life, and of the commonest objects in the country amused as well as pained us. She was very kindly received by all my friends and not alone for my sake, but for her own. I expended of the twenty-five dollars sent by yourself—traveling expenses and necessary clothing were sixteen dollars, I gave my sister four dollars, and the remaining five dollars is to be put in the bank for Mary Ellen's benefit. She will, if well, earn her clothes hereafter, in her ready way of helping in household affairs.

With thanks for your kindness,
I am very truly,
Mrs. C. C. Wheeler
122 W. 45th St.

* * * * *

Social reformist, police photographer, and *Tribune* reporter Jacob Riis, wrote the following courtroom description. Mr. Riis had a passion for the elimination of human suffering, and may have been one to exaggerate, but it supplies you with his firsthand account of what it was to be there in the courtroom:

> I was in a courtroom full of men with pale, stern looks. I saw a child brought in, carried in a horse blanket, at the sight of which men wept aloud. I saw it laid at the feet of the judge, who turned his face away, and in the stillness of that courtroom I heard a voice raised claiming for that child the protection men had denied it, in the name of the homeless cur on the street. And I heard the story of little Mary Ellen told again, that stirred the soul of a city and roused the consciousness of a world that had forgotten. . . . And as I looked, I knew I was where the first chapter of children's rights was written, under warrant of that made for the dog.

> ~Jacob Riis

Epilogue

WHATEVER HAPPENED TO MARY ELLEN?
By Dr. Stephen Lazoritz

*Child Abuse & Neglect, September (1989): "Whatever Happened to Mary Ellen?" Vol 14,
pp.143-149, Elsevier Science, Used with permission.*

In June of 1936, a schoolteacher named Florence Brasser from a suburb of Rochester, New York, wrote a letter to Mr. John J. Smithers, general manager of the New York Society for the Prevention of Cruelty to Children. (NYSPCC) The reply came quickly. The stationery bore the official seal of the society, and in the space after the sentence, "In replying please refer to Case No. ____," the number "1" was neatly typed in.

"Dear Mrs. Brasser," the letter began, "You realize, I presume, that the epic story of 'Mary Ellen' is known throughout the civilized world, and it was the inspiration of the movement for the legal protection of children, not only in this country, but throughout the Universe at large."

This might have been just another response to a request for information regarding the famous case of Mary Ellen, which resulted in the founding of the NYSPCC in 1874. However, in this instance the request was made by someone with more than just a passing interest in this case. It was made by Mary Ellen's youngest daughter, Florence.

Mr. Smithers' reply detailed to Florence how her grandmother, Frances (Fanny) Connor, came to the United States in 1858 from London, England. Frances married a soldier named Thomas Wilson, who died in the Civil War. In 1863, Frances Wilson wrote to her father that she was expecting a child, who was born that winter. Her mother abandoned the child, Mary Ellen, soon thereafter.

"The further circumstances you know, and it has been a profound satisfaction to this society to follow her later career, and to know that now, in the evening of her life, she has the comfort of daughters of whom she is proud," concluded Mr. Smithers.

Mr. Smithers was certainly correct in his statement that the case of Mary Ellen, and its profound and lasting effects on the cause of child protection, is universally known. The details of the rescue of Mary Ellen have been well chronicled elsewhere (Williams, 1980), but little has been written about the effect that this historic intervention had on the life of the victim of this terrible case of child abuse.

LIFE AFTER INTERVENTION

"What happened to little Mary Ellen?" asked Gertrude Williams (1980) in her chapter dealing with the plight of the little girl. "The former darling of the press, having served her purpose, was 'finally disposed of' by being reinstitutionalized."

When no suitable relatives could be found to care for her, Mary Ellen was placed in the Sheltering Arms, which was a home, not for young homeless children like herself, but one for adolescent girls, some of whom were troubled. Thus, the case of Mary Ellen was not only "the inspiration for the legal protection of children," but ironically it was also the first inappropriate placement resulting from such a case. (Wheeler, unknown).

Mrs. Etta Wheeler, the church worker from St. Luke's Methodist Mission, whose persistent efforts resulted in Mary Ellen's rescue, again came to the child's aid by expressing her disapproval with the placement at the Sheltering Arms to Judge Lawrence, who was Mary Ellen's guardian. Judge

Lawrence put Mary Ellen at Mrs. Wheeler's disposal, and in June of 1875 the little girl was sent to live with Sally Angell, Etta Wheeler's mother, on a farm outside Rochester. Mrs. Angell died of tuberculosis in September of that year, and at her request, her youngest daughter, Elizabeth, and her husband, Darius W. Spencer, who lived nearby, raised Mary Ellen. (Wheeler, 1913).

THE PUBLICIZING OF MARY ELLEN

As Mary Ellen was beginning her new life, the public did not forget her life as an abused child. In the nation's centennial year, 1876, a photograph of the ragged and beaten Mary Ellen was prominently displayed as part of the Society for the Prevention of Cruelty to Animals' exhibit at the Philadelphia Centennial Exhibition, alongside specimens depicting other abused members of the animal kingdom. This exhibit was hardly popular, though, being described by the *Philadelphia Times* as "about as pleasant to the senses as an inspection of a thriving morgue in dog-days" (Steele, 1942).

During the same year as the Centennial, Henry P. Keens, a songwriter and composer of little renown, published two musical compositions based on the life of the abused child. The first, whose sheet music was graced with a photograph of the beaten and abused child, was titled "Little Mary Ellen" and was "dedicated by permission to Henry Bergh, Esq.", the president of the Society for the Prevention of Cruelty to Animals. This song (Keens, 1876) began:

> See within that dismal chamber
> Clothed in rags and chilled with fear
> No kind father to protect her
> With no watchful mother near
> Weeps an infant, pale and feeble,
> Victim of her keeper's rage,
> Tender flower crushed and broken,
> Blighted in her budding age.

And the chorus went:

> Who will help this little orphan
> Left on earth without a friend?
> Who will shelter and protect her?
> Who will peace and mercy send?

The second song (Keens, 1876), published simultaneously, was "dedicated by permission to Hon. Elbridge T. Gerry", who was Henry Bergh's attorney who argued on behalf of Mary Ellen. He later became the president of the Society for the Prevention of Cruelty to Children. Entitled "Mother Sent an Angel to Me," the cover of the sheet music bore a picture of Mary Ellen with her cheeks filled out and her wounds healed. It began:

> There in sweet repose reclining
> See a child of fairy grace
> Well might angels look with wonder
> On the beauty of her face
> Tell me, maiden, who has changed thee
> From what once thou used to be?
> Who has healed thy broken spirit
> Saved thee from captivity?

And the chorus:

> Mother sent an angel to me
> Clad in virtue's robe of white
> Spreading wings of mercy o'er me
> Made my darkest hour bright.

It is not known how popular these musical compositions were, but at least one critic described them to be "full of deep pathos" (Steele, 1942).

MARY ELLEN, THE SURVIVOR

Mary Ellen thrived in the Spencer home and attended school through grammar school. In 1888, at the age of 24, she married a widower of German heritage, Lewis Schutt. Mr. Schutt was a gentle, intelligent man with a huge handlebar mustache. He had worked as a railroad flagman and gardener and had two sons, Jesse and Clarence, by his former marriage. In April of 1897, Mary Ellen gave birth to her first daughter, Etta, named for Etta Wheeler, and four years later in May of 1901, she bore her second daughter, Florence.

The Schutt family was a poor but loving family. Mary Ellen loved music, especially Irish jigs. Her favorite was "The Irish Washerwoman," which would always get her to tap her feet. She also enjoyed singing hymns. Mary Ellen was known to collect little things, such as scraps of string. These little things meant a great deal to her. Mr. Schutt's German descent enabled him to help the children with their German homework, and Florence recalls regularly walking one and a half miles to the railroad crossing to bring her father his lunch.

Mary Ellen worked hard to care for her family and at one point, took in another child, Eunice, to care for as a foster child for many years. Though she was not active in the child protection movement, Mary Ellen did attend the 37th Annual Meeting of the American Humane Association that was held in Rochester in October 1913. At that meeting, Mrs. Etta Wheeler presented a paper entitled, "The Finding of Mary Ellen," in which she described her role in the rescue of the abused child (Meeting announcement, 1913).

RECOLLECTIONS OF MARY ELLEN BY HER FAMILY

When her children and grandchildren would ask Mary Ellen about her childhood in New York, she would try to change the topic. "I suppose she had enough of it," reflected Florence. But Mary Ellen did provide some details of her miserable existence. She described Mrs. Connolly, her stepmother who brutalized her, as a "mean looking woman". Florence remembers her mother telling her of an incident when her mother was drying some clothes, and "she (Mrs. Connolly) got mad at something and took the hot iron and put it right on her (Mary Ellen's) arm . . . that was a burn!"

Florence described seeing scars on her mother, "on her arms wherever she hurt her." Eunice remembers scars around Mary Ellen's left eye, which were caused when Mrs. Connolly hit her on the face with scissors. "Grandma never knew when she would be punished, or for what, or how greatly," recalled Etta's daughter, Shirley Mehlenbacher.

Mary Ellen's daughter and granddaughter described Mary Ellen as being not much of a disciplinarian. "It wasn't her nature to spank very much. She might threaten you, but she would rarely do it." Florence described her mother as always wanting her to "be good and do the right thing." If they weren't? "She just punished us, that's all. Just spank us and that's as hard as it went. She would spank our little bottom." Eunice agreed that bad behavior might result in an occasional spanking, "but she had to catch me first," and recalled outrunning her foster mother. "She was just a real sweet lady."

FAMILY ACHIEVEMENTS

Perhaps the most remarkable and gratifying aspects of Mary Ellen's life were the accomplishments of her daughters. Both Etta and Florence attended college and became teachers. Etta was a well-respected teacher in the Rochester Public Schools. She had a deep love for working with children, and her teaching career spanned thirty-nine years. She died in 1988 at the age of eighty-four.

Florence also had a long teaching career, thirty-seven years, but one in which she achieved a unique honor. In 1955, Chili School 11, where she had taught since 1928, was officially named the Florence Brasser School in her honor. She continued to teach at the school that bore her name until her retirement in 1961. In 1967 the New York State Legislature recognized Mrs. Brasser for her lifelong accomplishments with a resolution in her honor. Mrs. Brasser died in 1993.

Mary Ellen herself died on October 30, 1956, at the age of 92. Those of us who work for the protection of abused and neglected children, however, will always remember her as she was in 1874; a child in need of protection and the inspiration for a revolution in her country's concern for children. But perhaps we should take a new look at Mary Ellen. We should look at the child who was able to thrive in a loving environment and to grow into an adult who had children of whom she was proud. Perhaps we should see Mary Ellen not as the victim of abuse, but as the survivor, and as a persistent reminder that the efforts of a few people on behalf of one child can make a real difference.

* * * * *

HENRY BERGH AND HIS SOCIETIES TODAY
By Charles William Bergh
With Eric A. Shelman

After the formation of the Society for the Prevention of Cruelty to Children (SPCC), Henry Bergh served as Vice President and one of the Directors as long as he lived. It was never his intention to run the SPCC, nor did he wish to take time away from his beloved Society for the Prevention of Cruelty to Animals, the passion that would consume the remaining 13 years of his life. From the beginning, the SPCC was maintained as a distinct and separate organization from the ASPCA.

The SPCC used space in the SPCA offices while they organized and worked to gain a charter. Bergh's pledge, which still hangs on the offices of the current *New York* Society for the Prevention of Cruelty to Children (NYSPCC) today, reads:

> The undersigned, desirous of rescuing the unprotected children of this city and State from the cruelty and demoralization which neglect and abandonment engender, hereby engage to aid, with their sympathy and support, the organization and working of a Children's Protective Society, having in view the realization of so important a purpose.

The three signatures at the bottom of the pledge are those of Henry Bergh, Elbridge T. Gerry, and John D. Wright, a wealthy Quaker who became the first President of the SPCC. Today, Elbridge T. Gerry Jr. sits as President of the Board of Directors, and Elbridge T. Gerry III serves as Secretary. Anne Reiniger is the current Executive Director of the organization.

Today the ASPCA has New York offices in New York City, Albany and Suffolk County. Others are in Los Angeles, CA., Champaign-Urbana, IL., and Washington DC. The ASPCA is supported by more than 475,000 members and donors and provides a national animal poison control center, the Bergh

Memorial Animal Hospital, and counseling services to help with pet loss. They actively advocate city, state and federal laws that promote animal welfare, have an active legal department, and provide humane education materials for grade schools.

Henry's wife and life-long supporter, Matilda, became bed-ridden, and after a long confinement in a sanitarium, died on June 8, 1887. His wife gone, Henry himself began to show the effects of age and many a cold night spent walking the streets of New York on the lookout for an overloaded horsecar or a fallen animal. The night of March 11, 1888 found Bergh alone at his home in bed while a great blizzard dumped a record amount of snow on New York City. His family doctor would find Bergh dead the following morning, March 12th.

Henry's funeral was held at St. Mark's church, where he and Catherine Matilda Taylor were to be married forty-nine years before. His casket was pulled by horses to Greenwood Cemetery, the same cemetery where a great helper of the ASPCA, Louis Bonard, was buried. One of the many floral arrangements at the funeral featured a picture of a St. Bernard encircled by white roses. The arrangement was inscribed, "Henry Bergh, Samson's Best Friend."

Indeed, Henry Bergh was a friend to all living things.

* * * * *

REFERENCES

George Sim Johnston archives. (1994) New York. *New York Society for the Prevention of Cruelty to Children.* various material, court transcripts.

Keens, H.P. (1876a). *Little Mary Ellen.* New York; William A. Pond.

Keens, H.P. (1876b). *Mother Sent an Angel To Me.* New York; William A. Pond.

Lazoritz, S. Whatever Happened to Mary Ellen? Reprinted from *Child Abuse & Neglect.* (1989) Vol 14, pp.143-149. Used with permission from *Elsevier Science*

Mary Ellen Wilson. (1874, April 10). *New York Times,* pp..2,8.

Mary Ellen Wilson. (1874, April 10). *The Sun* (New York) p.1.

Mary Ellen Wilson. (1874, April 10). *New York Daily Tribune.* p.2.

Mary Ellen Wilson. (1874, April 11). *New York Times,* p. 2.

Mary Ellen Wilson. (1874, April 11). *Buffalo Daily Courier.* p.1

Mary Ellen Wilson. (1874, April 12). *New York Herald.*

Mary Ellen Wilson. (1874, April 14). *New York Times,* p. 2.

Mary Ellen Wilson. (1874, April 22). *New York Times,* p. 8.

Mary Ellen Wilson. (1874, April 22). *New York Herald.*

Mary Ellen Wilson. (1874, April 28). *New York Herald.*

Meeting announcement. (1913) *National Humane Review*, 1, 192.

Steele, Z. (1942). *Angel In Top Hat.* New York; Harper and Brothers.

Wheeler, E.A. (1913). The beginning of child protection; "The case of Mary Ellen," *National Humane Review;* 1, 182.

Wheeler, E.A. (Unknown). The story of Mary Ellen", *American Humane Association,* Publication No. 280.

Harlow, Alvin F. (Unknown) *Henry Bergh: Founder of the A.S.P.C.A.* pp. 154-155. New York; Julian Messner, Inc.

Williams, G.J. (1980), Cruelty and kindness to children; Documentary of a Century, 1874-1974. In G.J. Williams & J. Money (Eds.), *Traumatic abuse and neglect of children at home* (pp. 68-77). Baltimore: Johns Hopkins University Press.

ABOUT THE AUTHORS

Eric Shelman was born in Ft. Worth, Texas, and has been writing for eleven years, with screenplays and several published short stories and articles to his credit. After reading a brief synopsis of Mary Ellen's case in 1993, Eric felt strongly that it was a missing piece of American history important enough to become his first book. He searched and found Dr. Lazoritz through the internet and the partnership was born, the book itself being written in two different time zones across the United States. The two authors only recently met in person. Eric has been married to his wife, Linda, for thirteen years, and lives in Southern California. Eric is currently at work on his third book, a novel.

Stephen Lazoritz is the medical director of the Child Protection Center at the Children's Hospital of Wisconsin, where he specializes in the care of abused and neglected children. Born in Brooklyn, N.Y., he became interested in Mary Ellen's case after reading an article about Henry Bergh and his work in the protection of animals. Obsessed with trying to find out "all there was to know" about the child's life, Stephen eventually had the privilege of meeting her daughter, Florence, and her granddaughter, Shirley. Stephen has been married to his wife, Mary, for twenty-two years and they have six children: Elizabeth, Megan, John, Christopher, Katherine and of course, Mary Ellen.

The scene that fills the background on the above pictures and on the cover is of Mulberry Bend, taken by photographer Jacob Riis. Columbus Park now stands where the bend once did.

Shelman and Lazoritz meet for only the second time since beginning work on the book over five years earlier. This was taken in October 1999 at the Museum of the City of New York.

From left to right: Eric & Linda Shelman, Mary and Stephen Lazoritz.

INDEX

Throughout this index the abbreviation *ME* is used for *Mary Ellen*.
Bold page numbers indicate illustrations.

IF YOU SUSPECT CHILD ABUSE, REPORT IT.

It's everyone's responsibility to protect our children. If you suspect child abuse is taking place, please act. For information on what you can do, contact the *National Clearinghouse on Child Abuse and Neglect.* You may reach them by visiting the web site at *http://www.calib.com/nccanch,* by telephone at (800) 394-3366, by fax at (703) 385-3206, or by E-mail at *nccanch@calib.com.*

You may also write them:

National Clearinghouse on Child
Abuse and Neglect Information
330 C Street, SW Washington, DC 20447

To quote Henry Bergh, *"No time is to be lost."*

* * * * *

ADOPT A GREYHOUND!

Why not give some thought to adopting an ex-racing greyhound? Whether you have a big house and yard, a condominium with a patio, or even an apartment with a porch, they make wonderful pets! Please call Greyhound Pets of America at 800-366-1472.

Or visit **http://www.greyhoundpets.org** on the internet today!

*"Until a person has known and loved a greyhound, a
part of their soul remains unawakened."*

DOLPHIN MOON PUBLISHING ORDER FORM

Fax Orders: (949) 380-7212   Internet: www.dolphinmoon.com

Telephone Orders: Please call and leave message. A representative will promptly return your call and take your order. (949) 380-7212.

On-line Ordering: Available at all online book stores

I would like to order _____ signed copies of *Out Of The Darkness: The Story of Mary Ellen Wilson* at $16.95 each.

Company Name: _____

Name: _____

Address: _____

City: _____ State: _____ Zip: _____

Telephone: (_____)_____

Quantity: _____
x $16.95: $_____
+CA tax (7.75%) $_____ (Only for California residents)
Shipping: $3.00 (1st book - $1.00 each additional)

Payment:
☐ Check
☐ Credit Card: ☐ Visa   ☐ Mastercard

Card Number: _____ Exp: ____/____

Name on Card: _____

Signature: _____